Another Place

An Ecocritical Study of Selected
Western American Poets

A N D R E W   E L K I N S

FORT WORTH:
TEXAS CHRISTIAN UNIVERSITY PRESS

Permissions
Permission to quote from the work of Peggy Pond Church courtesy
Kathleen Church.

All excerpts from *The Owl in the Mask of the Dreamer: Collected Poems*
copyright 1966, 1971, 1977, 1982, 1990, 1992 by John Haines. Reprinted
with the permission of Graywolf Press, Saint Paul, Minnesota.

Permission to quote from the following works by Jane Hirshfield courtesy
HarperCollins Publishers, Inc.: *The Lives of the Heart* (1997); *The October
Place* (1994); *Nine Gates: Entering the Mind of Poetry* (1997). From *Gravity
of Angels* courtesy Wesleyan University Press.

From *Making Certain it Goes On: Collected Poems of Richard Hugo* by
Richard Hugo. Copyright ©1984 by The Estate of Richard Hugo. Used by
permission of W. W. Norton & Company, Inc.

Permission to quote from the work of Adrian C. Louis, courtesy the author.

Permission to quote from authors in Chapter 2, "Hootin' and Hollerin' in
the American West: the Cowboy, the Land, and the Modern Reader,"
courtesy individual poets.

Photography Permissions
Peggy Pond Church. Courtesy Center for Southwest Research, University of
New Mexico.
John Haines. Courtesy Graywolf Press.
Jane Hirshfield. Courtesy HarperCollins Publishers
Adrian C. Louis. Photo by Ricardo Bloch.
Red Steagall. Courtesy Red Steagall.
Cover Illustration, "Sangre de Cristo Mountains," by Ernest l.
Blumenschein, courtesy of The Anschutz Collection, Denver, Colorado.

Library of Congress Cataloging-in-Publication Data
Elkins, Andrew, 1950-
    Another place : an ecocritical study of selected western American poets /
Andrew Elkins.
        p.cm.
    Includes bibliographical references and index.
    ISBN 0-87565-259-X (alk. paper)
    1. American poetry—West (U.S.)—History and criticim. 2. American
poetry—20th century—History and criticism. 3. Place (Philosophy) in
literature. 4. Wilderness areas in literature. 5. West (U.S.)—in literature.
6. Landscape in literature. 7. Ecology in literature. 8. Nature in literature.
9. Setting (Literature). I. Title.
    PS271.E45 2002
    811'.5093278—dc21

                                                                        2002002297

Designed by Carol Sawyer of Rose Design

CONTENTS

Mariae Helenae Uxori
il miglior fabbro

INTRODUCTION

No one needs to be told that the early European settlers of this land thought of the earth's natural resources as exploitable commodities, raw materials out of which to make a civilization in God's image. The land was here to be conquered and used for humans' ends and God's purposes. The current state of the environment in America is the result of centuries of this philosophy that theoretically urges use without abuse but that, in the hands of mortal humans, too often becomes rationalized abuse. Nor is it any secret that the nation's dominant religion, Christianity, enabled and even dictated this attitude by denying any inherent value, being, spirit, presence, or sacredness to nature. Lynn White, Jr., in his classic essay, "Historical Roots of our Ecologic Crisis," summarizes the process:

> In Antiquity, every spring, every stream, every hill had its own *genius loci*, its guardian spirit. . . . Before one cut a tree, mined a mountain, or dammed a brook, it was important to placate the spirit in charge of that particular situation and to keep it placated. By destroying pagan animism, Christianity made it possible to exploit nature in a mood of indifference toward the feelings of natural objects. . . . Man's effective monopoly on spirit in this world was confirmed, and the old inhibitions to the exploitation of nature crumbled (*Ecocriticism Reader* 10).

The sacred was taken from nature and lodged in the heavens, where humans were to seek it. Underfoot was mere nature; above was sacrality; between was the human, whose purpose was to wonder how he (or she) stood with God above, not with the spirit of nature below. Hence, nature was exposed and made vulnerable to human exploitation that was not only justified by God but that was very close to a human duty to honor God's benevolence when He placed all these wonderful natural resources within our reach for our use and His glory.

Today the ideas of respect for earth and responsible stewardship of natural resources are being taken seriously. At the same time, however, we have also come to believe that all value, truth, and meaning are socially or linguistically constructed. No value, truth, or meaning resides in the world itself but is constructed out of social conventions (something is good today that was bad yesterday) or linguistic sleight-of-hand (by calling it good, it becomes good). Princeton University scholar William Howarth summarizes some aspects of contemporary thinking in his essay "Some Principles of Ecocriticism":

> In the poststructural wave of discourse analysis, references to the natural sciences are almost entirely missing. Phenomena instead become cultural constructs, void of physical content and subject to cryptic readings . . . a bias echoed in New Historical readings of culture as shaped entirely by race, gender, class, money, and other factors of material life. . . . For deconstruction, on the other hand, all notions of order and structure become anathema, since language is assumed to have no stable meaning. This view is seen as mainly hostile to authoritarian rule, not as a new idea about nature or culture (*Ecocriticism Reader* 79-80).

Despite our new respect for the earth, the land remains in our contemporary intellectual culture a neutral site upon which humans project their values, which, fortunately, are now more likely to include recognition of the natural world's presence. Even so, postmodern nature remains in the tenuous position of surviving by humans' good graces.

Some would even question the continuing importance of place in human culture. Leonard Lutwack, in *The Role of Place in Literature*, contends that modern people have become so alienated from place (as a result of "the centralization of governing power and economic processes, the development of transportation and communication, the radical redistribution of dwelling places" [182-83]) that place has been displaced by movement as the significant fact of most people's lives. Place does not even count in the "peculiarly modern malaise called placelessness" (183). Places have become so standardized, the "Anyplace" syndrome, that place itself has lost its significance. Lutwack claims a "universal recognition" for this "new condition": the "dwindling importance of fixed places in the lives of individuals . . . the change from a life influenced by locations to a life governed by mobility and communications" (213). No one who has had to share a freeway with commuters speeding home while chatting on their cellular phones can doubt the contemporary importance of "mobility and communications."

Another Place is based upon a different premise articulated by professor of English Glen A. Love that it is time to recognize that "the current ideology which separates human beings from their environment is demonstrably and dangerously reductionist" for the simple reason that "the natural world is indubitably real and beautiful and significant" ("Revaluing" 213). A consistent theme in the poetry discussed here is that the West, as a land of imposing geography that varies from awesome prairies to towering mountains to crashing ocean waves with human-dwarfing deserts sprinkled about, has a spirit, or a variety of spirits depending on location. Furthermore, sensitive souls (such as poets) raised in or transplanted to places like the New Mexico desert, the Alaskan wilderness, or the Pacific shore absorb those spirits as part of their identities, and then the place's spirit—now integral to the poet's self—inevitably becomes part of the work that flows from the poet's creative spirit. Alaskan poet John Haines says, "I believe that there is a spirit of place, a presence asking to be expressed; and sometimes when we are lucky as writers, and quiet in a way few of us want to be anymore, a voice enters our own, becomes mingled with it, and we speak with a force and clarity not otherwise heard" (*Country* 19). In somewhat different terms, New Mexican poet Peggy Pond Church says, "One has to emphasize that the character of the land will determine the nature of the people who settle on it." Californian Jane Hirshfield puts the idea into poetic form, in "The Song":

> The tree, cut down this morning,
> is already chainsawed and quartered, stripped
> of its branches, transported and stacked.
> Not an instant too early, its girl slipped away.
> She is singing now, a small figure
> glimpsed in the surface of the pond.
> As the wood, if taken too quickly, will sing
> a little in the stove, still remembering her.

The girl, the *genius loci* of the tree, escapes to inhabit the pond to continue her song that the poet hears and that then becomes Hirshfield's poem. The poets of the West affirm Love's assertion that "the natural world is indubitably real and beautiful and significant." How does that affirmation get translated into poetry and what does it look like in verse?

Words and places, we now are beginning to understand, are reciprocally influential. Yi-Fu Tuan, who has done as much as anyone to create the modern discipline of geography, makes a powerful case that "Speech is a component of the total force that transforms nature into a human place" ("Language and the Making of Place" 685) at all stages of cultural development, from the hunter-gatherer phase through the exploration and pioneer stage, and beyond. Tuan seems bewildered that, despite the evidence of words' power, "people still find it difficult to accept the seemingly magical idea that mere words can call places into being" ("Language" 691). The idea can be twisted a bit to claim the equally magical idea that mere places can call words into being. John Elder quotes evolutionist Ernst Mayr's phrase "allopatric speciation," which Elder says Mayr uses "to indicate the way in which a given landscape's character has evolutionary influence fully equal to that of intra- or inter-species competition; the development of species must therefore always be understood in localized terms" (*Imagining the Earth* 39). In Elder's words, "Poetry, too, becomes a manifestation of landscape and climate, just as the ecosystem's flora and fauna are. A human voice becomes the voice of a place" (39). Conversely, a place becomes the voice of a poet. In the words of historian Donald Worster:

> The land has entered into western identity in more subtle and complicated ways than as property to be owned and fought over. . . . In a sense, westerners have long been conversing with the landscape as well as with each other, and their imaginations have been altered by that conversation beyond easy telling (*Under Western Skies* 235).

Margaret (Peggy) Pond Church
1903–1986

CHAPTER ONE

Sand, Wind, and Buttes: Peggy Pond Church's Lifetime Love Affair with the Desert Southwest

*M*argaret (Peggy) Pond Church (1903-1986), a native of Watrous in what was then New Mexico Territory, wrote eight volumes of verse, two biographies, and a children's tale while publishing poems in such magazines as the *Atlantic, Poetry,* and *Saturday Review* and carrying on correspondence with May Sarton, Denise Levertov, and Lawrence Clark Powell. Church occasionally lived outside New Mexico but in the early twentieth century most of her life and almost all of her poetry was a product of the Southwest when the region's culture and natural beauty were being discovered by the eastern literary establishment.[1] D. H. Lawrence, of course, moved to Taos, and others like Carl Sandburg, Ezra Pound, Vachel Lindsay, and the influential editor of *Poetry,* Harriet Monroe, visited and found the area beautiful. The transplanted midwestern author Mary Austin predicted the area would be the site of the next American Renaissance. Church was associated with the Santa Fe writers' group of the 1920s and 30s (including Austin; Alice Corbin Henderson, Monroe's assistant at *Poetry*; Haniel Long; and others) and, with Long, Henderson, and Witter Bynner, "actively supported" the local Poets' Round-Ups and "committed [herself] to supporting New Mexico Writers" (Armitage, "Heritage" 25). While Church's work has received very little critical attention during her lifetime and later, her poetry is as evocative a testament to the sensuality and spirituality of the land as has ever been written in the Southwest.

Church's vision of her relationship to the land is dualistic and spiritual: soul and body are separate entities, and the presence of something spiritual and timeless in the soul, reflected in the land's geology and its history, provides her hope of permanence, despite the acknowledged transience of her physical being. Church's conviction that her spirit's permanence is reflected in the apparent permanence of the landforms around her allows her to transcend or, as she says, "escape" the curse of mortality. She imagines herself returning to join the earth as a released soul whose voice will be added to the choir of the desert air. While embracing permanence of spirit, she develops her sense of self and self's place in the world through close observation of the land around her. In the modern era of anxiety, angst, and doubt in which she wrote the majority of her work, she manages to face squarely the harsh realities of living and dying. She says, "I am willing to accept extinction as the ultimate fate of all living species" while affirming life's value without becoming sentimental.[2]

Her early lessons in life were learned beneath the "bright familiar stars" of the plains, where she read of life and death on the marble gravestones of early settlers. Her father early put a bridle in her hands and taught her to gallop "with the wind and the sun and the power of a strong horse running" ("Return to a Landscape"). As she says in the same poem, her first air was "the midnight air of a canyon." Junipers, cottonwoods, mesas, dry arroyos, mountain trails, and other images of the Southwest dominate her poetry published between 1933 and 1985.[3] In addition to desert and mountain images we also meet images of the ocean, still fresh in her memory from the time she spent in Berkeley and San Francisco with her husband, Fermor. She describes San Francisco as "the only city with which I came to have an intimate acquaintance," but later, after returning to Taos to live, she reports primarily "a nostalgia for the ocean"[4] when thinking of her time in California. Despite her occasional residence in cities, then, the concept of place to the poet means the land outdoors—plains, streams, the ocean, and mountains—not streets, buildings, offices, or home interiors. In a March 16, 1978, letter to Lawrence Clark Powell, she says, "If you remain part of an environment long enough you become marked with the effect of that environment. The sun moving north in spring stirs something on your blood—in your body cells."[5] Even as an old woman, she reports in a 1985 *New Mexico Magazine* article that she still feels the "imprint" of the land "like rings that mark a tree's growth." "It's the land itself," she says, "that wants to be said" (Shearer 23). In Church's poetry readers get a lasting record of the ageless Southwest.

So attached to the land is Church that when she looks at it, she really believes she is looking at herself. At times, she feels almost like the earth's Siamese twin:

> And then I lay, a sage-swept plain,
> Slanted to riverward again.
> > "Foretaste"

At times, she so closely identifies with the external world that she temporarily loses track of her boundaries:

> I am on the verge of changing
> into something bewilderingly not human,
> a page from the metamorphoses of Ovid. . . .
> > "May 9, 1977"

Or again:

> The world I moved through
> all day
> seemed as much inside me
> as it did all around.
> > "Among the Holy Stones"

At another time, after she and her companion "lay for a time on the sloping tip of the landmark" (a basalt dike in the poem "Basalt Dike with Petroglyphs"), "The tidal movements/ within the earth swept through us." Sometimes, the union to place is less physical, more cerebral or emotional. For example, "one afternoon on Point Lobos," Church and her companion, presumably her husband of fifty years, Fermor,

> . . . thought, for the space of an afternoon, with the
> thought of rocks. The deep heart of the earth,
> muffled and unhurried, sounded through us.
> "I Have Looked at the Earth"

The harmony she feels between herself and the external world is not merely a philosophy for Church but a way of life. It affects her perception of even the most mundane of activities. In "Autumn Dusk," for example, she drives along a highway in the fall. The yellow of the turning foliage blends with the highway's painted "yellow margins" as the "motion of machinery," that is, the pistons of the car "hurrying" up and down, mimics the motion of the planet as it moves through the seasons. And, just as she sits in apparent motionlessness while her car speeds forward, so she imagines the earth's core "motionless" but really moving at the same speed as the planet. The image she employs to describe the earth's center could be used to describe her as she rides in the car: "speed quiescent at the heart of motion." She does not think of the car as a mechanical presence alienating her from the natural beauty of fall, nor does she seem to perceive any disjunction between human and non-human nature, the images of the one serving perfectly well as images for the other. The car, for example, of "Autumn Dusk" is described as "an arrow bearing our swiftness," while the swallows of "Enchanted Mesa" are described as "arrows from a tense bow."

The question to ask, however, is what does harmony with the earth mean? The phrase is usually employed as a catch phrase to suggest an author's love for the landscape, but with very little precise explanation offered. What does it mean for Church to feel this mystical identification with the earth?

First, when she sees the landscape or listens to the ocean's surf, she sees and hears time. The landforms attract her by their present beauty, of course, but in those forms she also sees the past, when the mesa was surrounded by a level plain. In "Morning on Tseregé," for example, she explores some ruins and discovers

> a wisdom of rocks and old trees, of buried rivers,
> of the great arcs and tangents of sky and mountain,
> and always the grass that whispered upon the ruins
> where a people had lived and fought, had died and
> had been forgotten.

The present she interprets as the culmination of all its history, as a tangible fact before her that is really a composite image, layered with its past and extending into history:

> Around the mountain,
> backward into a world behind time,
> landscape expanding like a dream,
> like rings that widen and vanish across water.
>   "Return to a Landscape"

The ripples of current events smooth out over time but never fully disappear from the landscape, which incorporates all time into its present.

Given her close personal identification with the land, we would expect her to understand her own psyche in similar terms, as a culmination of ages. Her present being is one terminus of all human history. While walking with her white dog one day, she says

> I could feel the primitive being
> who dreams in us all begin to stir within me,
> eyes, ears, skin-senses alter to
> the slope of landscape, the
> rustle of leaf and water, the
> mellow crisp of air.
> "On Seeing the Wild Geese"

She reminds us of Walt Whitman when he claims, in "Song of Myself" (section 44), "Immense have been the preparations for me." She contains her personal experiences, just as the land she sees now is defined in part by what she sees and hears happening on it at the moment, but both she and the land transcend the present moment. "Mountains," she says, "were part of me" ("Foretaste"). The stone she encounters on the beach one afternoon has lain there for "a day, a year, maybe a hundred years or more," and before that was part of a mountain ("how many millions ago"). She, too, has a history that stretches back into eternity:

> And where was I, I wonder—
> this little dot of consciousness called I
> that now after all these milleniums happens to stand
> by the sea and takes this particular stone in her
>   hand. . . .
> "Theme and Cogitations"

Her interaction with the landscape awakens her ancient self: "The sloping grasslands/waken ancient nomadic dreams"

("Return to a Landscape"). The land is both stimulus and image of what is ancient and valuable inside and outside herself.

The land also produces community, for all of us share its history and are implicated in its present: every human who has ever walked over this dust is part of the current dust; every animal that has climbed the mesa or walked the now-eroded plain that once stood next to the current mesa is part of that mesa's identity. The early inhabitants left something of their essence on the plateau: "The earth seemed alive with the human essence of those who had danced their prayers upon it" (*Otowi Bridge* 17). Similarly, the poet is not just Peggy Pond Church; she is all the human race, all its experiences and knowledge, condensed into one temporary human form. She feels this ancient time in her bones, just as she hears the ancient Indians' drums when staring across the empty plains. When she looks at the land, its vast openness suggests an eternity that incorporates temporal changes; when she looks into herself, she sees human history that transcends her brief time on earth. Therefore, when she looks at any feature of her beloved Southwest landscape, she sees herself and her ancient past as well as the land and its history. The land is to her an image of herself in all her depth and permanence. The desert whispers to her intimations of immortality. Her psyche echoes those whispers. Her poems are her attempts to unite in verse those inner and outer songs. In that act of uniting inner and outer, the poems become her constructed patterns that she hopes are in tune with the existing patterns of her psyche and the land. Her poems become landforms themselves, landforms of her psyche.

One of the best examples of this interweaving of external and internal, past and present, is the poem "Black Mesa: Dream and Variations." In the opening section of the six-section poem, Church tries to describe the mesa, so solid, yet so elusive, undoubtedly there, yet veiled this day in rain and clouds. The spectral image wakes some dream in the poet:

> The Black Mesa
> waked an old legend in us, tales of a black ship
> or a ship with black sails we could only half-
>   remember,
> an alien dream projected from a past world
> through our rapt eyes
> on the curtain of rain and darkness.

We may at first take this "alien dream" to be a simple memory of some old legend she has heard or a pleasant fantasy that fits the view the mesa presents today. As the remainder of the poem makes clear, however, the dream is the product of neither memory nor fancy but is, to Church's understanding, a fugitive image from her deepest self, a piece of her truest and oldest ground of being. The mesa has stirred a memory from her soul, not merely from her brain or imagination. When she hears Indians "dancing the Turtle Dance at San Ildefonso," the music, combined with the vision of the mesa, moves her deeply into herself:

> I slept in the labyrinth of myself.
> I went down through the vertical corridors of
>   heaped time
> with their indelible graffiti
> their coiled and unascended music
> down to the melt of the world and the unformed
>   crystal essence
> that would someday blossom and reflect light.

External stimuli inspire introspection, which conjures up internal images, which perfectly reflect the external world: the dark "crystal" at her heart corresponds to the mesa's dark form, the "graffiti" of her unconscious (all those "heaped" images of time beyond our individual life's years) reflect the Indians' petroglyphs (frequently mentioned in her poetry), and the "music" of her soul echoes the dancers' music.

The imagery of section three, a further description of the mesa, reinforces the connection between psyche and landform. The mesa is composed of "slow crystals," as she has a "crystal essence." The mesa, she tells us, is the "melt" of earth's "inwardness," as her soul is "the melt of the world." The poet, in her present bodily manifestation and in her ageless psychic depths, is truly a child of this place:

> I listened at the root of the Black Mesa
> like an attached child
> that hears only its own and its mother's heartbeat.

The internal mysteries Church discovers are also eternal, from the beginnings of "heaped time," so the mesa and Indian dancers are not only images of her inwardness but also of permanence. The mesa, the core of what was a plain, is an analog for what is eternal in her. However, while working with the fact that the mesa is what remained after its surroundings have been eroded, Church carefully goes beyond geology in her phrasing. The mesa is something sacred (the "Landmarked center of a universe, /terrestrial axis, /still body at the center of time's motion"), not just something old. The implication is that its internal image, her crystal essence, her soul, is also sacred, not merely antique.

Unlike a conventional image of sacrality, however, the mesa is dark, not light. Church emphasizes the color. The mesa is made of "cinders"; it is a "dark well"; it "seize[s]" and "devours light" rather than sheds light; its form produces "shadow" not illumination. Whatever it is down there in her psyche and out there in the world that corresponds to that internal mystery, it is dark. Her nature at first glance seems more akin to Hawthorne's than Emerson's, except that Church's dark landscapes are shrouded only in mystery, not in temptation, evil, or sin. The darkness is not a moral darkness; it does not conceal devils behind trees. Her darkness is an image of the whole of the world's light, condensed, as in a black hole, a locus of intense light so densely packed it appears dark:

> You are a lodestone,
> compact essence of extinct fire,
> a hand reaching
> out of earth's whirling depth to seize light
> and make yourself its darker habitation.

The light of the world compacted and held still is darkness. The dark mesa is neither enemy nor threat but, paradoxically, the repository of all light:

> The Black Mesa devours light
> like a collapsed star,
> drawing it down into the dark shaft
> from which her substance fountained.

And the poet's psychic core is also the dark place that contains light, the dark "womb" from which her life has "fountained."

Church is a Jungian by study and inclination, and the "womb," in psychological terms, is the Jungian collective unconscious that contains all that is necessary for life and light. Her apparent life is like the river that surrounds the mesa and "levels the land," "bearing our world away." She lives in this world of time and flux, but its aim is not hers: "The river's aim is only to flow onward;/the mesa's to remain." Her real self is the self corresponding to the mesa, the self that "keeps her fixed place," the hard-core sacred self that persists. That is what Church means by harmony with the earth.

How would one with Church's point of view understand the act of writing poetry? How would one so constituted approach the world in order to convert or transmute experience into utterance? Shelly Armitage asserts that Church had "the ability to see the poem as an act of relatedness rather than that of a lone ego" (*Church* 47). Church herself says something more metaphoric but similar in a 1972 journal entry: "A woman's work is not heroic but a weaving. The power to spin and weave, this is her alchemy."[6] This poet, then, approaches the world with respect, disinterest, and wonder. What precisely does that mean in the poetic process?

Before one can actually write a poem, one has to prepare oneself. The process for Church is almost religious, involving a series of ritualistic, mystical steps. First, she must put away her pride (and her eagerness to reach hasty conclusions that would enable her to capture and control the outside) and attune her rhythms to nature's. Many of Church's poems contain images of her lying down on rock, stopping her motion altogether to adjust her vision to the apparently immobile landscape around her. "Little Sermon in Stone" begins by describing a small hill in ambivalent terms. Some descriptors suggest infertility ("hard as stone," "earth's very cinder patch," "fist-big stones"), while some suggest fertility ("breast round," "dark red stones like blood"). Finally, she decides to slow down to the hill's pace, attune her heart to nature's time, and let the hill speak for itself:

> But we stayed there one winter afternoon
> hushing our man-proud thought, and stilled
>   our hearts
> to the slow beat of time's heart in a stone.

The result is a confusion of observer and observed or a breaking down of boundaries assumed to exist between inside and outside.

Once attuned and opened, the potential poet can hear the world's calls that had previously gone unheard. She develops new senses, poet's senses, that allow her to hear "beyond . . . mortal sense" ("Sandhill Cranes in February") and detect not only today's wind but the lingering notes of an ancient flute player whose tones once echoed among the rocks:

> Was it the wind we heard
> or the hump-backed flute player
> among the hidden rocks?
>   "Balsalt Dike with Petroglyphs"

In "She Will Want Nothing but Stones," she lies down one afternoon "among the slanting rays of winter" as the sandhill cranes fly over: "their cries fell/in a shower of shaken petals." She becomes a modern Danæ, bathed in the golden shower of the world ("caught in a golden vase of autumn"), refreshing herself in the world's beneficence.

This beneficence that one transmutes into poetic gold after slowing down from human time to world time is showered upon one; one does not wring it out of the world. Whatever the poetic process means to Church, it does not mean conquest or self-assertion. The land, the prime inspiration for and subject of her poetry, is not something to be conquered, fenced, possessed, or mastered either for the sake of creating shopping malls or poems. She consciously and consistently describes her creative process as one of cooperation with her subject (the earth), a cooperation she often contrasts with more aggressive, purposive, and, in her poetry, male activities. When, for example, in "Enchanted Mesa" she struggles to reach the top of the mesa, an activity that begs to be rendered as a victory of human over nature, she refuses the opportunity to celebrate her triumph. In fact, after proceeding "hand over hand" through the "slow talus" to the mesa's summit, she proclaims the mesa itself the victor: "But the bright edge/finally triumphs." She congratulates the mesa as her fellow climber, not her adversary. And while on top, she is, she realizes, held aloft by the very mesa against which she has struggled, an irony she appreciates and celebrates:

> . . . Only the strong
> skeletal firmness of earth holds
> sky on its shoulders.
>
> Holds us also
> that which we strove against
> in climbing.

Church abandons dreams of conquering nature's wildness because she understands wildness as the beauty that nourishes those who learn to abandon their need to control and as the source of much of her work. One night in the mountains, she sees "the beautiful horses,/shaking the moonlight from their flanks like water," as they dance on the ground's light covering of snow ("Horses in the Moonlight"). Her male companions miss the spectacle not simply because they sleep (and will not waken when she attempts to rouse them), but because they are not ready to see the moonlit world of beauty and miracle and would have been more frightened than gratified had they been present. The poet understands:

> Sleep and do not look on this strange scene, my lords
>   and masters,
> lest you feel them clearing the careful fences of your
>   own minds,
> possessing your unaccustomed hearts in breathtaking
>   beauty,
> and a wildness your hand cannot tame
> and a strength your knees can never master.

"Fences" is metaphorical, of course, suggesting the self-imposed mental and spiritual limitations to which the "masters" have accustomed themselves, and it is ironic, suggesting that the masters are those most closely fenced. The word also suggests the literal fences with which others demarcate the land into parcels of possession—their "poems"—the manifestation of an attitude antithetical to Church's, an attitude suggesting that the earth is an object best used or understood when confined. This is the attitude that sees value in a plat of land rather than a spread of land and that can therefore only see what is contained within the fences' limits. All inside the fence is beautiful; all outside is invisible. Such a world is small but safe. It is possessed and controlled. Better with that attitude, Church says, to stay asleep, to remain unaware of the wonders that will not fit into one's garden plot of a consciousness. "Lords and masters" becomes increasingly ironic as the poem proceeds: the men who sleep may think they rule her, the land, and the horses, but they are not even equipped to see the earth over which they claim to have dominion. They are better off with their dreams of domesticated land than the reality of wild nature.

The poet's world is consciously imaged, as a female world not tainted by the traditional male attitudes of hierarchy and control, and as a world larger and more beautiful because of the absence of those attitudes. The horses' vitality is celebrated for itself rather than valued because it is a freedom that the men can tame with their strength and thereby gain power from vicariously. Church recognizes that her attitude is not the dominant American response to the land in her time: "To the men of the age the land exists only to be exploited. They are 'captains of industry,' and farming has become an industry."[7] But Church does not so much associate the aggressive, acquisitive attitude with men exclusively as with what we may call the male principle in humans of either gender. While she can say "The attitude of man toward nature has been to possess it, to exploit it, to own it,"[8] she can also praise in Diego Rivera's work the "tenderness, compassion, surrender—all the feminine qualities so sternly missing from the American character. . . ."[9] And she can refer to "the exploitive side of the masculine in Mary's [Austin] own psyche which is the enemy of the land-loving husbandman within her."[10] Therefore, Church identifies the attitude as masculine but does not necessarily identify it as existing solely in males. Wherever such an exploitive relationship to the land exists, however, in whatever person, it produces no poems, in Church's understanding of the process. Art comes from love, as she makes clear in a 1968 meditation upon Mary Austin, the subject of Church's biography, *Wind's Trail: The Early Years of Mary Austin*:

> The poet's eye and ear, the lover of beauty, of the strange inhuman beauty of the landscape, the movement and color of it, the passage of its seasons, the movements of birds and small creatures. [Mary Austin], on one side of her nature, was as wedded to the land as her husband undoubtedly was. This was her woman side, her feeling side, the artist in her.[11]

Love of the land is a prerequisite of art, or at least of art that Church appreciates, and the "feeling side" of a human—male or female—she associates with the feminine in the psyche. Austin's husband apparently had more "female" within him than his wife, and hence he could allow himself to acknowledge his love for the landscape, which, in Church's opinion, Mary Austin only occasionally could do. When she does, as in *The Land of Little Rain,* the result is art.

"Blue Heron" can be read as a parable for Church's poetic method that results from her aesthetic philosophy. She describes her fortuitous observation of a heron fishing. She did not seek the bird but simply came upon it as she was driving: "I, driving around a bend in the road, and the world still in shadow,/with my own eyes suddenly saw the blue heron fishing." The world occasionally presents itself to us, as the cranes rained their music on her in "She Will Want Nothing but Stones," but we must be open, patient, and then attentive.

Church is all those; hence what she sees, as she watches the
heron "immobile as though he had been rooted there forever/
among the willows, long legs stretched and limber," is a picture
of what her poetic process is and is not:

> Not moving, nor pursuing, but waiting in the stillness,
> in the calm of the morning before the voices of
>   children
> shattered the air like glass, and men were driven
> against time and none could remember the blue
>   heron fishing.

The poet has to be patient and wait for these luminous
and numinous moments, able to arise early before the distractions of her domestic duties ("the voices of children") and able
to resist the impulse, once awake, to "drive" herself, in masculine fashion, to force the world to relinquish its treasures.
Although literally driving a car, she is not "driven" as her male
acquaintances are and will not pursue beauty as a conqueror
but will instead find beauty by patient observation. The heron
is outside the range of vision of busy, practical people who have
defined the world in such a way as to be able to see only those
phenomena that fit inside the fences constructed by that vision,
which is really a habit of being in the world of those who drive
themselves and who imagine the world as a place to be plun-
dered. To see earth's treasures, one must "walk quietly and
brush snow-cover from juniper," as Church and her companion
do in "Ground Juniper." Their reward is an image of their own
vitality, the "strangest and loveliest of evergreens,/semi-sepul-
chered beneath snowfall," the ground juniper, a reminder in
winter of the earth's fecundity:

. . . winter-imprisoned
upon earth's sleeping heart, green and undying
witness of life and summer.

By taking what comes its way, by nourishing itself on the melt from other trees' snowy limbs, the rare juniper stays alive on little and remains beautiful despite the harsh conditions in which it must live.

It is precisely the small beauty in the world, the beauty at one's feet, that provides the most intense pleasure for Church the poet. Imagining Prometheus chained to the rocks among the Truchas Peaks of northern New Mexico, Church knows the mythical being could have learned to ignore the view of the distant summits, despite their beauty, and could have learned to "endure all utter loneliness,/All silence and all longing for the world," but could never have recovered from the "pity of the flower/Blue as forget-me-nots, beneath his feet" ("The Truchas Peaks"). The flowers' small patch of beauty may seem to some pitifully insignificant next to the grandeur of their mountain host, but the poet understands that in just such small ways the world reminds us of its glory and holds us chained to its side. For Church, therefore, art is more than a process undertaken to create a timeless artifact. It is a necessary result of loving the world, and it is a way of life learned from, and most effectively practiced in harmony with, the rhythms of the beautiful things she sees around her. Our "mortal sense," our earthbound ears and other faculties, may tell us we are separate from the cranes, the basalt dikes, and the lichens of the world, but our hearts and souls ("We lay while our hearts listened") tell us we are participants in the "seasonal world," well within the "circled" and "centered" life of the planet. The world that looks so barren is

alive and numinous: all we need to do is listen well, with whatever it is in us that owes allegiance to eternity:

> This moon-white stone
> was inscribed along its brow with a cryptic writing
> like a musical notation,
> a message that seemed to speak, not to our learning
> but to a wisdom in us like the stone's
> that we read without knowing how to read.
>   "An Afternoon among Stones"

Church's vision always moves toward harmony, inclusion,
and a denial of boundaries creating alienation or separateness:
the human and the non-human, the holy and the mundane, the
past and the present flow into each other until "each other"
becomes a term of convenience rather than a description of any
real difference between one and the other. While flying kites,
for example, with a "medley of children" in "The Kites and the
Petroglyphs," she first feels a bit out of place for she knows that
today's kite field has been a ceremonial area where "Ancient
holy beings were glyphed onto the smooth rock." But then she
realizes that the glyphs of ancient sky beings and the children's
kites celebrate the same mystery of sky, air, and life. The modern kites are in their own way glyphs sent aloft in honor of life
(much as the sandhill cranes are flying petroglyphs), "a little
festival of stringed kites" that Kokopelli, the ancient spirit of
the place, would have enjoyed and laughed at.

If the stones contain angels, and we are admonished to listen to their message with the wisdom in us that is like a stone's,
then the clear implication is that we, too, contain angels. Therefore, we can talk back as well as listen, and that talking back is
poetry. "Little Sermon in Stone" illustrates the process. By getting

low and looking for truth on the ground rather than in the sky
("We lay upon the ground and felt the stone . . ."), by using all
the senses and then some to allow the imagination into rocks
and backwards into time (". . . and saw them with our hands;
and with our eyes tuned to chill/light's minute and fragile pulse/
gazed deep into the structure of the stone"), the human will see
what has been missed, will see, in this place seemingly "infer-
tile, inhospitable to life" "the stain of life upon the stones./ The
creeping lichens, live and unafraid. . . ." That vision becomes
the image of the act of creativity out of which poetry is created:

> The colored lichens take the world apart
> in their slow fingers. The bright mold of life
> moves like a web upon the unliving rock
> and seeks the imprisoned light and sets it free
> to live again in seed and stem and flower.

The poet, like the lichens, lets her imagination grow into
the apparently "unliving" world, working its way deep beneath
the surface, and there discovers not only life but the source of
life, light. As the lichens release "imprisoned light" and trans-
form it into life, so the poet releases gently and slowly (no pick
axes or dynamite images here) the light of the world and "sets it
free" as poetry. "Little Sermon in Stone" is a beautiful portrait
of poet as force of nature, as soldier of time, or, more appropriately, as lover of time, the slow courter who faithfully pursues
her intended's light, knowing it must exist somewhere, and then
releases it into the world. The vision is mutually life-sustaining:

> The winter birds
> pause and are fed. We too were fed
> through mind and heart upon stone's element.

The poet is the reverencer of earth, who observes with faith and love and who then creates a memorial in verse, the poem itself, to that constancy. The title ("Little Sermon in Stone") refers both to the poem and the landform that inspires the poem. That is as Church would have it: one phrase to describe the poet, the object of her love, and the product of that love. Elsewhere ("Basalt Dike with Petroglyphs") she describes the "Prayers" that "had been imprinted/long ago on these silent stones." Her poems are the releasing of those prayers, the act of praying, and the prayers themselves, all connected by imagery to the petroglyphs of ancient residents, the shadows of cranes, and the stains of lichens on the crumbling rocks.

The terms Church employs to describe nurturing relationships with other humans—terms of cooperation, complementariness, harmony, respect, and restraint—are precisely the terms she employs to describe her relationship to earth. This is as it should be, of course, for if she truly understands herself and other humans as intimately related to their land and the earth, then she is forced, logically, to attend to humans on the same terms with which she attends to plants, animals, and landforms. But logic often fails when dealing with our fellow humans, and Church shows us the conflicts we allow ourselves to fall into when dealing with other humans before showing us the true harmony that underlies all tensions.

Perhaps the most obvious place to look in a poet's work for illustrations of human relationships gone wrong is in those poems dedicated to depicting the marriage union. In several poems Church describes the plight of women tamed by domestic duties. The wildness the women once enjoyed, or perhaps only felt the subtlest hints of, they have given up to become wives. Armitage notes Church's lifelong awareness of "the disjunctive position between what society expected of a woman of her generation and her own creative and personal desires" (*Church* 46). In "Do Not Feel Sure," the poet warns the husband that his wife, apparently tame, has a wild streak in her, and that his security in her domesticity may be misplaced:

> Do not feel sure that she will be long contented
> In this house you have built for her.
> . . . . . .
> She was made to dwell
> Upon a stern dark edge of wilderness.
> . . . . . .
> How do I know?
> Well, I've known wild things bred a hundred years
> Till they forget the look of winter moons. . . .

The suggestion is that the wild wife may one day remember her wildness, which Church constructs as a refusal to conform to domestic expectations or to the female role as stereotypically understood, and the husband may find himself sleeping alone. These memories of "wildness" Church imagines are stimulated and stirred as the characters look outside, through windows or doors, to nature beyond the domestic threshold: "But the first, familiar shadow will waken her,/Or the first faint flicker of a star-sent cry. . . ." Memory, awakened by contact with the external, reinvigorates the women and makes them like the wild nature that inspires them: "She will make flight too swift for you to follow/Like a fear-fleet deer, or a wild, wind-driven swallow." Church the poet releases the women's wildness by linking them poetically, through metaphors, to the wild nature that they have temporarily lost or strayed from.

The sonnet "Bridal" also finds a restless and "wakeful" woman, metaphorically slumbering in her domestic duties, who has her wild side awakened by the "rustling feet soft-furred" and the "shadows of splashing leaves" that reside "beyond the door." As her husband sleeps, she listens to a "star-awakened bird" with whose freedom she identifies. We watch the bride perched on the edge of flight, imagining herself running, "moon-white, far up the fragrant lane/Of heavy-flowering trees," a magical, empowered being. Armitage observes, however, that when the woman in the poem "relinquish[es] . . . her personal freedom to marriage" she also loses "her magical stature" (*Church* 14). Soon her husband stirs and stretches "his arm beneath her head," and she is again trapped on this side of the door. The "slow wind rippled moonlight on the floor," and that was enough for the receptive woman to dream of liberation. The call of fulfillment comes to Church's women unbidden, with the powerful pull of an instinct, like a blood memory or an inheritance. The poet herself remembers something similar as she recalls her eastern pioneer relatives in "After Looking into a Genealogy." Her grandmothers were "beautiful," even though now they seem unremembered: "From granite stones the wind has wiped your names." Their "blood," however, lives in the poet, and, despite the fact that Church resides in the Southwest, the land outside her door continues to conjure memories, blood memories, of her grandmothers' lives, of "covered bridges over Vermont rivers." Church relates the strange sensation of looking at "a clearing in mountain country" and thinking, "One could build a house here./That slope would make a pasture." The grandmothers' strong, pioneering blood "leaps" through her veins, providing "I, the desert-born," with deep memories "of New England growing/Among New Mexico mountains." She listens carefully to her blood as it "stirs with [their] voices." These are the stirrings, leapings, and voices Church bequeaths to her female characters, the calls of the wild that she articulates for those mute domestics she draws.

In other poems, the "wildness" is more closely linked to a woman's imagination or creativity, which her husband cannot or will not understand. The woman in "Shadow-Madness," it is rumored, lives more in shadows than reality. She enriches her life by encouraging her imagination to work on the details of her dull domestic routine:

> In her room
> She tempted shadows with smooth surfaces,
> Loving the way the shapes of common things
> Bent into strangeness. Even orchard bloom
> Was only sweet when on her wall the moon
> Painted the silver image.

A harmless enough act of imagination, it seems, but her husband cannot reflect her creativity back to her. "He was not to blame," he simply "could not grasp intangibility," Church says. Hence, the woman's body remains imprisoned next to his, "but her thoughts became/Fleeting as images of blowing leaves/ Wind-blurred on water." That which is best in the characters, their wildness or their creativity, both really the same thing, is released upon metaphors from the outside world, figures of speech linking the women to the welcoming outside. Church's metaphors and images are not mere figures of speech. They reflect the deep understanding of nature that is part of Church's blood and that comes to her pen when she thinks of women trapped in relationships that deny part of their potential or humanity. Always nature accepts us. Nature is our nurturer, in sharp contrast to the way other humans too often treat us. Always nature gives us what we need.

It is not just that women struggle to overcome the conflict between their creative, "wild" side and their domestic, "safe" side, but that such a struggle is a violation of what Church understands as the ideal relationship, the mutually beneficial pairing that produces completeness in each partner and that ensures complete expression of each participant's soul. The proper relationship between two people is analogous to the proper relationship between people and their environment, a relationship in which each side benefits, both sides are respected, both are encouraged to exist in their wholeness rather than sacrifice parts of themselves to satisfy the other's needs. You cannot close the door on your wild side and expect to live happily ever after any more than you can plow and mine and log all the wilderness around you and expect to continue to live in a healthy, sustaining environment. Neither woman nor nature can live for long as a submissive member in a relationship with a dominant other. The goal is to release all that is present in the other, not to restrain or channel the other's potential. The poems indict men who dominate or deny their wives' inner selves, but they do not suggest that love is impossible, any more than Church suggests humans should stay out of forests or deserts. She shows us, however, that when you enter a landscape to control it or tame it, just as when you enter a marriage or relationship to control or tame the other, you guarantee the dissolution of that relationship. The battle is not, or should not be, one against the other, but two together in the interest of maintaining each other's wholeness. People should "see, with wonder on their lips,"

with eyes tear-cleansed and opened wide,
that struggle, each for his own soul,
was struggle side by side!
          "Whom God Hath Joined"

The poem is not Church's best because it relies so heavily on bald statement while her best poems transmute ideas into poetry through local imagery.[12] Even so, the statements are useful because they phrase in unambiguous terms the poet's conception of human relationships: they are battles fought side by side for both partners' wholeness. The identity and integrity of both man and woman have to be respected before the other, the intruder or the potential partner, can achieve a victory, and that victory can only be won with the full participation of the other as a cooperative effort, not against the other:

Or will your hands and his together hold the rainbow
the bridge between you, neither crossing over,
neither creating the other in his own image,
content to be to each other the bow and the
    bowstring
that speed to their unknown mark the future's
    arrows?
          "Prothalamium for Barbara"

Bow and bowstring require each other and fulfill each other. This is the image Church gives us of a life-sustaining relationship between two humans and between humans and their physical geography.

When the proper relationship is struck, it not only unites the people one to each other, but it also unites them as a couple to the world around. "On a Morning" is a beautiful poem about

mutual love in which the loved ones become indistinguishable
from each other and from the morning in which they love:

> On a morning
> when the mountains were walls of fire
> and the clouds like
> curled smoke,
> the blossoms of many trees were
> flames of another color.
> I stood with you
> breast to breast,
> pressed to you in an embrace without pressure,
> your mouth upon my mouth,
> out of us both, out of both our hearts a flame springing,
> separately rooted,
> arching over us,
> merging into one flame
> streaming upward,
> absorbing quietly
> the fire of the mountains,
> mingling with itself
> the burning blossoms.

The world presents a passionate face to the lovers ("fire,"
"smoke," "flames") whose passion unites them to each other
and then to the world. The three exist in a harmonious, mutually fulfilling relationship. The two humans "embrace without
pressure" and are "separately rooted." Neither forces his or her
self on the other, which allows both to blossom into flame
independently but as one loving unit whose two flames
"merge" into one and into the world. Everything present
retains its individual integrity while working together to make a

greater brilliance than any one (world, man, or woman) could make alone. The imagery—morning, blossoms, flames—suggests hope, beginnings, passion, and permanence (for blossoms in Church's poetry always foretell their own return). "Your mouth upon my mouth" is of course a kiss, but it is also the exchange of life's vital breath, their love enabling their lives. When done properly, relationships are mutually stimulating and tie one to the other as well as to the world in which one and the other reside. A relationship of this nature reminds one, or shows one, that one is not separate from the world, not alienated from it, but a part of a universe-sized, reciprocally fertilizing system of complementary beings.

The natural result of such an insight is joy that manifests itself in a desire to create beauty. "And Then There Was Light" describes the poet's luck one night at finding fresh snow for skiing. She and her companion emerge symbolically from a "maelstrom of black darkness" onto a summit of smooth snow and "white night." Some trouble has passed and the poet feels herself one again with the companion and the night ("I and the stars singing the same song"). Joy becomes creativity as she skis down the hill,

> cleaving moonlight,
> cleaving the still air,
> tracing the pattern of flight upon the smooth snow,
> over the arc of the white hill.

The poem she writes in the snow is her fitting result of this lovely night and her love for her companion. It is written "out of the joy in my heart," it destroys nothing, it adds beauty to the world, it commemorates without dominating or imposing. It is an embrace of rather than an imposition on the world.

The interdependence we share with the world and other humans, who are part of the world too, is overlooked at times, but comes rushing back in luminous moments on top of the mountain in the still night, near the stars, and in love. Fulfillment is a matter of being wholly oneself and recognizing oneself as part of another and then as part of an entire universe. One need not fear the transaction, because joining the other as one of two complete beings, neither seeking from the other what he or she does not have inside, enables one to return whole to oneself:

> A dog barked
> and shattered the chrysalis of silence.
> I came out of my dream
> and found the stars had moved
> only a handsbreadth down the indefinite arc
> of heaven.
> You and I were two people again
> contained in two bodies. . . .
>   "Shattered"

Establishing a mutual relationship with another human being, in Church's system, is part of the process of returning ourselves to ourselves, of making us whole inside. Church's thinking in this is influenced by her reading of Carl Jung, especially Jung's idea that we each enter life with vague intimations of a time when we, or when our ancestors, were psychically integrated beings, male and female selves living together comfortably within one skin, not like the iceberg beings we are now, great portions of our psyches buried in the cold depths of our unconscious, waiting their chance to emerge. In his commentary on *The Secret of the Golden Flower: A Chinese Book of Life*, a book Church and her husband read together (*Church* 29), Jung postulates that, initially, humans enjoyed a "unity of life and consciousness" (*Church* 103). In time, however, due to the tendency toward "dissociation . . . inherent in the human psyche, parts . . . split off" (111), creating "complicated fragmentary psychic systems" (110). "The unity once possessed has been lost, and must now be found again" (103). Our life, from this perspective, is an attempt to recapture psychological wholeness from a source deep in our collective unconscious that was once the human condition and is still our human potential. The search for our lost unity takes the form of a search for the ideal mate, the real-world fit for what Jung calls our "soul mate," the other who will complement our narrow psyche and make it whole. We are then like the androgynes, those half-male, half-female beings described by Aristophanes in Plato's *Symposium:* "Each of us . . . a token of a human being, because we are sliced like fillets of sole" (252), each of us seeking our other, complementing half. As C. A. Meier, one of Jung's clearest interpreters, put it, "Man expects and hopes to unite again with the opposite sex, and in such a way as to gain original totality," to create in our life a living image of "the male/female divine couple" (*Soul and Body: Essays on the Theories of C. G. Jung* 83).

Meier reminds us of the long life and importance of this image of a divine couple, called by Jung *syzygy*:

> There are the famous constituents of Chinese, and in particular Taoistic philosophy, the Yang and the Yin, the bright and the dark, the masculine and the feminine. In the Tantric system in India there is the eternal couple of Shiva and Shakti living in eternal embrace, and there is

the gnostic idea of Noμf (Nous) [mind] and Σοφί∂ (Sophia) [wisdom]. In the Christian religion, there is Christ and the bridal church. In the medieval period, the motif of *syzygy* was taken up particularly by alchemistic mythology, where *sol* and *luna,* or *rex* and *regina,* play exactly the same roles (*Soul* 87).

The image of a union of male and female energies is present in many cultures and many eras, suggesting a persistent human desire for internal harmony reflected in and achieved by an external relation with a member of the opposite, complementing sex. The importance of such a relation goes well beyond its role as a social arrangement or a union of two people in love. The male-female relationship of the sort discussed here not only completes the individual's quest for psychic wholeness, but that wholeness mirrors and reinforces the individual's harmonious relationship to the earth, and also provides a basis from which to perceive that harmony with the cosmos.

Church worked out the process by which our fragmented souls are made whole in her sonnet sequence *The Ripened Fields: Fifteen Sonnets of a Marriage,* the narrative of her fifty-year marriage to Fermor Church, whom she married in 1924 when Fermor was an instructor at the Los Alamos (New Mexico) Ranch School, the boys' school founded by Ashley Pond, Peggy's father. The middle sonnet in the sequence describes the human condition of duality into which each of us is born. Here are the opening quatrains of "Sonnet VIII":

> Once I was seed within my mother's womb
> and was at peace, unwakened, unaware
> until life's seminal arrow cleft that tomb

and split me from myself. So now I bear
the difficult pattern of duality
within my blood, my bone, and cry and strive
against the mute, the stern polarity
that while it rends, yet makes all life alive.

Any human life begins with duality. The female "seed" is split by the male "arrow." What was once single is now double, and the doubleness is a combination of male and female. Being brought to life by the fertilizing presence of the other is an abrupt wrenching from peace, but the value of the peace of the womb is undercut here with the womb/tomb rhyme. To be single (in an undifferentiated and unfertilized state) is, in this poem's imagery, to be at peace yet dead. There is the rub: one must leave this original state of bliss, this "unity of life and consciousness," in order to live, and then life becomes a process of searching for a way to return to unity while remaining among the living. Being born is the prototype event for being married: moving from singularity to duality, from peace to conflict, and, by implication, from "tomb" to "life." Whatever problems arise in a relationship between two people began in the womb. The image of the arrow suggests the violence of the confrontation between the two, fertilizing elements. This is the arrow that pierces calm, amniotic sleep and makes us die as unity only to be born as painful duality. The fact that Cupid is associated with arrows is not accidental or incidental to Church's poem.

The poem's conclusion builds on the opening quatrains:

So I have struggled with you endlessly
in outward semblance of the inner war
between the yes and no, the he, the she,

in my own elements. My secret core
opposes yours, and yet within your soul
I seek my severed self to be made whole.

The "he" and the "she" who combined to form infant
Church do not, in this imagery, eventually blend into one
strictly female person. She continues dual, part male, part
female, all her days. The "pattern of duality" refers, then, to her
persistent, not just her initial, androgyny. This "pattern" is
"within my blood, my bone" and, while it may be an identity
one forgets or denies, is not something one ever gets over or
grows out of. "War" contrasts with "peace" of the opening lines
and hence, as peace is associated with the death of the
womb/tomb, by extension war is life, or life is war. If the "inner
war" is inevitable, then the outward war is something one must
live with, or it is what one must have in order to live.

The visible war mimics the inner war and is the result of
that internal conflict, is necessary to life, or to her life, which
explains the lengths she goes to in order to maintain her marriage. Church's rhyming of "war" and "core" suggests as much:
the war is at our core; our core is a war. Any external manifestation (such as marriage) of that internal war will have the same
dual identity; it will be a life-sustaining battle. "The he, the she"
are linked within her, are linked outside of her in her external
relations through her union with her husband, and are linked in
the poem by the absence of any conjunctions to separate them.
Her "severed self," a clear echo of Aristophanes and Jung, is
"within" her husband's "soul" in the sense that he, too, is composed of "the he, the she," and therefore complements her dual
nature. He is dual yet single; she is dual yet single; together
they form a dual yet single being, the married couple.

The couple can only be a true couple, a mutually nurturing pair, if each member possesses the self-knowledge necessary to enter into such a mature relationship. But self-awareness is dangerous and requires a plunge into psychic depths to retrieve the lost or repressed portions of self. In that dive, described in Sonnet VII, Church encounters a dragon in her soul:

> The dragon in the soul is not a dream,
> nor an old fairy tale outgrown with time,
> no archaic reptile drowsing by a stream
> whose fossil footprint is safe-grooved in lime.
> The dragon is the thief that murders love
> to satiate itself. . . .

The image of the submerged serpent is an image of the fear that has to be overcome before we can recover the healing wealth from the depths of our own psyche. "The serpent in the cave," Jung tells us in "Lecture Four" of the Tavistock Lectures, delivered in London at the Institute of Medical Psychology (the Tavistock Clinic) in 1935, is an image from antiquity that "aroused fear and represented danger, but also signified healing" (*Analytical Psychology: Its Theory and Practice* 130). That is why "Asklepios, the god of physicians, is connected with the serpent" (*Analytical Psychology* 130). We must face the dragon of our fear and lack of faith before we can heal ourselves and release "the broken dove," the symbol of love. Church's dragon guards the secrets that will allow her to love.

What are the secrets? "The cave or underworld," Jung proposes, "represents a layer of the unconscious where there is no discrimination at all, not even a distinction between the male and the female" (*Analytical Psychology* 132). Hence, the image in the unconscious' "cave" that is to be recovered before healing and loving can take place is the image of the "male and the female principle which form the union of opposites," the image of "the primordial condition of things," "a most ideal achievement, because it is the union of elements eternally opposed" (*Analytical Psychology* 133). The image salvaged is an image of harmony, of Tao, the "ideal condition," the "complete harmony between heaven and earth" (*Analytical Psychology* 133). This is "the condition to be achieved by the attitude of superior wisdom" (*Analytical Psychology* 133). For Jung, then, and for Church, "The descent into the depths will bring healing. It is the way to the total being, to the treasure which suffering mankind is forever seeking, which is hidden in the place guarded by terrible danger" (*Analytical Psychology* 137). Dive into the dark cave of one's unconscious, there confront one's fear and pride, rescue from the dragon one's treasure—that is, the knowledge of oneself as a union of opposed elements, a union of all things contradictory but therefore vital to life—and then emerge strengthened and able to proffer and receive love, having loved oneself enough to gather both hard and soft, male and female, dark and bright of one's soul to oneself. This makes one whole, and, as Jung reminds us, "The meaning of 'whole' or 'wholeness' is to make holy or to heal" (*Analytical Psychology* 137). Thus whole and healed within herself, united with her primordial, androgynous core, she can achieve wholeness without and can heal her marriage.

Thus whole within herself, the poet can move toward the other and understand the true nature of love, a theme she articulates in "Sonnet XII," which begins, "To love. To know. Are these two then the same?" Loving, she decides, is knowing, the effort of the will that penetrates but does not possess, the act of humble submission before the unknown that does not imply subservience. As she phrases it:

> The effort of the heart, the mind, the will
> seeking to penetrate, not to consume. To name.
> To recognize. To touch. To fill
> oneself with knowing as the sea with light
> beneath the break of day. To know. To love.

Knowing is nominated as a synonym for loving because it suggests active embracing of the known phenomenon's complexity and duality: "To know. To love./To take into the heart the dark, the bright." Knowing is also suggested as a synonym for loving because it implies a complementary, mutually fulfilling relationship between the known and the knower:

> To love as we should love a star, a stone,
> not for our greed of light nor hope for bread
> but for the star's blind need of eyes, the tone
> of words within the rock none yet has said.

To have without consuming ("To drink the contents and yet be the cup"); to acknowledge the complexity of the other; to take as a means of satisfying one's own needs and as a means of satisfying the needs of the other; to need yet not to grasp out of need: this, Church now believes, is true loving and true knowing. If loving is knowing and knowing is loving, then that which we know we love. Hatred, strife, contention, evil are defined as negative forces, as absences of love and knowledge, as ignorance.

Church's vision allows her to see that love is not a matter pertaining merely to herself (her self-knowledge) or to her marriage (her understanding of Fermor). Rather, she says, again in "Sonnet XIII," she will be "toward *all things* the eyes, the voice"—understanding herself and her love has brought her to an attachment for "all things." Marriage to Fermor becomes marriage to the world, a love of "all things" based on knowledge of those "things." Or, as she says to begin "Sonnet XIV":

> Love is not gazing in another's eyes,
> finding another fair, nor being found,
> not tenderness to hush another's cries,
> nor strength that lifts one, fallen, from the ground.

Love is not simply one person understanding herself nor the union of two people looking at each other. Love is both personal and impersonal, two people together establishing a point of reference from which to view the universe: "Love is two faces set toward one star/that two who see may mark as their own north." Love positions one not just with respect to another, the object of romantic love, but with respect to the world, all the stars of the cosmos, all the "dark" and all the "bright" of the universe. Love is "two threads" weaving together a world ("a fabric") that contains both paradise ("the Bird of Paradise") and loss of paradise ("the ancient disobedience of Eve"). Love is a complex union of opposites which are really harmonized and whose union marries both to the world: "It is the tree that marries earth to sky/created of her dust, his blazing eye."

Love, then, as Plato knew, connects the human to the divine in the only manner possible for humans. The tree is the tree of Life, mentioned in this sonnet, but is also the Tree of

Knowledge, that symbol of humanity's hubris and fall and also our salvation, because knowing means loving which means being connected to the world and the heavens in the only way possible for fallen mortals. "The serpent twined between the Man, the Wife" makes us recall the dragon of "Sonnet VII," also associated with knowledge and self-awareness. Loving is a way of life one establishes by first recognizing oneself nakedly, which enables one to know the other, which initiates one into a loving relationship with the world.

What would a poet like Church make of death and her relationship to the natural world? And even if we think we know that she will approach death confidently, we have to question how sanguine one can truly be, no matter what one's philosophy, when facing one's own mortality.

Despite her love for and identification with the land, Church remains a dualist. She believes her perishable body and her eternal soul are separate entities, and she leaves no doubt to which she owes her first allegiance: looking through her bodily eyes, she says in one poem, is like looking through "prison bars." One problem with the dualistic position is that it can, in the wrong hands, become a position that elevates humanity above nature, a position that privileges the human, internal, spiritual, and subjective over the non-human, external, physical and objective. Scholar Glenn A. Love points to the problem when he claims that "the definitive pattern in American nature writing" is exemplified by Thoreau's passage on fishing in "The Ponds," from *Walden*: "The direct experience with nature, the fishing in this case, serves primarily as the raw material for the narrator's leap into subjectivity, a radical inward-turning, wherein the dreamfish in his head quickly assumes precedence over the real ones in the pond" (*ILSE* 3). Love goes on to connect his observation to that of critic Sherman Paul when Paul says that most American nature writing "doesn't challenge dualism so much as exploit it by giving the mind sovereign play" (*ILSE* 68).[13] Church, however, does not succumb to the temptation to use the earth as her imagination's plaything, nor does she think of non-human nature as merely physical. She is convinced, as Shelly Armitage says, "that wisdom [can] produce harmony rather than separateness or conflict" (*Church* 47) and that the entire world is endowed with spirituality. She and the earth are separate entities ("I am I and earth is earth"), but she is convinced that "the essence of the earth flows into me" (*Otowi Bridge* 69). Only upon our first encounter with her perspective does it sound self-contradictory: she speaks of her body as a "prison" she hopes to transcend or "escape" some day, and simultaneously imagines her imperishable soul residing in the land after her death. Church distinguishes her body, however, as one temporary form of physical reality from the earth, the collection and final resting place of all such forms. She knows that the separate landforms, mesas as well as mountains, like her body, are perishable, but she thinks of the great earth, the whole of all physical forms, as an imperishable entity, as close to an eternal thing as we are ever likely to encounter. Transcendence to her means leaving her body to join the earth. Keats and his poetic heirs feared that being "human and mortal" means being forever alienated from the earth, a typical dualistic position, unless one is content to become a "sod." Church clearly disagrees about the inevitability of alienation, but even if she were in agreement on that point, she still would not mind becoming a "sod." In fact, that is her hope:

When we are dead we know this one thing will become
    of us:
We will go into the ground; our bodies will surely
    crumble and feed tree-roots, or blow as dust on the
    wind or be rain-washed at last into the ocean.
        "I Have Looked at the Earth"

She holds the same hope for everyone. "For a Mountain Burial" describes the dispersal of a friend's ashes "under the low-bending branch of a fir tree" near "a granite ridge." The tree, Church knows, will draw "mineral nourishment/from bone cells/and crumbled granite," that is, from both the friend's remains and the remains of the granite ridge, the two becoming equals now that the human body has died and released its prisoner. The poet reminds herself to let her friend enter her new domain, not to "strive to keep her/captive to any mind/or heart-formed image," because she has faith that death is a release and a joyous beginning:

    May all ghosts take the form of birds
    and begin singing
    among the birds of daybreak.

Church makes no special case for humans. Even her beloved dog Poli-kota[14] must depart, and her demise, particularly the fact that she has to put her to death (not, she realistically reminds us, "to sleep"), combined with her increasing years, challenges her serene acceptance of transience:

    Nothing remained
    but this complete cessation,

and I, an old woman, clutching at a dream's end
wordless in the steep shadow
of my own death.
    "On the Putting to Death of an Old Dog"

Despite her terror at the shadow of death surrounding
her, she is calmed by Poli-kota, who was unusually serene for a
trip to the veterinarian's table—"this time you did not flinch . . .
nor draw back. . . ." Death and life, she sees, "go hand in hand
together" for all beings, including the wild mountain mushrooms Poli-kota had earlier trampled randomly and indifferently (a bit like Dickinson's beheading frost at play) in "White
Dog with Mushrooms." She "cannot mind long" the loss, for
she finds at her feet a bone,

perhaps a steer's vertebra
once hidden in gliding flesh.
Now weathered and whitened
it lies in my hand
like a wordless metaphor
in the shape of a butterfly.

The earth speaks to her in wordless metaphors reminding
her of the cycle of existence in which she is a willing participant. The dog, too, brings her a message of calm acceptance:
"It seemed as though you withdrew of your own free will/and
shut the last door between us." The "wordless metaphor" of
the steer's vertebra and Poli-kota's graceful departure remind
her that the "gliding flesh" of the entire world must one day
be shed.

Her sympathy for the living and her faith in the hereafter finally take the scare out of death for her. As she watches

a willow tree in her garden "die back a little more each year" ("Elegy for the Willow Tree"), just as she must have watched Poli-kota's vitality fade and just as she has seen her own youth disappear, she decides to "grant . . . a quick death" to the "aged dancer/who can no longer keep up with the strong music/that summer and the winds weave." The chain saw does its job until all that remains is a "rough trunk" standing "at the edge of the lawn like a monument." The parting is painful ("Trembling I hid from the sound of that execution"), and she knows she is doing the right thing, but she resists the facile optimist's temp-tation to tell us glibly that death is not to be mourned or grieved. The earth is portrayed as almost savage, but its hunger has a purpose, to complete its sacred obligation to produce new life: "Under my feet the hungry earth is waiting/with its many-mouthed creatures to taste this sacrament." Church cannot avoid considering her own mortality, and the final lines of "Elegy for the Willow Tree" convey both horror and excitement at the prospect:

> Oh earth, air, water, fire!
> Oh essence of bright summer!
> I stand on the threshold of what mysteries?

Church's cosmic optimism is symbolized in the poems by the occasional appearance of an "angel" who accompanies the poet on her trip through life and into the beyond. The angel does not so much guide the poet (who most often refers to her movements in the world as "meanderings") as look after her. In "On Seeing the Wild Geese," Church and Fermor supposedly are out looking for migrating geese, although the birds appear nowhere except the title, and are "lured" by the "angel" into Santa Clara Canyon. The canyon is a time machine, taking them back to their childhood (the rising and falling topography makes the poet and companion feel like children again, the "terror and joy within us/of the pushed swing looping upward/ away from the level earth") and propelling Church imaginatively forward toward her death. The calm of the canyon is achieved by images of cottonwoods, chamisa, streams, a bed of sand, and the white Poli-kota who follows the poet when she takes her own way from her husband after lunch. All is peaceful and still. The dog wanders; Church, "beckoned by golden leaves or/a rosier seed plume," meanders; everything seems in its place. Yet most of the images are of death or decay, culminating in the final image of Church standing still, flanked by graphic evidence of dissolution:

> On the one hand the delicate water
> was eating the cliff away;
> on the other the golden
> leaves kept on slowly falling
> free from the tree forever
> to their own doom.

"Free" and "doom" are linked in the poem's peaceful tone to present a picture of death as delivery, no raging, no violent tearing away from earth, but a simple falling into "forever" at one's appointed time. The angel who has led the poet to this spot makes the passage from life to death acceptable. The angel is Church's passion for earth which, oddly, makes leaving earth easy. She celebrates all of earth's life forms, down to the smallest random stones, and can therefore leave her body with assurance that she will be delivered to the earth, as the leaf falls from the tree, its temporary skeleton, to the earth, its permanent home. Church, like the leaf, sees herself one day making that gentle journey, carried on the winds, to her true home, the earth. This "doom" is her freedom, and her love of earth ushers her from life to death, rather than encourages her to cling to life. Leaving life when one is brown and sere is equivalent to moving to the new "mystery." Being on the tree is certainly not bad, but leaving at the proper time is the true goal of the leaf. "Leaf subsides to leaf," she understands, but with a tone of stoic celebration absent in Frost's poem. "Grief" is replaced by freedom.

Such a merging with the land, however, if that were as far as it went, would offer only the intellectual solace of knowing that one's ashes will nourish trees. Church believes there is more. During her life, several "moments of unlimited happiness" give the poet insight into, or at least hope of, a more consoling continuation of her self, what could be called an earth-bound transcendence:

> Each of these moments was like a sudden dying,
>   a brief escape from the body, an instant of being
>   the beauty
> Which, living, we only taste a little.
>   "I Have Looked at the Earth"

The implication is clear: the beauty tasted momentarily in these epiphanic moments, including an afternoon at Point Lobos, we will taste forever after dying. We will not simply decay into compost but will remain, in Church's system, sentient entities forever tasting joy. There is something of "The Fall of the House of Usher" in this, but the tone is opposite Poe's melancholy, self-indulgent sensuousness.

Another moment of "unlimited happiness," a "day that stood up around me, blue," is related in "Foretaste." Again,

Church feels temporarily relieved of her physical prison ("I was not body-bound this day") and carried out of herself:

> And suddenly this curious thing:
> A spinning earth I seemed to sing.
> A spinning earth I then became
> And whirled through space like a clear flame.

The image at first suggests an otherworldly, or at least high-altitude, transcendence, but Church quickly pulls readers back to earth:

> Oh then I saw what death might be,
> What keen, unfettered ecstasy
> To be the earth, not just to see
> Blue light spilled over hill and tree;
> To feel the rain tread on my heart,
> Not watch it shine, a thing apart. . . .

She does not imagine a simple merging of her dust with earth's. She imagines herself retaining some ability to feel, see, or in some way perceive more fully and more intensely than she enjoys while alive. She transcends to become a sentient part of the earth. Her human mortality is no barrier to achieving harmony with nature but an absolute prerequisite for full integration with the earth she loves, an integration that she plans to have the faculties to enjoy.

Church means this fairly literally. In her "Introduction" to *Wind's Trail,* Shelley Armitage quotes from a letter Church wrote to Mary Austin on October 8, 1929: "My dearest ambitions are fulfilled in any experience which comes through the avenue of the mind of the senses. For while we may develop other faculties for experiencing after death, that they will be just these is doubtful . . ." (xii). The poet takes no hard stand but certainly leans toward the perception of an afterlife as part of the earth. The poetry bears out this conclusion. While surveying the New Mexico landscape after an absence, in "Return to a Landscape," she remembers her early experiences with family, canyons, and plains. Her thoughts turn, as they often do, to her death:

> When I die I would like to return to this earth that
>   made me
> and be part once more of its substance,
> the smallest crystal
> that still holds the memory of a human lifetime
> in a minute circuitry.

Church cannot accept the possibility of an entire lifetime of memories and emotions irretrievably lost to dust. Instead, she imagines human beings nurturing the earth in their deaths. As each of us dies, we give our "minute circuitry" to the trees and streams and add a new note to the wind's song and the hawk's cry. Voices, that once were poetry, become new tones in the summer breeze, poems of the world: "The air I have breathed will someday be shaped into another music." To conclude the poem, Church asks, "Does an essence linger/that is sentient still to music?" Her answer, given by implication in her entire body of work, is yes.

Fermor died in 1975, and "Sonnet XV," the final sonnet of *The Ripened Fields,* written two decades after the penultimate, is

Church's elegy to her husband. Like any honest account of human endeavor, *The Ripened Fields* and all of Church's poetry ends in death and raises the question as old as Adam that colors successes: given the fact of human mortality, how rewarding can any of earth's temporary joys or accomplishments be? Church answers that question in the final sonnet's final four lines. The world has not disappeared with her husband's death, it has simply become very quiet, and it seems as if the only two people remaining with the elements are Peggy and Fermor Church:

> Nothing seems lost—light's changes, wind-swept
>   silence,
> the arid land reflecting the shape of water.
> I gather pebbles feeling your quiet presence
> companion me still in all we loved together.

The four elements (light/fire, wind/air, land/earth, and water) and the two lovers take a final stroll. "Still" suggests both continuation and quiet. The act of gathering pebbles is a small act to symbolize her memories and his legacy. The final word "together" is just right. And the use of "companion" as a verb tells us that theirs was an active relationship, never static. Action amidst stillness, the personal gathered within the universal: all are companioned together in a final vision of loss in which nothing essential is truly lost. Her answer to the challenge of mortality is that the eternal lives within her, that she has discovered it, and in that discovery she has touched what connects her to the now and the forever. "Sonnet XV" releases the reader as gently as the poet releases her husband—feeling no loss.

Death to Church was nothing to fear. Death was a passage, as she says in *The House at Otowi Bridge,* while waiting for Edith Warner, to succumb:

> I felt as though we were waiting for a birth as much as for
> a death, as though the passage from life were not after all
> so different from the passage into it, as though Edith's
> spirit were only in labor to be free, like a child that must
> be delivered from its mother. Why have men made such
> an enemy of death, I began to wonder? (117)

Church took her own life, according to the precepts of the Hemlock Society, of which she was a member, on October 23, 1986. Neither the end nor the beginning, her death, as she understood, was one event in the continuing series of lives granted to her.

Red Steagall
1938–

CHAPTER TWO

Hootin' and Hollerin' in the Rocky Mountain West: Cowboy Poetry, the Land, and the Modern Reader

Cowboy poetry has few admirers in the academic community, perhaps because the cowboy poet consciously eschews all those traits the academic critic has been trained to associate with quality poetry, including experimentation or at least boldness in style and formal matters, indifference to the traditions—of rhyme, meter, and stanzaic pattern—ambiguity, sentiment but no sentimentality, complexity, allusiveness, irony, wit, angst, and the other critical chestnuts of the modernist period. To a true cowboy poet, these traits smack of eastern elitism and pinheaded intellectualism. The genre demands that all its participants toe several lines, one of which is the portrayal of the poet (and through the poet, the cowboy) as a down-to-earth, practical, straight-talking hombre who would have nothing to do with the truth-told slant and who would associate most of the other rhetorical flourishes of modern poetry with sissy stuff. The poet, whose worst fear—right next to losing his favorite horse to a prairie dog hole—is to be embraced by an academy can hardly expect (nor does he) more serious critical attention. To give the poetry its due, however, merits discussion for two primary reasons: first, it continues even in its contemporary form to be a body of work with a central and culturally important generic purpose, that is to champion the virtues of laboring on the land, especially as those virtues are embodied in America's last mythic figure, the cowboy;[1] second, despite (or because of) the irrelevance of that cowboy figure and outdoor labor to most modern Americans' lives, the poetry's popularity grows annually. The two phenomena are related: the poets' portrayal of the cowboys' strong, unwavering sense of self keeps alive a heroic icon of the culture, and *that* self-assurance and integrity provide modern readers a source of hope that somewhere, under the wide open skies, someone is still living the good life. And, as in so much western American literature, the determining factor in the cowboy's sense of self is his understanding of his relationship to the land—a traditional working relationship to Mother Nature in a time when most readers' relationship to the American landscape is a vicarious one.

All cowboy poets sooner or later acknowledge their love of the land, the "good old girl" who "treats everybody fair," as Owen Barton characterizes it in "Mother Nature." And all readers of the poetry recognize that "nature," broadly defined or, more often not defined at all, has some role in the verse. As Rebecca Carnes says, "the cowboy's emotional ties to nature are clearly shown through loving description" ("Cowboy Poetry"

47). One of the acknowledged consistent themes of the poetry is, in Anne Heath's words, "the love between man and land" ("Cowboy Poetry" 46). Heath goes on to claim that, "There is something about the big sky and living close to the elements of sun and wind that invites the mystical, a contemplation of nature" ("Cowboy Poetry" 46). The cowboy in cowboy poetry defines himself, and comes to know who he is, through his role as laborer on the land. The poet asserts that the cowboy has a special knowledge of the country and of his connection to it based upon his working relationship to his place. The puncher in this formulation has much more in common with the cow than with the cow's owner—he is on the range, in the mud, in all weather, trying to survive, right there with his "bees" and his faithful horse. This special knowledge (the "something" occasionally referred to in cowboy poetry) ennobles the cow puncher and creates his sense of self-worth, despite his lowly economic position in society. For Thoreau's "I am determined to know beans," we may substitute, "I am determined to know cows," for just as Thoreau worked in the soil as the medium of his knowledge in his attempt to "know" beans and, from them, himself, so the cowboy works in the mud as the medium of his knowledge in order to "know" cows and the land and, from them, himself. Thoreau extends the formula, however, by saying, after a long day hoeing his beans, "It was no longer beans that I hoed, nor I that hoed beans." It is not the cows or beans themselves that are important but the manner in which the physical labor returns the cowboy to himself (the true self that presumably exists under the layer of cultural accretions that is sweated off on the prairies) and paradoxically takes him out of himself, away from the ego-centered world of concerns in which we modern humans reside most of the time. The cowhand does not truly possess the land and is traditionally not a landowner. But he does claim to be its spiritual owner and, in turn, is possessed spiritually by the land, which is an earned result of his labor and sweat in fertilizing the prairie. No wonder many contemporary cowboy wannabes have found a powerful message in the verse.

The cowboy does what he does because of his love for the activity and the place where the activity occurs, but the fact that the labor is more than a pastime is important to his sense of self. Never be tempted to conclude that the vocational nature of the cowboy's labor is accidental or incidental. "A *cowboy*," Blake Allmendinger reminds us in his study of the cowboy's various forms of self-expression, "is defined by the work he does," and the cowboy's forms of expression, his poetry as well as his other constructed artifacts, "all reveal cowboys to be men who are culturally unified by engaging in labor routines that they think of as cowboy work" (*The Cowboy* 3). The puncher's reward for his labor, his personal insight, is "no easy gold at the hand of fay or elf," as Frost says in "Mowing," nor "gift of idle hours," but is specifically the result of his physical activity as an employed ranch hand. He is doing a necessary job, one that he occasionally talks about as if it had been going on forever as an eternal feature of the land. The cowboy claims his role on the land as one of essential labor, as God's work, deriving its validity from the same source that makes the land sacred. And, as is true for other western poets, the cowboy's understanding of his special relationship to the land is the paradigm for his understanding of relationships in general, including his relationship to other individuals, his society, and the cosmos. For example, the cowboy's attitude about his special place on the land explains the odd observation that the enemies one would expect him to castigate—bad or unpredictable weather, hostile

Indians, mangy coyotes and other predators—he tolerates with respect as other rightful inhabitants of the land. They are obstacles but not obstacles he curses, because they too belong rightly to the land. He deals with them as one deals with a respected and worthy adversary, without rancor and without bitterness.

Therefore, when Marcus Crowley hears a coyote giving a "war whoop/From up on yonder hill" ("My Friend, the Coyote"), rather than reach for his rifle he praises the animal as "a creature of the wild frontier" with "magic" in his music because the wild and free quadruped, like the cowboy, is "truly so symbolic of our West." Even a specific coyote that has caused damage can be respected. While riding home on old Punch after a day in Butte Valley, for example, the speaker in Eric Sprado's "Our Range" comes unexpectedly upon old Three Toes, "Daddy of all coyotes that had ever/Eaten one of my lambs." While pausing before making good on his vow to "put a hole in him/For every lamb he ate," the speaker thinks:

> Somehow, in those seconds, I came to understand
> How he and I, both renegades,
> Belong to the very same land.

The title acquires a new meaning with Sprado's realization: "our" had initially meant cowboys, but by the poem's conclusion it means all valid residents of the plains and prairies. The speaker can never shoot Three Toes because "We both belong here, you and I," the coyote "by birthright," because he and his kind have been born for millennia to the land, and the cowboy "by a strangely human rite," something typically inexplicable but based on the fact that he has worked the land respectfully and reverently.

Nor can one rage against the weather, no matter how bad it gets, because the weather, like the coyote, belongs to the plains naturally. Despite the fact that a hailstorm wipes out the family's harvest and brings his father to tears, the speaker in Colen Sweeten's "Hailstorm" feels only pain and not bitterness:

> Soon the hurt was healing.
> There was no bitterness.
> There was no blame.

Red Steagall shares Sweeten's attitude toward the weather when he writes:

> Wouldn't change things if I had the chance.
> The weather don't matter, I ain't goin' nowhere.
> There's no place I'd trade for this ranch.
>   "The Weather"

Even the Indian, the traditional cinematic cowboy enemy, is given his due. L. Gough, in "The Red Man," uses the occasion of General Ranald Mackenzie's 1874 campaign to subdue the last Comanches as inspiration for a lament of the Indians' loss of freedom that could, with a change of a few words, be a lament for the cowboys' loss of freedom: "The west was once the land of the free,/When the Red Man roamed o'er the lone prairie." The Indian followed nature's cycle, as a good cowboy does, and was, in this account, peaceful until forced by the white invaders to become hostile:

> But the white man crossed the ocean wide,
> The Red Man's wigwam then he spied,

And began to drive them mile after mile;
Then soon the Indians became hostile.

Gough capitalizes "Red Man" while leaving "white man" lower case, making his intentions clear, but he cannot help his inherited diction when later he notes that only after "many a thousand battles were fought" did the white man manage to remove "the savage."

By contrast, the cowboy is no lover of the farmer or the miner, for the interlopers see the land as a piece of property from which to extract riches through slow or not-so-slow destruction. Novelist Larry McMurtry remembers his cowboying ancestors this way: "To the McMurtrys, the plow and the cotton patch symbolized not only tasks they loathed but an orientation toward the earth and, by extension, a quality of soul which most of them not-so-covertly despised" ("Saddle" 38). And John Lomax, a patriarch of cowboy poetry collectors, reveals a common attitude when he sneers at the fact that "The trails are becoming dust covered or grass grown or lost underneath the farmers' furrow . . ." (*Cattle Trail* xi). It should not be surprising to discover that cowboy poets' references to farmers and miners are usually pejorative.[2] One of the farmers' sins is believing he can improve on God's handiwork by plowing it. The cowboy, by contrast, does God's work and reaps eternal validation for his efforts by respecting and preserving the land. The holy image of most cowboy poets is of open range before the arrival of fences presumably erected by farmers. Bob Fletcher celebrates such a time and castigates those whose arrival marked the end of the free range ("Open Range"):

Western land was made for those
Who like the land wide and free,

> For cattle, deer, and buffalo,
> For antelope and me;
> For those who like a land the way
> That it was made by God
> Before men thought they could improve
> By plowing up the sod.

The worst thing that can happen to a cowboy is to look up one day and find himself surrounded by farmers, not Indians: Robert Carr ("The Old Cowboy's Lament") wants to move out now that "The range's filled up with farmers an' there's fences ev'rywhere," just as Arthur Chapman, in much the same language, bemoans the fact that "the plains are full of farmers, with their harrows and their ploughs" ("The Cow-Puncher's Elegy"). Carr's poem was published in 1908 and Chapman's is from a 1917 book of verse, indicating that one of the earlier recognized facts of cowboy poetry was that the cowboy's way of life was already lost.

Another more contemporary example of this anti-agrarian dream is "The Pistol," by Rod McQueary, in which the poet focuses his attention on a .44 abandoned on the untilled prairie by a rider killed by an Indian hunting party, probably "Out for deer, beyond the butte." The rider makes a valiant defense but still succumbs. Even so, the Indian attackers are never vilified and the wording suggests that the poet understands their attack as a matter of natural course. About a hundred years later, however, in the summer of 1987, "some worried, weary farmer," who has turned the land into an alfalfa field and is now out on his "old swather," runs over the rusty pistol. The farmer's response illustrates the cowboy poet's perspective—hostile Indians are preferable to weary farmers. The farmer picks up the gun and throws it away with such angry force that he rocks the threshing machine he is working from. As he curses the "old-timers" for not picking up their "crap," he demonstrates his lack of appreciation for how the gun came to be there.

The old-timers were busy leading real lives, one step ahead of Indians, while the modern farmer is simply putting in his time, one step ahead of the bank. The contrast between a worthy partner (a Native American hunting party) in pursuit of the true life and a degrading ally (the banker) in pursuit of the land's destruction is clear. The Indian hunting party and cowboy were doing what came naturally to them on the open plains, and the rider of the nineteenth century dies without rancor. The farmer, by contrast, cannot even appreciate the land and seems to hate every pass he makes on his old swather.

Miners, if possible, are even less respected. As far as Chapman is concerned, they ruin the neighborhood more than the sod-buster does. In "The Cowboy and the Prospector," he tells of entertaining a drifting "minin' feller" in a cow camp. The miner tells tales of scratching and digging in the hills, being unable to understand why the cowboys were "punchin' cows fer ten a week." The misunderstanding is mutual, and Chapman concludes: "He might be right, but I misdoubt/If such a chap could be a friend." Anyone who plunders Mother Nature and drifts without roots is immediately suspect. A more recent example, by Wallace McRae published in 1979, resorts to irony to the same end. In "Crisis," McRae gives the coal miners' public relations man a voice to speak about the environment as he sees it with plentiful clean air and water. The coal mining man would have us believe that he can improve the environment by digging it up, if we'd just give him a chance.

McRae, because he has been raised on the land and learned its lessons first-hand, resists the miners' siren song of greed by telling himself that he is on the right side of this fight. He uses italics in his poem to indicate, one assumes, the cowboy's words that are thought rather than uttered regarding his deep conviction in the rightness of his beliefs. This is a curious rebellion of silence that one meets in other contemporary cowboy poets. The bitter silence hides a deep sense of outrage, as McRae illustrates in "The Land," where the anti-miner and anti-farmer attitudes are connected to the cowboy's worldview, in which the land is a woman and a mother, and plowing, mining, or otherwise defacing the land is equivalent to a sexual assault. McRae says that the miner and the farmer exhibit a "mindless lust" for the land. Not only do the miner and the farmer not have a love of the land; they do not respect it the way a cowboy does.

Finally, although the cowboy loves and respects the land, he disdains non-cowboy nature lovers, even when they share some of his ecological concerns. This is presumably because the nature lovers have only a distant, theoretical, or aesthetic relationship to the land, and their attitudes toward it must therefore be false. Or, when that is impossible, to claim that because the attitudes parallel the cowboy's, then the nature lovers themselves must be denounced as fakes. In fact, in most cowboy poetry, "environmentalist" is used as a dirty word, and no explanation or defense of the attitude is ever required for the initiated reader:

> Environmentalists complain
> Of methane gas and over grazin'.
> Animal rights and granola types
> Would reduce the size of herds we're raisin'.
> Dan Bradshaw, "Runnin' Fer Office"

Cowboys all claim to love the land and want to protect it just as environmentalists do. Some cowboy poets' speakers even claim to be willing to die or kill to protect their "mother." In "The Land of Magic," Rob Blair points our attention to "the big, dizzy mountains" he loves while proclaiming, "This land has raised me up,/and for this land I'll kill." No Greenpeace member could take a stronger stand, but no cowboy poet would ever admit to inhabiting common ground with an environmentalist. The hostility to environmental activists, it seems, is less a matter of differences of opinion about land policy that has been reasoned and considered but is more a hostility based on the cowboy poets' suspicion that politicians', environmentalists' and others' beliefs are based on theory, rather than sweat, and in that way devalue the cowboy by devaluing his special knowledge based on experience and labor. It is not the philosophical position one reaches, the cowboy poet suggests, but the road one takes to reach it that matters. And the only valid road to reaching a position from which one can honestly speak for and from the land is the road of toil, which teaches one love and identification.

One of the clearest illustrations of the cowboy's self-image and its origins is "Anthem," a well-known poem by Buck Ramsey, recognized as one of the leading poets and somewhat of a patriarch of the clan until his death in 1998. The poem begins in the morning with the speaker on horseback. He feels himself blend with the elements of the landscape:

> I lived in time with horse hoof falling;
> I listened well and heard the calling

The earth, my mother, bade to me,
Though I would still ride wild and free.
And as I flew out on the morning
Before the bird, before the dawn,
I was the poem, I was the song.

"Bade" may be a bit unusual for a cowboy character, but the rest of the stanza is a perfect example of cowboy transcendentalism. The speaker does not walk through the woods and feel himself a transparent eyeball, as Emerson does, but he rides over the plains and in the press of the motion ("as I flew"), a motion connected to horse and vocation, his psyche becomes indistinguishable from the spirit of the earth, and he, in his action, becomes the cowboy poem. Sitting and meditating would produce different results, as would riding for pleasure. In the act of vocational labor out on the prairie the cowboy discovers his identity, and that identity is not separate from his activity or the activity's location but is fused with both. The recognition is more than ontology; it is a statement of ethics. This state he achieves is a pure and ethical state of being, a state whose purity cannot be understood by those unfamiliar with the activity and, furthermore, a state that is only achievable in the midst of the activity: "Those horsemen now rode all with me,/And we were good and we were free."[3] As one rides, one is good and one is free. When one stops, one is something else, and, Ramsey suggests, something less.

The knowledge is impossible to impart to the uninitiated, but it can be hinted at to those who care to listen. In Waddie Mitchell's "Where To Go," a young cowboy goes to an older "pard" for advice after letting his life become too busy ("my fire has too many irons"). The old friend "squatted on haunches"

and "with a stick started scratching the earth" before responding. The aged mentor thus gets close to the source of his
knowledge, scratching his mother's back as it were, patiently
awaiting her help and asking her advice before offering his
own. After a homily or two, the older man tells the youth that
he has to find his own truth, and he can only do that on horseback and alone:

> Now saddle up with the things that I've told you,
> Leave man's little world far behind.
> Find sanctuary out on the cow range,
> Let the wind do its thing on your mind.

Out on the range, the seeker will find his knowledge,
which will return him to his true identity: ". . . search for that
trail/That will help you find out who you are."

Another clear example of a cowboy poet's claim to special
knowledge based on his labor in the open is Darrell Arnold's
poem, "There's Somethin' That A Cowboy Knows." The burden
of the poem is explaining what the "somethin'" is and the
source of that knowledge. Cowboy poets assume a rhetorical
stance of close identification with the audience that allows
them to eschew explanation, especially of abstract terms (such
as "somethin'"), assuming the audience knows already what
the "somethin'" is. Most poets are content to assert, with Dan
Bradshaw, "Ya know ya can't explain it/To someone who's never
lived it" ("Loafer Mountain"). Arnold participates in this stance
to some extent (referring to "a need he can't explain") but is
more helpful than most of his confederates. The "somethin'"
seems to be first a matter of particular experience of particular
sensory phenomena:

There's somethin' that a cowboy knows,
A scent born on the air
Of sage, and sweat, and leather,
And of smoke and burnin' hair.

Other phenomena the cowboy knows as a result of his laboring life include "the pain of choking dust" and the "pledge of springtime" as it is manifested in "tiny, shiny wobbly calves/ A-dryin' on the ground." The experiences are not always pleasant ("He knows the blast of winter storms/When cold cuts like a knife"), but suffering, as a part of doing one's job with integrity, is an important component of the cowboy's self-image. If range life were easy, one suspects the cowboy would look elsewhere for work. In other words, whatever the cowboy possesses that makes him feel special and that is central to his sense of self and his self-knowledge comes from his meaningful (that is, vocational) participation in the outdoor life of the prairie. His work produces experiences that, after appreciation and reflection, he understands as the basis of his unique self. Humility and elitism exist comfortably side-by-side in the formulation. The cowboy suggests he is special (the "somethin'" is what "the cowboy" knows and you do not), while also suggesting that he is sublimely satisfied with simple pleasures phrased in homey images.

Despite Arnold's distrust of abstraction, however, a distrust that is typical of the genre, the poet claims more than a simple acquaintance with particular phenomena. Like Ramsey, he claims ontological implications for this experience. What he knows makes him who he is, and one who has not worked the range as he has and gained the special knowledge there that he has gained cannot be the same type of person:

There's somethin' that a cowboy knows
That poorer men will not—
Like ridin' circles all day in
A fast, ground-eatin' trot.

The knowledge threatens to make the cowboy solitary, living apart from all others:

There's somethin' that a cowboy knows,
A kinship with the wind
That causes him to live alone,
His horse his closest friend.

Some suspect that cowboys are closer to their horses than to their wives. In his humorous poem, "A Broken-hearted Cowboy," Chip O'Brien tells of meeting ol' Buck in the bar and discovering that the cowboy has just buried his "darlin'." Assuming that Buck is mourning his wife, the speaker treats him to a comforting drink or two until Buck is too drunk to drive. After offering him a ride home, the speaker narrates the following exchange:

"Naw, my wife's commin'."
"I thought she was dead!"
"Weren't my wife. It were my horse."

McMurtry, again remembering his days growing up with cowboys, corroborates Arnold and O'Brien when he remarks, ". . . I do not find it possible to doubt that I have ever known a cowboy who liked women as well as he liked horses . . ." ("Saddle" 39). Max Brand knew enough about cowboys and the popular taste to know that, in a good (or bad) B-Western, "There has to be a woman, but not much of one. A good horse is much more important" (quoted in Rainey 18).[4]

Not all poets go so far as to suggest that the only being with whom the cowboy can be psychologically intimate is his horse, but the tendency, that Arnold takes to the limit, is clear: cowboys learn the land in a way that no one else can, and that knowledge becomes such an essential part of the cowboy's psyche that he cannot share his life with anyone who does not possess the same knowledge and the resulting sense of self and self's place in the world. When one does meet a kindred soul, however, as in "A Rare Find," by Randall Rieman, the recognition is immediate and joyful:

> It's a wonderful thing,
> Though it's hard to explain,
> When you meet a new friend on your way,
> And you know, in no time,
> There's a reason behind
> The ease that your friendship's obtained. . . .

The "reason" is simple: the new cowboy

> shares your same love for the land,
> For horses and cattle,
> For life in the saddle
> And nights underneath a clear sky.

The imprint of working the land is on both, and the result is a "sameness in spirit that goes beyond words." The new cowboy friend, then, is recognized, as Sprado recognized the coyote Three Toes, as a compatriot, one with whom one shares "somethin'" special. Always there is that suggestion that if you need "words" to understand the vague "sameness," then you do not have it. This is a difficult position to relate to, as Arnold understands: "His choice, a life that only he/And God can understand."

California rancher and poet John Dofflemyer, the editor of *Dry Crik Review*, as close to an official journal of cowboy poetry as exists, makes the same claim for a sort of elitism of working stiffs in "'Til I Depart":

> Few men feel these hillsides breathe
> or hear the heartbeat underneath,
> 'cept those that live here day to day
> and nature's beasts can hardly say
> a thing. . . .

No one who does not work on the land can hope to understand it, and nature cannot be expected to explain herself. Cowboy poets are not as unskilled as they pretend or their critics assume. Dofflemyer, in a technique typical of the genre, employs his vaguest word ("thing") in the most important spot in the line to indicate precisely his point: if you have to have the "thing" explained to you, then you do not know what it is. Furthermore, the poet is reluctant to tell you what the "thing" is, because your ignorance suggests your unsuitableness for the knowledge. If you really want to know the "thing" that nature can tell you, then you should go out and punch cows. If you simply want to be told it from the poet or hear it on weekend trips to nature, then you are a cultural exploiter, and the cowboy poet is reluctant to talk to you. Dofflemyer is like the shaman who refuses to let the outsiders get at the community's secrets or ritual words. The ironic connection here to Indians protecting their tribe's secrets from marauding culture-hounds from white universities or suburbs is not so ironic. Most cowboy poets do not reveal resentment in their verse for the Indian residents of the land but accept them as native people who, like cowboys, belong on the plains and people who would easily understand the "thing" to which Dofflemyer refers.[5]

Resentment directed toward city residents, however, is much more common, contending with pity for the dominant attitude toward urban folks. There is probably no way to, or no desire to, reform or educate those who live in towns. Transplanting them to the country will not necessarily rejuvenate them, although our literary tradition, going back at least as far as the Puritans' diaries and Crèvecoeur's famous letters, suggests that transplantation to a new climate or environment will make new men of old. Dofflemyer does suggest that city slickers can at least appreciate the outdoors when they are shown it by a good guide, such as himself. In "Blackrock Pass," he describes a mighty thunderstorm that catches him and a group of dudes unawares:

> we pulled our slickers on
> and baled off the western slope
> and at the second switchback
> zeus tossed his yellow rope
>
> not too far from where we paused
> and roared in the canyon walls,
> then tossed another to the other side
> and loose rocks began to fall.

The classical allusion and the eccentric capitalization (or lack thereof) are about as "fancy" or idiosyncratic as cowboy poetry allows itself to get. The sentiments themselves, however, are strictly generic. After weathering the storm and reaching their destination, the men pause and the poet concludes:

> we finally make pinto lake
> to dry beneath the fly,
> and i'll wager these successful men
> would like to return as much as i.

The cowboy exposes the "successful" (ironically so) men to the world's true elements, which are not the clear skies and sunny days of travel brochures, but something only the real cowboy can guide one to, the beautiful harshness that makes the West so nurturing of individualism and all the other well-known components of the cowboy myth. The cowboy will never be "successful"—he will never have money or power— but the cowboy will have what no "successful" man can have: his secure self-knowledge, based on his labor and the various deprivations associated with that labor. Note also that the cowboy does not go to the city in order to get in touch with something real. The city vacationers come to the cowboy's range and there get a glimpse of the "thing" that cowboys know as part of their daily lives. The cowboy-shaman is pleased that his charges are impressed by what he has shown them, but he is being uncharacteristically charitable to urbanites when he suggests they would like to do it again. The cowboy in this circumstance can afford to be charitable (whereas in other circumstances "successful men" are lampooned), because here the cowboy knows he has assets the "successful" men can never reap.

✧

One of the dilemmas this complex of attitudes forces upon the poet is blinking occasionally at the profession of his personae. It would be difficult, even for a poet dedicated to keeping alive the myth of the cowboy, to pretend that running cattle on formerly open land is anything except an intrusion of the human and a subjugation of nature, just the sorts of things "they" are accused of wanting to do to "our" land. McRae, in "Things of Intrinsic Worth," a classic of the genre, wants to set up a dichotomy between the way "we" formerly treated the land, understanding its intrinsic worth, and the way "they" now treat it. While remembering the past, McRae paints an idyllic picture of a time when folks lived in harmony with nature, contrasted with the present when different people abuse the same loved locales. As if speaking to family or old friends, the poet recalls a rock on "Emmells Crick" where "Dad carved his name." That rock is gone now; it has been dynamited into rubble and obliterated by the strip mining "dragline machine." McRae also nostalgically recalls late night raids by kids on "the old Milar Place" for melons. This too is gone now. "They" burned it down to get it out of the way. All our old familiar places are not just gone, but ruined by the destructive acts of miners who do not understand or do not care about what they have done.

Little things (carving initials, stealing melons) are acts of love or playfulness; conscious despoilings (blasting the rock into rubble, burning down structures to get to the soil) are acts of exploitation and greed.

Of course, "we" ignore the cattle we introduced to the land, as if their presence did not profoundly change the area's ecosystem. Why does McRae turn a blind eye to cows? Because the theme here is that the land is a phenomenon of "intrinsic worth," a fact "we" can understand because we have sweated on it but "they" cannot comprehend because all they ever do is extract profit with the use of dynamite and bulldozers. McRae describes a scene where he is asked how things are going. His reply is "Great!"; things are fine eve though the miner is destroying the land around them. McRae seems appalled that this situation would not be obvious to anyone. It seems there is hardly anyone left who cares about the destruction being wreaked upon the land; the destruction of "things of intrinsic worth."

No attempt is made to correct or even protest the abuse of the land. The poets dissemble and say "Great!" But they also claim special knowledge of the true worth of "The Earth" because of their relationship to it. The reasonable conclusion is that if the earth is of intrinsic worth, one would simply live on it and enjoy it or leave it alone and enjoy it. Where cows fit into that formula is not immediately clear, but the cowboy would lose a lot (including his name and his identity) without the cattle industry, so that industry's effect on the earth is ignored when convenient or necessary. The attitude is easily labeled selfish, suggesting as it does that everyone except "us" vacate the land or never come to it to begin with. "We" will have our things of intrinsic worth, but no one else can have a piece of the action. But then, in this formulation, no one else has earned that right. The education that is a prerequisite for any claim to a right to belong is garnered on horseback behind a herd of cattle. No bureaucrat or professor or environmentalist or Nashvillian on plastic pony can appreciate what only the cowboy can understand. It is no accident, then, that one of the dubious benefits of bulldozing in McRae's poems is a new school that has made the rest of the state envious. Who needs that school? Not the cowboy, who learns his lessons outside, and who, by implication, is the only one who deserves to be here anyway.[6]

The knowledge of self as part of place has further ethical implications, as Buck Ramsey in "Anthem" notes. Because place is more than a simple brother or sister and is really part of one's own identity, disturbing it is tantamount to self-mutilation:

> This knowing gave us more the care
> To let the grass keep at its growing
> And let the streams keep at their flowing.

Ramsey goes one step farther and suggests in a statement that would seem highly ironic if it were not so sincerely phrased that no one can own the land. This from a cowboy who works for someone who owns land:

> We knew the land would not be ours,
> That no one has the awful powers
> To claim the vast and common nesting,
> To own the life that gave him birth,
> Much less to rape his Mother Earth,
> And ask her for a mother's blessing,
> And ever live in peace with her,
> And, dying, come to rest with her.

"Peace," now or eternally, cannot be yours if you pretend to own what gave you your identity, much less if you "rape" that same fecund source of your life. Ramsey, to his credit, at least asks the question his verse suggests. If the land cannot be owned because it is our life-source, then are we not guilty for working it so that its owners can profit?

> It was the old ones with me riding
> Out through the fog fall of the dawn,
> And they would press me to deciding
> If we were right or we were wrong.
> For time came we were punching cattle
> For men who knew not spur nor saddle,
> Who came with locusts in their purse
> To scatter loose upon the earth.

The greedy owners are explicitly described as those who do not know how to ride. Their greed is one indictment, but their lack of knowledge of spur and saddle, where one learns who one is and how to treat one's "Mother," is the crowning charge. The problem is that, despite Ramsey's statement that the "old ones," the wise old men of so many myths, "would press me to deciding" if what they were doing was right or wrong, the poet reaches no conclusion. He does not press himself to decide. Instead, he feels remorse (or self-pity?), and changes the subject:

> The old ones wept, and so did I.
>
> Do you remember? We'd come jogging
> To town with jingle in our jeans. . . .

And then he recounts younger, wilder days: when faced with a real dilemma that admits of no easy solution, short of challenging the economic base upon which the cowboy myth and lifestyle rest, nostalgia is the dodge most often chosen by the poet.[7] The cowboy is the last repository of true knowledge and true values, the owners having become consumed by "raw greed," but the puncher cannot repudiate the owner, or he will lose his job. It is much more than a job, it is his source of identity. Perhaps one reason the poet is given to "nostalgic views of the past and to melancholy feelings that things will never be the same" (Hurst, "Connections" 32-33) is that the double-bind of modern capitalism has even the cowboy in its grip. The cowboy cannot quit the range any more than the factory worker can leave the mill. Even when he attempts to face the dilemma, as Ramsey does here, the inescapable conclusion, that one cannot remain pure ("and we were good and we were free") in the present tense while working in the service of "raw greed," has to be escaped. So it is:

> Some cowboys even shunned the ways
> Of cowboys in the trail-herd days,
> (But where's the gift not turned to
>   plunder?). . . .

The parenthetical justification reveals its weakness. Ramsey cannot even give this logic a good look but has to hide it inside parentheses. Everything gets sullied, he says, and then he hopes that we, too, will blink at the moral self-deception included in that sentence. Nonetheless, the cowboy can at least claim that his vocation produces a valuable, perhaps sacred, knowledge because it places him into contact with the true and elemental facts of the earth. He at least has that. Ramsey concludes the poem by repeating the first stanza, now placing it in the future tense. We have this, he says, and I will cling to it for as long as I can:

So mornings now I'll go out riding
Through pastures of my solemn plain,
And leather creaking in the quieting
Will sound with trot and trot again.

The "long plain" of stanza one has become "solemn," but the hope remains: "Those horsemen will ride all with me,/And we'll be good, and we'll be free."

Most poets, not just Ramsey, feel the threat that modern life poses and make the phenomenon a theme in their work. The threat is so great because it not only endangers the land, it also threatens the sacred cowboy working life lived on that land. In "To a Cowboy's Grandson," for example, Gene Randels spends the first forty-eight lines describing the experiences he has had on the prairie. He finds himself moved by and recalling not large events as much as a range of small images derived from daily events. He recounts various animals he has seen (turtledove, spotted pony, whippoorwill, badger, deer, and, of course, cattle), the area's fickle weather ("a late spring blizzard," "the tornado's awful wrath," the "killing drought in thirty-one"), and relics of the place, both natural and human-made ("twilight in the evenin'" and "an unglazed pot" presumably crafted by a Native American). He has become who he is by his long and loving association with the land and its facts, which he lists affectionately while making no attempt to push home a point until stanza thirteen, when he says,

But can it survive
the dreadful hand
Of the destroyer God
called modern man?

What he sees, hears, and knows is who he is, a breed apart, not a "modern man," although by definition he obviously is a man and is modern. By "modern man" Randels means something else: he means people raised in other places with other values and different self-images resulting from different relationships to the land upon which they grew or became themselves. He means, in fact, everyone who is not a cowboy.

He does not really fear for himself—he has had his life and now he has his memories—but he fears for his grandson, who tells grandpa "of troubled schools,/of children's hate,/Of atomic bombs,/the doomed world's fate." If the child remains in those schools (presumably in towns or cities) he will learn only of destruction and hate and will grow up to be one of those who leaves his spent rifle shells on a hillside, in other words, a "modern man." The antidote for the grandson is to ride the range. The speaker can, and does, tell the boy things ("tell him of the morning star,/and great steam trains"), but only the actual experience of living and working close to the land will make the lessons hold:

> Let him grow his roots
> into the land,
> Then foursquare, rooted,
> he can stand.

If the boy is allowed to "glory in life/to his fingertips," the experience of working with his hands and feeling something earthy as he labors, then he will be spared the horrible fate of growing up to make "micro-chips," which, in the cowboy poet's world-view, are less noble than cow chips. The result will also be a self-knowledge and self-image strong and "rooted," able to withstand the chaos and destructive energy of the modern world:

> Then he can look in the face
> of any man
> And say, "This I think,
> and this I am!"

The modern world is a temptation, a serpent in the cowboy's garden that may occasionally tempt him away from the true life. The "collision of past and present" (Hurst, "Connections" 34) is perceived to be "destroying much of the 'big high and lonesome'" (Carnes 48). A city slicker, therefore, raised to embrace "progress," can never really hope to become a cowboy, but a cowboy who has once lost his way may get back to the range. Henry Real Bird (a Crow, one of the few Indian cowboy poets), after being "Lost on the road," gets back to the ranch in the nick of time:

> The return to cowboy wages
> Turn back the pages
> Thought from where wildflowers grow
> And peaceful fires glow
> Around teepee rings,
> Sweet smell of sage
> Among the pine. . . .

His "shattered dreams" had perhaps prompted him to try the road to California, but "the truth" showed him the way back to the range. His ranching dreams may have been illusory, but they were at least true, while the lure of the non-cowboy world was a lie that, no matter how successfully one worked it, would always be untrue:

> Nothing'll last
> If you believe in lies,
> Traded dreams
> To break at seams,
> Lost all my tokens
> For this economy
> Where soft words were spoken
> In lost autonomy.

He was in danger of losing everything (all his "tokens") while attempting to gain the world, "this economy" where lies or "soft words" are the standard currency, and where one's freedom, one's "autonomy," is the only real product one has to sell. Better to remain poor but true, Real Bird says ("The truth/Is what you know) and return to cowboying, getting "up before the sun."

The simple fact is that there is no better place than under the stars on a horse, and while cowboys, powerless as they are and as they must be if they are to retain their special identity, cannot change the facts of modern life, the cowboy poet can deem those facts to be ultimately unimportant. In the great pasture beyond, the cowboy will be acknowledged. "Bullhide Chaps and Memories" is Jim Shelton's eulogy for Thad, the wearer of the chaps. After recounting their times together, the speaker apostrophizes the departed friend:

> Pick a place in heaven
>   That has wild oats by the score;
> Pick a mountain, grassy valley;

Open wide your cabin door,
For Madge and I will meet you
On the cowboy's golden shore,
And we'll give back this piece of leather
And the bullhide chaps you wore.

This surely supports the assertion that cowboy poetry often hearkens "back to an idealized rural culture" (Carnes 50). Heaven, Shelton assures us, will look like a ranch, which means that the cowboy obviously has the ideal life here and that death is only a temporary interruption in the cowboying life. "It truly was a Paradise," Wesley Beggs says, referring to the range of the late nineteenth century, and death, it is hoped, will return the faithful to their prelapsarian plains. There is a definite sense that the buckaroo believes God has touched not only the land upon which he works but himself as he works the land, because he works the land. While discussing Bruce Kiskaddon's "Judgement Day," Blake Allmendinger says the poem continues an earlier tradition (illustrated by such anonymous nineteenth-century poems as "A Cowboy's Prayer" and "The Cowboy's Dream") in which the puncher represents himself as being "judged by a different standard than the Lord's other petition-ers," having "earned God's special treatment or favor" (*The Cowboy* 46). The cowboy is doing God's labor on God's land. The place and the work on it are sacred. The cowboy is Adam on horseback, minding God's pastures, as in "For Jeff," by Jon Bowerman:

It's either too hot, or too cold when it's not,
But you're out every day just the same.
Glad you can be where the wind's blowin' free
With the smells of the wide open plain.

In this land that God saved for the juniper and sage
And critters and drifters like me,
He set it aside for the buckaroo,
Where everything's still wild and free.

There are too many cowboy heaven poems to cite, but their existence demonstrates the belief in the value of the labor on the land. In "Judgement Day," another Kiskaddon poem, after St. Peter (the "top hand angel") has judged all the other mortals, he turns to the cowboys, "that grizzled wild brigade." But before the "boss of Heaven" can judge the buckaroos, he has to call for "the range law book." Why? Because "You could never judge a cowboy/By another feller's laws." The cowboy has his own laws, a special covenant with God, reminding us here oddly of the Puritans, because he has done God's work. Or, as Stephen Wilhelm puts it in "Is There A Cowboy Heaven?"

This is yore reward, good cowboy,
    Fer yore lovin' o' th' plain
An' yore deep respect fer Nature
    An' yore brave disdain fer pain.

No wonder Howard Norskog can suggest that "God's a cowboy" ("Cowboys Heaven") and Al Summers can rest contented that "I know we'll meet the Range Boss there up yonder in the sky" ("Let's Keep on Ridin'").

It is no wonder that the cowboy resents any attempt by government to regulate the land: he leases directly from God. The changes in the landscape made by "modern men" naturally become a subject for lamentation by cowboy poets of the generation that has seen the prairie transformed. There are perhaps even more instances of nostalgia for the good old days before roads, subdivisions, and especially fences than there are examples of the cowboy's promised life in the hereafter. A few examples give the flavor. In Ernie Fanning's "The Vanishing Valley," a cowboy rests atop a "big rimrock" while out chasing cows and wonders, "Where the hell did the valley go?"

> Whatever happened to the fields of spuds
> And onions that the old degos used to raise,
> And where have gone the lush green meadows
> Where the fat cattle used to graze?

When he can manage to see the valley through the smog, all he sees are "mounds of steel and gray concrete." Resignation is the typical response: what can the cowboy do, for "that was yesterday." Before long, some poets suspect, the cowboy himself will be a memory. The 1990 national census reported that fewer than one percent of the people in Wyoming, The Cowboy State, list their primary occupation as ranch laborer. Buck Wilkerson has already eulogized the cowboy, in "Saddle Tramp," describing the "old cow puncher" in "Levis, boots and a Stetson" whose day is gone:

> This ode is set down in his memory;
> He was one hell of a man in his day.
> He has vanished—he's no longer needed,
> His breed has just faded away.

The "aeroplanes" and trucks have taken the saddle tramp's job, and the gain in efficiency is marked by a loss in identity.

There are still people, Ross Knox claims, who would become cowboys, who would choose the life lived hard and the sense of self earned openly, if they were given the chance, which he admits is unlikely:

> What I'm trying to say is in twenty more years
> A cowboy could be a thing of the past.
>
> And what about the youngsters that want to
>   punch cows,
> Now and then you'll find one or two. . . .
>   "The Dying Times"

Again hopeless in the confrontation with time, Knox can only conjure up an impossible dream, a time machine "like I seen on T.V./That would turn back the pages of time," affirming the suggestion by one commentator that the poetry "calls up the old values" (Shepperson and Winzeler 262) and makes a matter of dogma its refusal to "embrace the optimistic belief in perpetual progress" (Shepperson and Winzeler 263).

Cowboy poets, however, have always felt their way of life threatened, and the theme of loss is hardly a contemporary one. In Wesley Beggs' "Twenty Years Ago," the poet is already afraid in 1912 that "cow-punchin' days were over." And in "The Cowman's Troubles," a poem by Gail Gardner included in his 1935 book, *Orejana Bull for Cowboys Only,* the poet laments:

> With the bankers and lawyers and the forest officials,
> The land office men and inspectors as well,
> A-ridin' the cowman all over the country,
> No wonder his business has all gone to Hell.

In the early twentieth century, however, cowboy poets were working in a culture that by and large embraced ideas of progress, cultural evolution, and getting ahead. They were in that respect out of step with the larger culture that dreamed of happiness in material terms. Bitterness has always been an element in cowboy poetry. Perhaps it is more pervasive now—more poets are more bitter—but it has always been present, and the poets have always known their enemies: prosperous materialists or any others who, for various reasons, have seen the land as a commodity to exploit for money or politics or other forms of self-interest. Now we see specific new enemies added to the list—environmentalists, animal rights activists, vegetarians, lawyers, and anyone associated with Washington and the eastern liberal establishment.

What is more clearly new is that the bitterness over a sense of innocence lost has spread to the culture as a whole, giving the general population in the twenty-first century more common ground with cowboy poets than any differences in vocations would at first suggest. The cowboy poets have always stood for a way of life lost, but now the bitterness, animosity, and adversarial stance heard in their poetry connects to the culture's general sense of anger at the despoiling of America's potential as a pure, clean, well-lighted place. This new common ground not only keeps the genre relevant in an age that is daily further and further removed from the nineteenth century cowboy way of life, but it actually makes cowboy poetry more popular than it ever could have been when life under the stars was its only message and ranch hands were its only audience. Indeed, the verse has experienced a pronounced resurgence of popularity in the last decade. The first Cowboy Poetry gathering at Elko, Nevada, in 1985, attracted forty-two poets and 400 listeners. *People* magazine and *Newsweek* both covered the event. The titles of *Newsweek's* article, "Get Along, Little Doggerels," and of *People's,* "120 Rhyme-Stoned Cowboys Show

How the West Was Spun," suggest that the popular press took the gathering less than seriously. Since 1985, however, the event has become an annual one, now attracting several hundred poets each year and several thousand listeners and spectators. In his introduction to a recent anthology of cowboy poetry of the late twentieth century, Warren Miller writes that,

> It may surprise the reader to learn that there are more cowboy poets now than ever before. As I write [1994] there are annually more than one hundred public gatherings of cowboy poets around the West, each a festival presenting dozens of cowboy poets and reciters to eager audiences. Literally hundreds of cowboy poets have published books of their original poems, either as privately published chapbooks or through established publishing houses. Several periodicals exist solely to publish cowboy poetry, which is now heard regularly on radio and television, on recordings, and on the lecture circuit (*Cattle, Horses, Sky, and Grass* x).

At precisely the time when cowboy poetry's ostensible subject matter—buckaroos and horses—is less relevant to most readers than ever, and just when academics, in the name of truth and responsibility, are being asked to reevaluate traditional attitudes toward the cowboy myth, cowboy poetry is more popular than at any time in its history.

The audience's new connection to cowboy poetry is made through the figure of the "Other," the one who comes from the outside to disrupt the cowboy's idyllic relationship with the land, to make the cowboy feel less independent, to enforce upon the cowboy's consciousness the fact that he is only a powerless hired hand with little control over the land's or his own fate, a pawn in the way of larger historical forces. A relatively large segment of the American public now also senses the presence of the Other in their daily lives. The cowboy has long recognized himself as an outsider or orphan, as Allmendinger substantiates, although to some extent the cowboy's outsider status was, and still is, a matter of pride to him. More and more, however, the poets' readers and potential readers also interpret these Others, who are insiders, as standing between themselves and their true or potential identity, keeping or threatening to keep all of us off the range, which to the cowboy in real terms and to readers in symbolic terms is the place where one's identity is established. Ironically, the insiders help the cowboy to establish his identity by assisting him in being the outsider. However, being outside can also mean losing one's vocation, when the vocation itself is threatened by those Others who would have Americans turn to vegetables or chicken, who would regulate public land use more closely, who would "interfere" with the cowboy's freedom by introducing other regulations on grazing or pesticide use, or who would do anything else that impinges upon the cowboy's vocation. Being outside is fine, as long as those inside leave the cowboy alone. Americans in general, one may suggest, feel more and more alienated from their lives and place the blame on those more powerful or more wealthy. We now have come to share the cowboy's resentment of losing our sense of self to others who seem to have gained strange control over our lives while we were napping. This loss of control has always been felt by cowboy poets; the rest of the culture is now catching up to the poets. In addition, being "managed" by bureaucrats is a particularly acute body blow to the traditional sense of the cowboy's identity, his hardiness, and his masculinity. As Waddie Mitchell, one of the best known and most successful of the new poets, says in his poem "The Throw-Back":

> But nowdays they've throw'd us some ringers,
>> New problems that's kick'd in our slats,
> Like computers, the futures, and unions,
>> And worst of all . . . bureaucrats.

To have one's "slats" kicked in by something other than a bronco or a bull is downright embarrassing. And when the kicker is a bureaucrat, popularly pictured as an effeminate pencil-pusher, the insult is doubled. The cowboy, that last image in our American myth of the lone individual creating his own destiny, speaks clearly to those readers who are angry to realize that they are in the industrialized and capitalized twenty-first century. To the cowboy poet this means that the world is controlled by Others who tell the cowboy that he is irrelevant, and that his skill, his special knowledge, and his very sense of himself as a child of the land are obsolete, unimportant, of no value in a world of money, technology, and big government politics. The nostalgia for the past, the golden days, the unspoiled era, the days of the American Garden, that has always been associated with traditional cowboy poetry and that has manifested itself at various times in both bitterness and sentimentality is a large part of the current appeal of new cowboy poetry. "We"—poets and readers alike—would be pure, golden, cowboy Adams and Eves if only "they" would let "us."

This must sound familiar to any inhabitant of contemporary America. How many Americans today feel oppressed by outside forces they feel are running if not quite ruining their lives? Today it is no news to say that many Americans—regardless of where they live or what they do for a living—feel their "political and economic independence to be sorely threatened" (*The American West* 139), precisely the characteristics of the audience Karl Doerry in *The American West* identifies as being most receptive to westerns. Therefore, it should be no surprise that cowboy poets, like all things western, from movies to miniseries to hats and boots, are doing very well. People buy them or watch them or read them for images of a nonhierarchical community life free from schedules and bureaucracies, a world where one's courage, skill, and virtue are acknowledged and rewarded, where a meaningful vocation that is not alienating is possible, and where people somehow seem nobler and more powerful than the darker forces surrounding them. The cowboy poets in this formulation make a bargain with their readers and listeners: the readers agree to believe that the poets are real cowboys (when most are really professional entertainers who usually have had some experience on the range) and that the history and values they are selling are real; the poets allow the audience to enter and enjoy a mythical realm of time (a past when cowboys sang while they rode herd, a past when honesty and effort were all that mattered) and a mythical place (the land of the cowboy, an egalitarian, God-fearing realm where skill matters, where fate is character and character is fate).

As we listen or read, we get to imagine that there really once was a place where the alienation at the root of our culture from all things big never existed, and we are allowed for the moment to overcome poetically, or at least to ignore, our own alienation by entering the world of cowboy poetry where the only thing big is the sky. Author William Kittredge writes, "Many of us, in our comfort-bound existences, like to think of ourselves as radically individual, addicted to living on edges, staring some devil dead in the eye. Inside our circumscribed routines, we yearn to lead clean, well-lighted lives—like the cowboys" ("Introduction" 67). Poet and audience come together at the annual gatherings to reinforce each other's self-image, to assure each other that they still exist, that such "clean, well-lighted lives" exist, and to lick the wounds of the twenty-first century American (usually the male) made small by bureaucrats, ignored or exploited by Washington, mocked by intellectuals, made to feel stupid and obsolete by technology, and dwarfed by big money. As Kittredge continues, "It won't work, of course." But he concludes, "Still, we ride on into a solacing dream" ("Introduction" 67). The futility of the dream is perhaps even recognized by its dreamers. One ironic twist that may not be commonly recognized is that the same alienation from the vast panorama of futility and anarchy that is modern history, as described by T. S. Eliot, a decidedly non-cowboy poet, is at the root of both cowboy poetry and traditional modern poetry, the verse written by sissified eastern poets that no self-respecting cowboy poet would admit reading or liking or even allowing in his bunkhouse. The hatred or at the very least distrust of civilization also ironically connects the poets to what might be called modern and contemporary "nature writers," also people the poets would not want as poetic kin. John Elder, for example, in *Imagining the Earth,* notes that a "characteristic circuit in [Robinson] Jeffers' poetry" is "love of the wilderness and hatred of civilization feeding on each other" (8).

Examples of the anti-civilization attitude abound, but particularly illustrative is "Rancher's Revenge," by Bob Christensen, in which a group of cowboys, after working all day branding calves, sit down to rest, smoke, and talk about "how this cattle ranching's changed." One man offers his opinion:

> "Some say that beef's too high,
> Some say it causes cancer;
> Any bureaucrat you ask
> Will have a different answer.

And when I think of government
And all the funds we've spent
To get the public on our range,
And then they raised the rent.

They pay a man to raise no corn;
They buy another's cheese;
They pay you not to milk your cows
And to turn loose half your bees.

Then Pete says on the radio
They broadcast Tuesday night
That there are just too many cows:
That is the rancher's plight."

Then another fellow, Joe, begins to fantasize: what if the
nine million head of cattle currently on the range were condensed into one big cow?

"He'd have his off hind foot near Buffalo,
The front one in Tacoma,
The near hind foot in Jacksonville,
The fourth one near Pamona.

And after he ate all that hay,
Wouldn't it raise a fuss
If that steer did to Washington
What Washington's done to us!"

Note that the rancher is the victim of Washington, and the
after-work chat becomes a sort of around-the-campfire, out-on-
the-prairie version of a talk show. We are not the problem:

everyone else is. The pronoun usage in cowboy poetry is always
instructive: "they" are the ones in Washington who have done
"this" to "us." The cowboy refuses to identify with his government, preferring to establish himself, at least in the poetry, as a
victim, struggling to get by despite "their" incomprehensible
policies. The imagined revenge is also instructive. No one in
the poem suggests he will take arms against this sea of troubles
or that he will resist in some less violent fashion. They all will
continue to participate as victims, but show their disdain for
Washington in their verse. The image of a huge cow flop covering the Capitol dome may be attractive, in its own way, but it
suggests an emasculated rancher who is unable to respond
directly against his oppressors and who has lost even the gumption to refuse his subsidy check or price support.

The point of the poetry is that utopia used to exist before
"they" took it away, as Howard Norskog makes clear in his
poem "Takers," in which he describes the pitiful plight of an
aging rancher:

> The government took all his horses,
> And the bank hauled his cattle away,
>
> They told him the land was going for forfeit
> To pay some back taxes come due.
>
> . . . "Vacate the premises now,
> If you cannot pay up with all speed!
> We're coming to take everything that you have."

Big government and big money "take" while the poor
rancher (burdened enough, it would seem, but also given a flu

by Norskog) has spent his life giving to the land. The government, of course, goes in for overkill and calls out the National Guard to evict the old guy. Norskog cannot quite urge the old man to shoot the Guardsmen, even though he sits by his front door with his rifle and "twenty-odd shells." Instead, the rancher becomes a martyr to the cause, the ultimate in innocent victimhood, as he sits on his porch, while "the soldiers in battle dress came through the trees." He "raised up his rifle;/but he never fired at all," and of course he gets gunned down. His act of rebellion? He leaves a note telling them that "he's at last traveled home." Small compensation for a bullet-riddled body, perhaps, but the rancher maintains his purity against the marauding Huns of the acquisitive and insatiable culture of the East.

The motif of the "last stand" has always been important in western art and western culture. One of the best expressions of the theme is the painting by Frederic Remington, *Fight for the Waterhole,* in which white soldiers line the slope leading to a small waterhole somewhere on the semi-arid plains. The soldiers are armed, and hostile Indians circle the site. The white men may force a stand-off for a while, but we know they're doomed. Karl Doerry reminds us that this "last stand" motif was popular in western art and literature at the turn of the century, during that period of "widespread and violent labor unrest, strikes, and riots" ("The American West" 144). Doerry continues that "It is surely no accident that the Western [film genre] experienced a renaissance after World War II, when the country again felt its values threatened by the postwar economic boom, the external threat of the Cold War, and the internal challenge to democratic American values posed by McCarthyism" ("The American West" 145). Film historians Arthur McClure and Ken Jones agree:

> . . . it is entirely possible that in the midst of the confusion and uncertainty created by the Depression and World War II audiences sustained many of their "faiths" by identifying with such admirable and powerful symbols of straightforward righteousness as seen in the "B" westerns. (*Heroes, Heavies, and Sagebrush* 11)

The western movie, Doerry claims, and one could say all things western, including cowboy poetry, may be interpreted as "appealing to audiences by offering an alternative to their morally ambiguous and problematic present" (*Heroes, Heavies, and Sagebrush* 145). Today, in another period of cultural uncertainty and ambiguity, the last stand motif returns to a central position in cowboy poetry: we are taking our stand at our waterhole, holding off the savages. The waterhole is the West, or the myth of the West, in which the cowboy figures so prominently. The guns are transformed to poems. The Indians, oddly enough, have been replaced by other "savages": intellectuals, politicians, bureaucrats, and bankers. The Old West and its values are always, from the beginning, it seems, under siege by hostile, outside forces, and the only one left standing to fight the good fight is the cowboy, as Dick Gibford makes clear in his poem "The Last Buckaroo." First, Gibford paints a grim picture of modern life: "The urbanite/Has taken flight/Not knowin' where to roost"; "Super powers . . . lie for hours,/Right to each other's face"; and "The truth seems lost." The modern world has gone to hell. We are surrounded by the new "savages," this time in three-piece suits and sporting law degrees. Who will save us? Who else: "Ridin' lead to Armageddon/ Comes the last buckaroo." From his experience roping, branding, and doing honest labor under the sun and stars, the buckaroo knows "truth indeed" and, at this apocalyptic moment in history, he comes riding on "his steed." The final image in Gibford's poem is of "the last buckaroo/. . . standing in his place." Exactly what the last buckaroo does to save us when he arrives is unclear, but at least he will stand firm and true to his principles.

While much of what we hear in cowboy poetry sounds innocent, good-natured, or simply benign and sentimental, much of the complaining originates in an anger born of perceived helplessness and victimization and is more mean-spirited than it appears to be on the surface, often directing its anger toward the members of the opposing camp. Mary Jane Hurst, to mention one commentator, notices the humor in the poetry, and she notices its characteristic target, but she maintains that its tone is more innocent than it really is. Focusing on Baxter Black's "The Vegetarian's Nightmare," she says that it "links up with contemporary culture because it deals, albeit ironically, metaphorically, and humorously, with real issues— vegetarianism and movements for animal rights—which affect cowboy life today" ("Connections" 35). The cowboy not only feels "affected," however, but abused, and his poetry is only humorous on the surface while often being contemptuous and combative underneath, at the subtextual level. Shepperson and Winzeler are even more disingenuous than Hurst when they claim that, ". . . the use of truly hostile language is limited. Few voice broad social protest; few emphasize political, ideological or controversial subjects; few really find someone to blame" ("Cowboy Poetry" 264). On the contrary, the entire genre is underpinned by social protest, although that protest is disguised somewhat and superficially softened because the expectations of the genre (that the cowboy speaker be polite and

respectful, controlling his emotions as a real man would)
demand as much. Nonetheless, to the initiated reader, the
protest and blame are quite evident, especially in contemporary
examples of the verse. The poem, "The Papers Say," by Vess
Quinlan is a good example. The poem sounds innocent enough.
The speaker is complaining about cattle prices, attributing the
usual problems to the usual suspects:

> The interest rate has doubled,
>   And so's the cost of gas;
> Now the B.L.M. is trying to raise
>   The price of grass.
> . . . .
> The trouble's these new notions
>   Of what folks ought to eat:
> There's a growing crowd around
>   That frowns on good red meat.

No harm done, one might say, although some animosity
does peek through in the final stanza:

> I talked to all the cowmen:
>   We're going to stand and fight.
> If folks won't eat our good red meat,
>   We'll run cattle just for spite.

The subtext in these poems, however, is always clear to the
faithful readers of the genre, no matter how innocuous the surface may look, as is evident from the illustration by Joe Beeler
that accompanies the poem's text in one edition (*Cattle* 78) and
that expresses the true, underlying hostility of the poem better

than the words' surfaces do. The illustrator portrays a street scene, with a cowboy on the front left quietly leaning against a building as a group of motley protesters, oozing disreputability, pass on the right. In the illustration, the cowboy looks clean and well-scrubbed. He sports a trim physique and is neatly dressed in jacket and white hat. The protesters, this group of Others, are slovenly and unshaven, with hairy armpits, backwards caps, long hair, and stubble on the women's legs. They are raggedly dressed in shorts and patched jeans, and several wear tattoos. These are stereotypical "old hippies," carrying placards with a variety of slogans which suggests flighty idealism and a lack of touch with reality (one man even has his eyes closed). No matter how benign the poem sounds, the illustration makes clear the hostility and antagonism that underlie the words. The cowboy is a reasonable adult and superior to the unwashed, unshaven, misguided protesters who are allotted all the respect of children throwing a temper tantrum. If these people suddenly were run over by a pick-up truck, neither the poet nor the cowboy would grieve. There is no hint of the possibility of, or desire for, the sort of rational discussion between opposing forces that we associate with democratic discourse. Quinlan and the other poets expect that the reader will, as illustrator Beeler did, pick up on the attitudes expressed so gently, even humorously, in the poems.

One step beyond the contempt of Beeler's illustration and Quinlan's words is the actual violence suggested by Baxter Black's poem, "The Cowboy and the Lady." In the story, a buckaroo, trying to be gentlemanly (as he understands that term) encounters a woman he sees as "seductive," "limber," and "lean." From this description, we quickly sense that whatever follows will be her own fault. The cowboy's impulse is to take off his hat, reach for the door, and offer to hold it open, but when the woman demurs (in a rather exaggerated manner), we learn a lot more about Black's attitudes toward women than about any real woman we may have run across. The lady exclaims that she has no need of any "cowboy" who would take her to be a "frail fräulein," and as the cowboy attempts to "impress" her with his "sweet talk," she confronts him. She knows what he is and what he wants, since "all men" are only "after one thing." With his honor bludgeoned, the affronted cowboy has no choice but to avenge his wounded masculinity. When she gives him "an obscene gesture," he lets the door "slip" from his hold, and it hits her "square in the face."

As we feel the door hit this seductive ne'er-do-well, we get a visceral sense of the thinly disguised hostility and violence in many of the new cowboy poems, a result of the way the poet sees his way of life, or the way of life his genre typically celebrates. His sense of self is undercut by forces beyond his power, but these forces will not be turned the way a herd of cattle can be.

It is clear that the current popularity of cowboy poetry is one more indication of middle-class anger and resentment at being passed over, minimized, made to feel small, made to feel economically and personally and spiritually insecure. As Stephen Tatum says, when we go see cowboys or other "exotics," we are evidencing our "desire to 'see' what we have 'lost' as a result of living in a devitalized, banal urban present, and in doing so displace our anxieties into the very act of looking, one which gives pleasure to the extent that the hungry eye is gratified by the visual possession of commodities (*Eye on the Future* 62)." When one recognizes that reading cowboy poetry satisfies the same need as seeing a cowboy in action at a rodeo or virtually any other cowboy theme show, for example, then Tatum's analysis be-comes relevant to the phenomenon of cowboy verse. The poetry speaks to the deep insecurity, sense of helplessness, and loss of power that run through the middle class now the way hope and optimism did in the post-World War II generation. The immediate result is a victimization, a posture of passivity that does not reduce the anger but only produces it in greater quantities. The further result is the intolerance evident in the poems, a phenomenon that dovetails nicely with the many other examples of increased intolerance evident in our culture today. While the cowboy poet's anger is directed at powerful people, his most venomous attacks are reserved for the less culpable or for those simply related to the bad guys. So while we do hear nasty remarks about bankers, the feminist gets hit in the face with a door. And while we do hear discouraging words about bureaucrats, the environmentalists and vegetarians are pictured as unwashed, barely human, placard-carrying protesters. The powers that be seem too powerful, so the poets' anger is displaced onto those who are vulnerable, the easy targets who are always chosen for backlash.

It seems, therefore, that despite the poetry's valuable function of giving a voice to the phenomenon of human receptivity and responsiveness to nature, a receptivity that modern citizens desperately need and want to absorb into their culture, a sadness lurks beneath the poetry's smiling face and the celebratory mood of the gatherings. Both poet and reader, trapped in a world that assaults their sense of self from all sides, are forced into the ironic position of parodying themselves in order to save themselves. The cowboy's real life—either while working or while doing non-cowboy activities—is probably no more heroic and noble than anyone else's, but to tell the tale of that existence would be death to the poet's career. His real life has to be pushed aside, just as the reader pushes aside his when he loses himself in the pastoral visions of the poetry, and the poet has to show his reader instead the stereotypical version of the cowboy's life. In Tatum's words, "the 'natural' gets displaced by representation, in the sense that one defines one's authentic subjectivity by imagining the way others will regard and consume one's constructed self-image"(*Eye on the Future* 63).

The poet willingly participates in this objectification of the cowboy's life in order to reap material benefits—a career as an entertainer—while the reader participates to reap psychological benefits. The poet has to distance himself from real cowboys, whose lives are not particularly heroic, and turn them into objects to be employed to create a consistently heroic image of a character, a lifestyle, and a world that the audience will pay to listen to or read about, while the reader has to distance himself from his real concerns and any possible real-world solutions to them. Thus the cowboy poet oddly participates in his own commodification in which he packages and sells himself by first denying or altering for market demands the details of his and his subject's reality, and his reader participates in his own alienation, which he is supposedly attempting to transcend or resolve by turning to the verse and its images of a rooted, meaningful life of outdoor labor. The cowboy today, as Larry McMurtry notes, "very often . . . becomes a victim of his own ritual" ("Saddle" 39). McMurtry could have added that the reader falls prey to similar, self-consuming if not self-defeating rituals. The poet sells himself to the tourist gaze to enable visitors to the West (real or printed) to feed on the life and character of a hero, to feed on the heroic that is missing from their lives. The cowboy's life, then, is ironically objectified and commodified just as the Indian and his life have been, as objects for a tourist economy, for alienated, disenchanted, romantic, nostalgic, middle-class couch potatoes who find themselves out West, or in the western section of the bookstore, looking for some stability and meaning to their lives.

Photo Credit: Peter Iseman

John Haines
1924–

CHAPTER THREE

A Terrible Beauty: The Alaskan Wilderness and the Poetry of John Haines

For John Haines, nature is a world apart from the prairies of the cowboys or the desert landforms of Peggy Church. Haines acquired his particular poetic vision as a result of years spent in the Alaskan wilderness, when there still was such a thing, just after service in the Navy from 1943 to 1946. He went to Alaska in 1947 but, after building "a small cabin . . . with dirt floor and mossy roof poles" ("Homage" 42), returned temporarily to the mainland in 1948 to continue his studies.[1] He recalls thinking of his small house and wondering why he had left it (Sims 34). He returned to the homestead in 1954 and remained an Alaskan year-round until 1969 (the year he was named the state's first Poet Laureate) and then intermittently until

1992, when he left, unhappy that the wilderness had become so thoroughly domesticated: ". . . now in order to look down on the river itself I have to cross the highway and climb a guardrail, where once, years ago, I looked directly down from the house to see five wolves trotting downriver on the spring ice" (Sims 34). Haines also found it difficult to make ends meet in Alaska and left the state periodically to take visiting professor or poet-in-residence posts at various universities. He was reportedly collecting unemployment in Fairbanks in 1991 ("Poet Can't Eat Laurels" 12). He has since returned to the state and lives in Anchorage. Haines began his long-term affair with America's last wilderness when he left behind what we call civilization and set up his home seventy miles from Fairbanks, at Richardson near Banner Creek and the Tanana River in the Tenderfoot area, a region that at the turn of the century had been populated by speculators with gold fever but by mid-century had been largely abandoned. His homesteading at first recalls Thoreau, but Paul Zweig in "Messages in a Bottle" reminds us that, "Unlike Thoreau, he went more than the symbolic mile from home" ("Messages" 281). Haines describes the area he encountered: "By the time I came there in 1947, only six or eight of the older residents still lived along the creeks, or in the hills above the Tanana" (*Country* 8). He trapped, hunted, and managed to raise enough food to survive. There must have been compelling reasons for anyone to homestead for two decades in a land where cold and dark are much more real than warmth and light, where, even in September, "the immense sadness/of approaching winter/hangs in the air." Haines supplies the reason when he explains that, as a child, his family moved from place to place (his father was in the Navy). "It would naturally follow that I nourished in myself a great wish for something more permanent. . . . I think I knew then that I would have to find a specific place and be born over again as my own person" (*Country* 5).

At Richardson, Haines was "born over again." That sounds religious, and it is, but it is also aesthetic. In Alaska he found his way of expressing his relationship to the world by expressing his relationship to a particular place in that world: "As a poet," he says, "I was born in a particular place, a hillside overlooking the Tanana River in central Alaska. . . . It was there, in the winter of 1947-1948, that I began writing poems seriously, and there many years later that I wrote my first mature poems" (*Country* 4). For some reason, a reason that Haines himself admits is probably impossible to pinpoint, the landscape of Alaska at the time in its history when a man could walk from his "homestead at Richardson all the way to the Arctic Ocean and never cross a road nor encounter a village" (*Country* 5) was exactly the place he had always been dreaming of: "From the first day I set foot in interior Alaska, and more specifically on Richardson Hill, I knew I was home. Something in me identified with that land-scape. I had come, let's say, to the dream place" (*Country* 5).[2]

"Dream place" may carry misleading connotations. For Haines, the world is a beautiful place in which he feels right at home, but it is a dangerous and bloody place, too, not the comfortable home of hearth and slippers but the realm of hunted animals' entrails and blood-spattered snow. His nature is a world red in tooth and claw but correctly, not regrettably, so. He feels himself brother to the moose, bear, and goshawk, as well as to the rabbit and field mouse that serve as prey for the world's predators. The danger, violence, and terror of the wilderness are necessary and proper, and only those who fail to or refuse to see their own teeth and claws are able to regret the natural slaughter that purifies and cleanses the world, that at base is not only survival (of the individual, the species, and the planet) but that is also an expression of passion of the same sort that writes poems, makes love, and, when misunderstood or denied, builds missiles and clear-cuts forests. Haines himself asserts that, "deprived of the opportunity to hunt birds and beasts we are inclined to hunt one another and, as Shakespeare put it, 'make perforce a universal prey'" ("The Lure" 16). Of all the American poets who have felt the need to be intimate with death in order to, in Whitman's words, understand "the klew" to it all, Haines has the bloodiest hands.

The Alaskan wilderness and his life in it provide him with the armature upon which to fashion his art, a core around which to synthesize into poetry his experiences, passions, and thoughts: "Many things went into the making of those poems and the others I've written since: the air of the place, its rocks, soil, and water; snow and ice; human history, birds, animals, and insects. . . . But it was finally the place itself that provided the means of unifying all of these into a single experience" (*Country* 4). Despite having lived in cities pursuing employ-ment, the wilderness experience is in his poetry from the beginning poems to the latest ones. The experience of living off the land, knowing what blood and skin and death really mean, and feeling them as palpable presences in one's life, has never left the poet, which he readily admits in several essays. In the early poems, the presence of Alaska is most obvious and explicit, but even in his later work, even when the subject is a painting or a sculpture or an anti-war rally, Alaska and that homestead at Richardson are always present behind the lines, in the tone, in the imagery, and in the poet's understanding of his place in the world. Haines expresses the basis of that rela-tionship quite succinctly, emphasizing the words "rapture" and "veneration," which replace the more typical modernist impersonality and alienation:

> Clearly, on the evidence, something has been lost in the art of nature study in this century; not simply curiosity, or even excitement, but a better word: rapture. It is an emotion that comes, not merely from looking at things, but from seeing them with a kind of veneration, as if within these objects, these vistas of water and mountain, something of the impenetrable mystery might be sensed and named, and before which one might be, not designing or dominating, but quietly attentive ("Attention" 76).

This rapture or awe cannot be obtained by being an observer of nature but only by "having lived acutely in a physical world" ("Attention" 77).

One of Haines' earliest published poems, "If the Owl Calls Again," from his first volume, *Winter News* (1966), introduces several recurring images. The speaker, at dusk in the cold of Alaska, waits for the owl to call again, inviting the speaker to join the bird in an evening hunt. The two "will not speak" but will sit

> in the shadowy spruce
> and pick the bones
> of careless mice.

After the hunt, "fulfilled," each will float "homeward as/the cold world awakens." In "A Moose Calling," another poem from the same volume, the speaker is hunting a moose whose siren call lures him on:

> Who are you,
> calling me in the dusk,
>
> O dark shape
> with heavy horns?

The moose participates in the "ruse of the hunter," and the hunter acknowledges the moose's partnership in a life-affirming act. Haines' understanding of the human existential condition becomes clear early in his poetry: alone in a cold world, man the predator awaits the world's invitation to take part in a dark, silent, and violent ritual of initiation and perpetuation.[3]

The attitude toward the "careless mice" or deceived moose might seem a bit callous or bloodthirsty to those who get meat in plastic wrappers. Zweig has said with praise that at the center of Haines' character resides "a kind of sober murderousness" ("Messages in a Bottle" 282). Elsewhere in Haines' poetry it is clear that the prey is as respected as the predator, and the two are complements in a symbiotic relationship that keeps the earth clean and its resident species alive. In "Prayer to the Snowy Owl," for example, the predator owl is the "preserver of whiteness." Again, in "Dream of the Lynx," the lynx in the speaker's dream, its "life risen/to the surface of darkness," awaits its meal "beside a narrow trail in the blue/cold of evening." Approaching somewhere in the forest is the "unseen, feeding host." That final word, combined with the image of the lynx's "life risen," suggests the sacredness of the prey in the prey-predator relationship. The prey becomes a communion host, the body of a deity that is willingly offered to "life risen" and then humbly consumed to perpetuate life. The prey in this formulation is perhaps even more respected than the hunter, who must rely upon the prey for his life. The predator survives, but the prey nourishes and, as life-giver, is apotheosized. The needy hunter must call the god's name (lure the prey to him) or await the god's call (listen for the cry of a mentor predator to instruct him), go to the dark woods as supplicant, and beg for a vision or sight of that which will nourish and save him. Poet Gary Snyder makes the same point in *Earth House Hold*:

> To hunt means to use your body and senses to the fullest: to strain your consciousness to feel what the deer are thinking today, this moment; to sit still and let your self go into the birds and wind while waiting by the game trail. Hunting magic is designed to bring the game to you—the creature who has heard your song, witnessed your sincerity, and out of compassion comes within your range (quoted in Elder 43).

In "Prayer to the Snowy Owl," the supplicant implores, "Descend, silent spirit,"asking the owl/spirit to reveal itself. In "Horns," he writes,

> I went to the edge of the wood
> in the color of evening,
> and rubbed with a piece of horn
> against a tree,
> believing the great, dark moose
> would come, his eyes
> on fire with the moon.

With patience, we may be allowed a glimpse of the sacred that is always around us but usually hidden. And when the deity emerges from hiding and enters the clearing of our consciousness, the sight is awesome:

> His horns exploded in the brush
> with dry trees cracking
> and falling; his nostrils flared
> as, swollen-necked, smelling
> of challenge, he stalked by me.

After the moose emerges, the speaker stands transfixed

> in the moonlight,
> and the darkness and silence
> surged back, flowing around me,
> full of a wild enchantment,
> as though a god had spoken.

The light breaks as the god reveals itself briefly and then disappears. His "roaring" breath is the breath of vitality, connected with the many images of wind in Haines' poetry, which communicates the mysteries in silence, the only voice being the sheer breath of the life-force itself as if we are alone in the world with it.

Haines engages in a dialogue with nature, calling to it, listening for its response, beckoning the gods of the forest to step forth. The persistent use of personification is more than a method: it is a point of view that says that the line between species is not nearly as distinct as we would like to believe. We are alone in the darkness, calling our muses and deities to us, who stomp forth enraged and clamorous but depart peacefully and silently, leaving us as before, in the dark, surrounded by silence, but now with the knowledge that such wonders exist. That a god responds occasionally when we make ourselves vulnerable (meeting it in its territory) is about all the reassurance we get in these poems. In this wild world, if we remain humble and patient, then perhaps the sacred, clothed in the rugged skin of the profane, will emerge:

> We are still kneeling
> and listening,
> as from the edge of a field
> there rises something at evening
> the snort of a rutting bull.
> "Book of the Jungle"

The moose feeds the hunter and then its rotting carcass feeds "the small pilots of the soil," the insects who traverse the stripped moosehead for their survival. The moonlight that accompanies the moose's appearance in "Horns" is repeated in the "faint glow of phosphorus" that still resides in the "black water" of the moose skull in "The Moosehead."

Black water and phosphorus: from darkness comes light, from blood comes salvation, from silence comes communication of the most intense but inarticulate mysteries of life and living. Haines' perspective is that of the man who has lived in extremes and seen them connect. The hunter hunts for the nourishment that is both physical and spiritual. The "rutting bull" of "Book of the Jungle" is the god, and visits the earth with the same ferocity and divinity as the one who raped Europa. Haines agrees with Wordsworth, who says in "Nutting" that "there is a spirit in the woods," and he would accept the suggestion that we must therefore move through nature respectfully, but he would disagree with the Romantic poet's suggestion that such respect also means that we must "move along these shades/In gentleness of heart; with gentle hand/Touch." Wordsworth laments his gathering of the hazelnuts from the "virgin scene" because he sees himself as human, as distinct from the grove as nature. Haines understands that human and nature are one thing, not two, and that no living scene is "virgin," for if it is living then animals and insects and plants and trees themselves have reproduced there, which always means growing out of the death of some other element in the scene. Haines' nature is a wilderness in which human and nonhuman elements reside mutually: "We speak of nature, of the natural world, as if that were something distinct from ourselves . . . seldom noticing that we are in nature and never out of it" (*Fables* 129). Wordsworth's nature is a grove from which we humans have been expelled.

Go ahead and nourish yourself from the nuts, Haines would say. It is only your delusion of alienation from nature that turns that feeding into a "merciless ravage." Haines is a hundredfold more bloody than Wordsworth or any other Romantic poet would dream of being, but he is never a ravager and never merciless, for he understands that his prey are his kin. The role of predator is not without guilt ("I am haunted by/the deaths of animals" he says in "On the Divide"), but the guilt is inevitable and amoral—perhaps transmoral, the burden the hunter must bear to participate in the sacred life cycle, just as the prey's burden is its doom. These moose and mice are very much earthly and earthy gods—gods who show us in their lives the intersection of the sacred and the profane, the still point where the divine touches the temporal. Again, Snyder makes a similar point about the relationship between hunter and hunted: "Hunting magic is not only aimed at bringing beasts to their death, but to assist in their birth—to promote their fertility"4 (quoted in Elder 43). John Elder in "Imagining the Earth" explicates Snyder's words: "Hunting, within such an understanding, is a sacrament; it brings men closer to nature, rather than estranging them from it" (Elder 43).

While Haines' wilderness gods live, suffer, and die, they are always respected and always maintain their dignity and divinity. They are tenacious. They preside over an injured, frozen world, as in "The House of the Injured," in which the speaker stumbles upon a "small, windowless, and dark" house in the forest. The interior emits a reek of the "suffocating odor of blood/and fur mixed with dung." Yet the speaker pushes himself inside and discovers "an injured bird/that filled the room." A wild bird, even a small one, if trapped in a dark house would certainly seem to fill the room and command all one's attention. Yet the hint here is of something beyond the literal, of something noble in this dank hut, something grand commanding this house of the injured. The bird is not in peak condition (its "beak was half eaten away" and the feathers "ruffled"), yet suddenly the speaker "sank to [his] knees—/a man shown the face of God." Haines' God is itself injured in this world of walking injured—all of us who are mortal are injured—not a Mt. Olympus eagle but one of us, an image of our own decrepit state, one step closer to death and decay with each moment, but an image of the divinity that persists in that always dying body. It is a small house of a world and even its reigning god is wounded, but it is that tenacious animal vigor, grand in the stench and rot of its physicality, that touches the spiritual for Haines.

There is nothing cute and fluffy in Haines' nature: no cuddly stuffed bears or purring lap cats. Donald Hall remarks, when describing why Haines was chosen to receive the 1991 Lenore Marshall/*Nation* Poetry Prize, "this landscape is not a Sierra Club calendar" ("Lenore Marshall/*Nation* Poetry Prize" 677). Haines gets as far as possible from the romantic or sentimental in his depiction of nature. When he tells us, in "Winter News," that winter approaches and "the voice of the snowman/calls the white-/haired children home," this is no image of jolly Frosty but the warning, carried on the frigid air, of hypothermia and frostbite. The cold season has its beauty (while fishing for salmon, in "Poem of the Wintry Fisherman," he describes the fish as "blood-red, green and orange,/in the ice-blue glacier water"), but if one lingers too long while being sentimental, one will become the prey:

> Along the darkening river,
> ravens grip their iron twigs,
> shadows of
> the hungry, shuddering night.

The spawning salmon deposit the beginnings of a new generation and then die: Haines will nourish himself off their life-generating death throes; the foxes patrolling the shore will gather the remnants; the night itself is alive and hungry: everywhere in this harsh wilderness we are reminded of the life and death struggle that existence is; the terrible beauty that comprises the world. The world's indifference to his existence occasionally frightens the poet, but it scares his dogs, too:

A drowsy, half-wakeful menace waits for us in the quiet-
ness of this world. I have felt it near me while kneeling in
the snow, minding a trap on a ridge many miles from
home. There, in the cold that gripped my face, in the low,
blue light failing around me, and the short day ending, in
those familiar and friendly shadows, I was suddenly aware
of something that did not care if I lived. Or, as it may be,
running the river ice in midwinter: under the sled runners
a sudden cracking and buckling that scared the dogs and
sent my heart racing. How swiftly the solid bottom of
one's life can go (*The Stars* 104).[5]

The world he shows us is indifferent to all its children,
humans and nonhumans, making the poet feel more at home
though not more comfortable. The anthropocentric vision gets
us into trouble, thinking ourselves central and then feeling
alienated when we discover we are only one element in nature,
not its nucleus. Close observation of the sort enforced by wilderness existence teaches that everywhere "are life's victims/cap-
tives of an old umbrella,/lives wrecked/by the lifting of a stone"
("In Nature"). It is a harsh world but not an unfair one, and it
is the world we belong to despite its resistance to let us or anything survive easily. The harshness of the tundra is evoked by
mention of its landmarks, which Haines describes in such a way
as to let us see that the beauty of the place carries just under its
skin the threat of death:

> In the tangled lakes
> of its eyes a mirror of ice
> is forming, where
> frozen gut-piles shine

with a dull, rosy light.
    "The Tundra"

The tundra is a living body, "full of blood," a living, sacred body that one worships with fear and respect.[6] Winter we expect to be hard, but even spring is no softy. In "And When the Green Man Comes," the chaotic profusion of spring is captured in the image of a green man, with "the clamor of bedlam" in his beard, strolling across the thawing tundra. However, he also packs death in that beard, which Haines will not let us forget: ". . . and in his beard/the maggot sings."

The land's harshness becomes commonplace ("It is minus sixty degrees," he says, flatly, in "Fairbanks Under the Solstice"). It is sometimes used as a symbol of welcome deliverance from the unnecessary distractions of a warmer climate, as in the image of the "ghostly newsboys" in "Fairbanks Under the Solstice" "delivering . . . word of the resurrection of Silence." Even the poet's diction is spare, minimal, as if the speaker is preserving his energy.[7] Silence and cold are our true modes of being, for under the weight of the winter cold, heavy snow, and gray sky, we are forced inward, where all the real action is anyway. So while Haines acknowledges the "great black-/and-gold butterflies" around "the crowded feet/of summer," his real admiration is reserved for the mole, the "one/who in the dead of winter/tunnels through a damp,/clinging darkness" ("The Mole"). The butterflies are "intense" but also "brief," flourishing only in the best and easiest months, while the mole persists, "unnoticed," through the most trying of times. Never ignore the butterfly, but never forget his darker and more permanent counterpart the mole, who comes closer as a figure to representing the answer to the question of the poem "What Is Life?":

There are no roads
but the paths we make
through sleep and darkness.

An invisible friend: a ghost
like a black wind
that buffets and steadies
the lost bystander
   who thinks he sees.

The first stanza sounds rather like egotistical rough-and-ready individualism, but, with the addition of "sleep and darkness," is really an image of our wandering lost and virtually sightless in a dark world with few directional indicators except the ghostly black wind that both "buffets" and "steadies" us. Our only mistake is the sin of pride, thinking that we know where we are or that we can see clearly what is in front of us. Wiser to burrow on mole-like, trusting our instincts until, if we are lucky, one day we may be able to emerge "blinking at the sun" and drying our "strange, unruly wings" ("The Mole"). Thoreau shows us armies of ants dying neatly by the thousands. Haines shows us the red interior of a gutted moose, dead and alone, a bloodier and colder world but oddly a calmer and cleaner one, too.

A primitivism lurks not too far beneath the surface of many of these poems. The suggestion is always implicit that we have lost touch with our true, deep, and ancient self, buried beneath layers, generations, or even millennia of culture. Returning to the life of a primitive hunter is Haines' way of acting out, or living up to, his poetry's suggestion that a subterranean and older vital life force lies within us all. It is, however, very difficult to return to that self, as we hear in "To Turn Back," which begins with an image of "the grass people," or the grass personified, bowing their heads in the wind. The grass, rooted in earth, suggests some earlier state of consciousness when humans pursued more basic ends, living simply rather than accumulating wealth, busying our minds with electronic images, climbing corporate ladders, and doing the rest of the things we moderns do. The grass is planted in a reality that is enduring and simple, and reminds one again of Thoreau's concept of "economy," or cutting back on the superfluities of our lives. Haines wonders if we humans can be as simple and focused on living life as the grass is:

> How would it be
> to stand among them, bending
> our heads like that. . . ?

He gives no answer ("Yes . . . and no . . . perhaps . . ."), but he does declare that

> to be among them
> is to have only simple
> and friendly thoughts,
>
> and not be afraid.

Humans obviously cannot return to a grass-like condition (Keats' sod again), but elsewhere the poet says we can and must be aware of the deep and primitive self within us, the one that links us with the blood of the hunt and the frigid breath of the winter.

Sometimes, oddly enough, we see that primitive self most clearly in a city, as in "The Snowbound City," from Haines' second book, *The Stone Harp* (1971). The stifled city is likened to "a beast with broken spine/its hoarse voice hooded in feathers/ and mist," corroborating the suggestion that even when away from the wilderness Haines sees with the angle of sight he learned in the Arctic. When the city is snow-covered, its façades that normally cover nature are themselves by nature obscured. Then the city's walkers, used to navigating by man-made landmarks, those stone and mortar attempts to hide from the primal truth hidden beneath them, are lost and have to feel their way home by relying upon their older instincts to guide them:

> When evening falls in blurred heaps,
> a man losing his way among churches
> and schoolyards feels under his cold hand
> the stone thoughts of that city.

To the adult, these thoughts are vague intimations of some truth he has lost. Only the children, unencumbered yet by the adult's defenses and still closer to the truth of things, can really move:

> impassable to all but a few children
> who went on into the hidden life
> of caves and winter fires,
> their faces glowing with disaster.

The "hidden life" in Haines' vision is always there, just covered. What to the adult is chaos and bafflement, to the children is possibility. Their faces glow because what is from the adult point of view a snowy "disaster" is to the children a chance to shine. These children remind us of the blundering mole who moves forward in the darkness by trusting his inner eyes, his internal communication with the "hidden life."

The "hidden life" is symbolized with an image from the landscape: "The Hermitage" (from *Twenty Poems,* 1971) is a "secret home," a place in the forest "below the stairs" where the speaker can go to retreat into himself and keep everyone and everything else at bay. Perhaps this external place exists— people often have special places to which they retreat—but the poem certainly uses the "crevice stuffed with moss" as a symbolic place, an internal place, one's secret home or hidden life or whatever one chooses to call it, the place where we feel most ourselves, at our deepest spot "in the roots" of our being. It is the source or locus of what Haines calls "passion" (in "Panorama"), a libidinal energy that sometimes is sexual ("this hand stroking a breast") but more often is turned to other activities ("pulling a turnip from stubborn soil,/cracking a bone, driving a nail") that are manifestations in the world of our deepest psychic impulses, our "full and divided nature" that is both good and evil, "violent and generous,/cunning and naive,/stalking and lying at rest. . . ." We are bloody and forgiving, but for the most part, Haines suggests, we do not see or understand our full nature, a combination of impulses that frightens us and that thereby makes us, if we ignore it, its victims, turning the passion to self-defensive and destructive ends (in Haines' words, "bombing the Kurds" or "selling junk bonds" ["The Lure" 16]) that seem out of place with our other more benign activities (listening to "fieldmice squeaking in the grass"), which are part and parcel of the same "full and divided nature." Haines' driving motivation, correctly identified by poet and one-time Alaskan Robert Hedin, is "a profound desire for wholeness" (192).[8] The poet uses a landscape term (panorama) as a title for his work about the complex human psyche, suggesting again how closely tied to place is his understanding of his humanity.

We try to flee or destroy this divided face because it seems horrible to us. "Yeti" is a poem about the abominable snowman dwelling within us all, the "maimed and shaggy captive" of our consciousness. Sometimes the mountain climber, alone and with his mind open to possibility, his normal routine no longer protecting him, hears the "snow-filled cry" of the beast, but most of us are never that vulnerable to ourselves. "Something will always/be hidden," he says, the "force behind our face," the force that is passion that we drive away, "like a wise ape/driven to the snows." Our daytime consciousness Haines calls our "sleep of reason" from which we have banished all "emblems of blood," reminders of our primitive Yeti-self that lives with us until we dress up and act civil. We have an internal wilderness ("Wilderness survives at the camp/we have made within us," "Victoria," from *Cicada,* 1977) that Haines knows because he has lived thoughtfully in the external wilderness. We are part wild, here imaged as "a forest willed up with night," a frightening place but as necessary to a living world as the sun that "climbs again" every morning. Night's existence does not negate the sun's warmth and light. Until we realize this, we will not "be at home/again on earth." We will walk around each of us individually like a "great bale of straw/smoldering in the darkness," in an image reminiscent of Eliot's hollow men, stuffed with straw.

At some level, we do seek reunion with our exiled passion:

> This rain of particles,
> random sparks catching fire,
> blowing out in the stellar drifts,
> each one seeking the other.

We have inside us something like the "great shark" whose fossil Haines examines in "The Fossil" (*News from the Glacier,* 1982). The internal shark reminds us that "life is beaked and nailed/and armed with teeth," a fact we are forced to acknowledge "sometimes in our sleep," when we see the image of this cold-water self in "the lips of living men." Again Haines suggests that we try, tentatively, to recapture this deep self ("night after night/the heart's wide nets are cast"), but again he cannot tell to what extent we as a culture and a people will be successful. The shark image is different from his earlier lynx image, due to a new life experience (viewing the fossil in a museum), but the terms of the earlier poems persist, again reflecting the permanence of the impression of Richardson Hill.

Whatever the prognosis for others, Haines shows us his own journey of self-discovery, again in the images of the place that formed him. In "Cicada," he speaks through the narrative of the long-buried insect's awakening. The bug finds itself buried ("I sank past bitten leaves") and "in the dark" when a voice within it calls it to life:

> A whisper, dry and insane,
> repeating like a paper drum,
> something I was,
> something I might become.

The whispers of mortality are painful to heed ("a little green knife/slitting the wind upstairs") for crawling out from under one's protective coverings is frightening. Yet the cicada has to obey its urge to life and is rewarded with "loud acres of sun" when it emerges. The emergence of hidden life reminds us of the concluding anecdote in Walden, when Thoreau tells the story of the bug trapped in a farm family's tabletop for years, only to emerge into light and life. Haines' emergence of course was in Alaska:

> I was born to this crowded waste,
> came late in my time
> to know the knot in my belly.
> > "Hunger" (*News from the Glacier*)

In the rocks and among the "faces like broken bowls" he has read the "body and book of stone" and there seen his most primitive self,

> an animal stripped
> of all comfort,
> not able to speak my name,
>
> a terrified creature
> gnawing at roots.

Going to Alaska was, as Haines says, being born anew, returning to the part of himself that he had never known. From that knowledge, he gains a perspective from which to "read the soil," that is, to understand the world through new eyes, with bifocal vision that now incorporates the dual nature he discovers in the forest.

The metaphor most commonly used for this undiscovered, primitive portion of the psyche is that of depth: the deep within us. Haines employs that device, but also uses a distance metaphor to the same purpose, as in "Ancestor of the Hunting Heart" (*New Poems,* 1990):

> There is a distance in the heart,
> and I know it well—
> leaf-somberness of winter branches,
> dry stubble scarred with frost,
> late of the sunburnt field.

This distance is akin to a collective unconscious, a living memory of our racial past. It is "a distance/never cropped or plowed," that is, a distant time in our psyches before we were domesticators but were hunters, a time recalled to us "only by fire and the blade of the wind." The distance is the "seed-strewn whiteness/through which the hunter comes." The distance is the internal, psychic "ancestor," as the title suggests, of the ancient hunter's heart. It is the primitive heart in us that is our heritage although too often ignored. It is also a vision, remnant, and reminder of the eternal. It is what "the dead see dying," as he says in the final section (IX) of "Meditation on a Skull Carved in Crystal" (*New Poems,* 1990):

> a grain of ice in the stellar
> blackness, lighted
> by a sun, distant within.

The paradox of "distant within" is Haines' way of suggesting that the ancient and timeless, the products of living under the sun and on the land, are within us and beyond us, part of all humans. As he says about going out to break trail and set traps: "It was far, far back in time, that twilight country where men sometimes lose their way, become as trees confused in the shapes of snow. But I was at home there. . . . I entered for a time the old life of the forest, became part fur myself" (*The Stars* 31).

Living in the wild, then, as a hunter, not a domesticator but a stalker and killer, is Haines' ideal occupation for or vocational representation of his quest. The hunter is the primitive heart in touch with the bloody side of his dualism, and, at least in Haines' case, the hunter is the respecter of his prey, the blood-letter at the religious font engaging in a spiritual as well as a physical act. The hunter antedates "field" and "furrow" and "woodlot[s] patched with fences." He walks in the unfenced and untamed cold while "the rest are camped indoors," safe ("Ancestor of the Hunting Heart," *New Poems*). Hunting is "a last-ditch defiance in the face of an impending global unity of mind" in which "we re-enact something fundamental in our being," as the poet proclaims ("The Lure" 16). The activity can quickly degenerate into murderous guys with guns shooting up the countryside. Even the healthy attitude about re-enacting something fundamental in our beings can be twisted into frustrated executives running around the woods naked getting in touch with their warrior side.

Haines, however, cannot be written off that easily. He is not speaking of all this academically or recreationally. He does not merely venerate the prey from the safety and comfort of an armchair or re-enact his primitive side with paint balls and protective goggles. In his life in the wild he has been the prey, as he shows in "The Dream of February," when he finds himself "In the moonlight,/in the heavy snow" one night, hunting. Suddenly behind him he hears "the quiet step/and smothered whimper/of something following . . ." a "lynx/with steady gaze." The action of the poem occurs in a dream setting, but the fact remains that the poet has exposed himself to danger and has been aware of his role as potential prey for some of the area's predators. His voice, therefore, has the credibility of one who has been pursued. He was no weekend warrior but a hunter in residence for over two decades in one of the most forbidding landscapes in North America, and his quest is a life's work that pervades all his later poetry, not a part-time activity. Plus, the activity is never engaged in for egotistical "glory" (C. Allen 32), and the poet always credits the land—a land that got into his bones—with his awakening. That profound relationship to his place in Alaska moved him to seek the deeper truths, an effort that became part of his being and his later work:

> It would be easy to say that something of the cold and clarity of the land . . . just somehow got into the poems I wrote while I lived there. In a way, this is true, but there is more to it. It was an awakening, profound and disturbing. Everything was so new to me that it was like finding myself for the first time with my feet on the earth. To the extent that it was possible for me, I entered the original mysteries of things, the great past out of which we came (*Country* 9).

We can predict that the poet would have little nice to say about contemporary American society, constituted so differently from the society he formed for himself by moving to the wilderness. When the consciousness and sense of self he formed while living at Richardson crash into late-twentieth-century American materialism, the result is predictable: Haines, the poet of the wind, blows news to us that we are scuttling our future, creating a society based on superfluity, whereas he has learned by cold necessity that one's soul is nourished by the essential. He considers it his job as poet to confront what he believes is wrong with his culture. He frequently criticizes contemporary poets for neglecting this historical duty: "We poets have handed over a critique of society to journalists and writers of nonfiction. Yet it has always been true of great poetry that it contains, or embodies, a critique of life, of society and its values" (*Fables* 31). Haines can become quite irascible when berating what he sees as "a poetry of increasing isolation and narcissism" and asks, as if confused, when this loss of "ethical passion" came about: "When did we stop taking our words seriously, and cease to believe that what we had to say really mattered" (*Fables* 31). What current poetry needs to give it some "tension" is a bit of "moral outrage" (*Fables* 32). Taking himself seriously, he shows us in "The Stone Harp" a wilderness invaded by men and machines: "A road deepening in the north,/strung with steel." The oil being pumped to keep alive the lower forty-eight is likened to Alaska's blood, as if the wilderness were a living animal:

> Now there is all this blood
> flowing into the west,
> ragged holes at the waterline of the sun—
> that ship is sinking.

The more we (as predator) drain from Alaska in order to keep the consumer culture alive, the less alive that beast is, and the less alive will be the land whose blood we are draining, the prey. This is entirely the wrong relationship to ensure health. The culture is "an uncoupled train" "rolling back from the blocked summit . . . with no hand on the brake," rumbling

down the slope, "gathering speed in the dark" ("Rolling Back").
The tone is apocalyptic as Haines plays Cassandra, the ignored
prophet, joining that line of American antinomians who suggest
that only constant vigilance on the part of the individual will
enable us to keep our spirit alive in a culture that encourages
spiritual death. Haines clearly recognizes the threat:

> The way we live nowadays seems intended to prevent
> closeness to anything outside this incubator world we have
> built around us. Within it, individuals face an increasingly
> impoverished inner world (*Country* 16).

One can take, as a hunter takes, but only what one needs
and then one gives back. Haines is no noble savage, but in some
places he sounds a bit like Natty Bumppo, knowing instinctively
the right and wrong way to treat nonhuman nature. He ran a
trapline for twenty years but says that from the beginning he
understood some basic conservation principles: "I understood
quite early that I should not trap the country too hard. . . .
Though my awareness of these things was still half-formed, I
seemed to have had it in me as an instinct to care for the country that I might live in it again" (*The Stars* 23). Whoever ran the
Alaskan mining industry, whose detritus litters the landscape,
obviously had no such instinct. Mining is a perfect example of
the sort of extractive industry that takes and takes and never
replenishes in a losing game. What is waste to the hunter is
food for other animals, but the miners' waste is just waste: "a
strand of barbed wire," "a line of boxcars," "the scattered iron/
and timber of the campsite" ("The Train Stops at Healy Fork").
No wonder that the "coppery tribesmen/we looked for had
vanished."

If it is true that immersion in an accumulative culture threatens to obliterate our soul, it is reciprocally true that losing touch with one's soul hastens the culture toward destruction. In "The Lemmings," we are meant to see the creatures massed at sea's edge and think of ourselves as a culture huddling together waiting to fling ourselves over the edge of destruction. The individual lemmings are completely detached from the source of their happiness ("No one is pleased with himself/or with others"), and therefore "In each small breast/the hated colony disintegrates." No society can survive if it is composed of despairing and distressed individuals who have lost touch with their souls. What may look on the surface to be peaceful and prosperous is in turmoil in some buried, unseen spot:

> In this darkness beneath
> a calm whiteness
> there are growls and scuffles.

We are the herd that has lost touch with our "darkness beneath," the source of vitality and health, and are therefore, in Haines' diagnosis, on a blind, unconscious march to destruction. The land returned Haines to his darkness and spiritual health. Now we simply plunder the land to feed our "calm whiteness" that can only mask for so long the underlying darkness that, unexamined, becomes an internal toxin. He hopes for a purging, as he shows in "The Flight":

> It may happen again—this much
> I can always believe
> when our dawn fills with frightened neighbors
> and the ancient car refuses to start.

Dawn here is the beginning of a new era after all we have accumulated has overwhelmed us and crushed us under its weight. The pointlessness of our materialism is summarized by the image in "The Flight" of "a refugee cart/overturned in the road,/a wheel slowly spinning. . . ." Our scurryings for money and property are so much wheel-spinning to the poet.

Many of Haines' poems from the late-sixties and seventies are fairly formulaic political protest verses with little of the animal vitality that characterizes his early and later work. The middle poems are transition poems, as some critics have noted,[9] both a transition from solitary poems to social poems and also a transition from living alone in Alaska to becoming part of an American culture that had alienated many of its more sensitive and intelligent souls. In this work, Haines sees humanity "strolling like an overfed beast/set loose from its cage" ("The Way We Live") and all he can think of is getting back to his private economy: "a man may long for nothing so much/as a house of snow." We become the prisoners and mirrors of our creations. Having created a culture based on petroleum, we become tar babies: "Wherever we walk on earth/bits of tar/cling to our footsoles" ("Tar"). Having let our billboards speak for us and define our dreams, we have become mute and can only offer slogans in which the future may read "of the paradise defaulted/and the vision tamed" ("The Billboards in Exile"). We have heard vague intimations of the culture's destructiveness. "For a long time now/we have heard these voices' singing along eroded wires," ("Rolling Back"), but we make so much noise ourselves that we cannot hear our own conscience: "They tell us what we partly know/hidden by the noise we make" ("Rolling Back"). We fool ourselves with our money, as if coins and bills had some inherent value.

To a man used to living among the real currency of moose and bear, tangible and inherently valuable means of exchange, the seriousness with which people perceive dollar bills is ludicrous: "It is ash, it is air,/then nothing, nothing at all" ("The Autumn of Money"). We have become as colorless and characterless as paper plates: "Their manhood and womanhood/was crushed, bleached/with bitter acids,/their fibers dispersed. . . ." Like paper plates, we have become "porous and identical," "made to be thrown away" ("The Legend of Paper Plates"). Yes, the political poems do become didactic and heavy-handed (most political poems, by any poet, do the same), but at least we hear Haines' sincere concern for his fellow humans who are turning themselves into identical, throw-away, purchasable items, and we hear his concern for himself. Having to make a living, he returned to teach and found himself caught in a culture that swallows all who enter. His only way to protect himself, to keep the darkness within alive and thriving, is to write, to declare himself not yet vanquished. No matter where his later poems are set, his imagery returns to the forests where his consciousness was formed. Of all the consumer products he could use as a symbol of our spiritual malaise, he uses paper plates and connects those lifeless, domesticated objects to their history in the forest, where they were once "proud, bushy, strong." That image is his reminder to himself of what he wants to remain and retain.

Even though the protest poems are formulaic and suffer when taken out of their anti-Vietnam War context, Haines can be effective when he focuses his criticism on individuals—when the criticism becomes sympathy—rather than letting loose at the entire culture—when the criticism remains only criticism and turns arrogant. And, to Haines, individuals are the key anyway, because individual despair is at the root of the culture's headlong rush toward self-destruction, and individual regeneration will or can save us, an idea central to our literary tradition and dating back to the seventeenth century. Critic Larzer Ziff, discussing the works of the American Renaissance in his study of Puritanism's legacy, describes succinctly a continuing theme of American literary history: "In their works there is no middle distance, as it were. Filling the foreground is the psyche, and filling the background are the workings of a divine plan, be it malignant or beneficent, while between the two the institutions of the human community are dwarfed" (305-06). Haines would have no argument with the analysis. In "To A Man Going Blind," the poet shows us a lone man watching his days pass, watching the "evenings/coming on steeper and snowier," his internal landscape growing darker and darker:

> . . . you wait
> like a leaning flower, and hear
> almost as if it were nothing,
> the petrified rumble
> from a world going blind.

We see the petrified man, one of Thoreau's lives of quiet desperation, unable to move, unaware of what he could do to move and change his life, the blind cause and the blind product of a blind culture in a dark time. More than bitter and more than didactic, the poem makes us sympathetic while reminding us that there is really nothing we can do to save other blind men. Haines moves from the individual man to his street to his entire world, and we feel the emptiness of the concentric circles of experience. When Haines is less effective, he generally begins a poem with an apocalyptic image ("The houses begin

JOHN HAINES ☀ 131

to come down"), proceeds to an image of the culture collapsing of its own weight, as if it were just too gluttonous to support its bulk ("There are too many stories,/rumors, and shadows:/like hordes of grasshoppers/they eat up the land"), and concludes with an image of himself escaping to a stripped-down life like the one he had before he came to town to make a living ("I must make my life into/an endless camp,/learn to build with air,/water, and smoke . . ."). He seems homesick as much as disgusted.

We have allowed ourselves to become rotten within, he suggests, by tending only to external matters, as encouraged to do by the materialistic culture we have created, and ignoring the internal, the core where life truly resides. We look healthy, we look sound, but we are hiding from each other and from ourselves the hollowness we have covered over. Haines, being Haines, uses an image from nature to make his cultural diagnosis and criticism. His "Poem About Birches" is Eliot's "Hollow Men" and Yeats' "Second Coming" translated through the poet's Richardson Hill experiences:

> But too long withheld, the heartwood
> sours and slowly rots; the tree
> totters within, though its white bark
> shines and seems to hold.
>
> Until one day, just a little wind
> on a load of snow,
> and that hollow life breaks down.

Despite the apocalyptic tone, his poetry, even in this stage, remains hopeful. First, he believes nature can recover from man's onslaught. "Of one thing we may be certain," he declares: "Nature will cure everything given sufficient time, and neither the earth nor the cosmos requires our presence to fulfill itself" (Sims 35). In "The Rain Forest" he depicts the forest as "a green ape," a King Kong of flora, fauna, and fecundity. He does not mention in this poem the cities of men gnawing at the forest's edges, but he does show the green life of the planet as tremendously resilient, a vaguely threatening presence that will not be ignored. The ape/forest, in fact, seems ready to take its revenge on puny man:

> Though the ape has not yet spoken,
> I listen this evening
> to drops of water,
> as one might listen
> to a tongue growing green.

The forest is rooted ("his broad feet clenched in a soil") and ready for a comeback, while humans seem to be transients looking for a way to destroy ourselves.

Second, he believes, in the long tradition of the Puritans, Crèvecoeur, Franklin, and Thoreau, in the possibility of self-renewal, of making oneself new, the Adamic strain that runs throughout American literature. One image, directly connected to his Alaskan days, of the hope for individual regeneration that may lead, one person at a time, to cultural regeneration is the hunter in the woods, the one who lives respectfully and skillfully on the land. Few real hunters or opportunities for real hunters remain, of course, but that does not entirely daunt Haines, for he is more concerned with the hunter's attitude toward the world than his vocation. He knows his experience in Alaska has been unusual, not an experience easily replicable by

the middle-aged man in his La-Z-Boy. But he does think that
the values learned there are transplantable. In a poem written
at the height of the Vietnam protests, he uses the imagery of
Alaska to link war protesters, who in this configuration apparently have seen something of their own darkness and been
saved from the culture's siren call and error, with images of the
ancient hunter. "In the Middle of America" (1967) describes a
meeting of protesting students planning their strategy as if the
undergraduates were a gathering of hunters around a wilderness campfire:

> In the middle of America
> I came to an old house
> stranded on a wintry hill.
>
> It contained fire; men and women
> of an uncertain generation
> gathered before it. The talk
> was of border crossings,
> mass refusals, flag burnings,
> and people who stand or fall.

The wonder to Haines is that this scene occurs "in the
middle of America," in the middle of the forces aligned against
individual discovery and meaningful life. These people are
gathered for a purpose the poet can validate, and so he does
validate them by linking them imagistically to winter hunters
sharing lore, doing the community's true work. His image
allows him finally to feel at home and hopeful even when cut
off from the source of his hope: "I moved among them,/I listened and understood."

✧

We never lose track of the fact, however, that Haines is a poet and that any understanding of himself and the world that he gathers from his Alaskan experience is also going to become a foundation of his understanding of the poetic act, his aesthetics. This is obviously true for Haines because he began writing poetry seriously in Alaska. For one thing, the land compelled the newcomer to attend to facts or starve. That enforced observation seems naturally to have evolved into a poet's vision: "I was forced to pay attention. . . . Words began to fasten themselves to what I saw" (*Country* 6-7). He was forced to do what any good poet must do, to see, a simple enough sounding task but one that Haines thinks our culture is killing by making the world a less intimate place where the facts and forces of nature have become less important, if not entirely unimportant, to our survival: "To see what is here, right in front of us: nothing would seem easier or more obvious, yet few things are more difficult. There are unmistakable signs that something may be dying among us: that capacity to see the world, to recognize the 'other' and admit it into our lives" (*Country* 17).

In another way, his experience living off the land shapes his understanding of his poetry's method and goal. Several times in his collection of essays, Haines refers to the relationship between dream and actuality, between the inner, intangible, spiritual world, and the outer, tangible, physical world:

> There is the dream journey and the actual life. The two
> seem to touch now and then, and perhaps when men lived
> less complicated and distracted lives the two were not
> separate at all, but continually one thing. I have read

somewhere that this was once true for the Yuma Indians who lived along the Colorado River. They dreamed at will, and moved without effort from waking into dreaming life; life and dream were bound together. And in this must be a kind of radiance, a very old and deep assurance that life has continuity and meaning, that things are somehow in place (*Country* 27-28).

Modern men and women, he suggests, have lost the ability to move smoothly between the realms, something the hunter must do if he is to be at home enough in the woods to survive as predator and not become the prey. This ability to live in both the physical world (the raw material of poetry, the sights, sounds, smells, and other sensual facts) and the spiritual (the world of imagination, of the interior of things, and of value) is the ability to make poetry and to live as a poet. The callings of hunter/primitive woods dweller and modern poet become one activity of living rather than one activity of keeping the body alive and another of nourishing the soul. The interaction between the inner self and the outer self creates a true life and a true poetry:

It [the Alaskan experience] gave me a way of perceiving the world that I might not have acquired otherwise, and not least, a solitude in which I could learn to listen to my own voice. But as I have tried to show, I do not think that place, outer place, alone can account for this. There must be another place, and that is within the person himself. When that interior place, formed out of dream and fantasy, and by intense imagination, finds its counterpart in a physical landscape, then some genuine human reality can be created (*Country* 13).

The place where dream and actual life speak to each other is the "genuine human reality" where poetry is made. It is the realm in which Haines lived, not simply wrote, in his Alaskan days.

The hunter's identification with his prey and his interior experience of the weather and other facts relevant to staying alive, on the one hand, and the poet's identification with his subject, on the other, become analogous activities, exercises in moving freely from dream to reality, from external facts to internal connections. He feels the caribou herd's exhaustion in his own bones ("The Field of the Caribou") and knows himself bathed by the same "red mantle of dawn" that "sweeps" over the bodies of dead animals ("On the Divide"). When the door opens and the cold enters, Haines is not simply chilled: "I feel/its breath deep in my bones," he says ("The Visitor"), and the "shaggy frost-fog" is like a human visitor who "bounds across the floor" and tries to lure him outside of the safety of the cabin, one brother to another. When the south wind comes blowing cold, he does not look at the thermometer outside the kitchen window to know the temperature has dropped; he feels the "invader" in his dreams and awakes "in the ruined kingdom/ of frost" ("South Wind"). Winter is a living being: "the unfinished, the abandoned,/slumped like a mourner" ("The Sudden Spring") whose presence the poet feels even in the middle of spring. Maggots are not only seen as "wrinkled white men" ("The Insects"), their activity is written of in respectful, human images ("building a temple of slime"). Even the inanimate, like stones, are given not only existence: "They are dreaming existence./One is a man, and one/is a woman" ("The Stones") but also a history:

> And the life within them became
> an expanding shadow,

a blue gravel on which they fed
as they changed. . . .

Haines' poetry is the product of an observation (that implies a distance between the subject and object) that becomes identification (that implies no distance) as a fact of life, a means of living, a passage back and forth from dream to reality. As one critic notes, the poetry moves toward an "inseparability of subject and object, land and speaker, until it can be said that Haines fulfills William Carlos Williams' dream to 'reconcile the people and the stones'" (Hedin 194). The poetry comes out of the life and is as natural a product of the life as the rotting gut piles of the tundra, although the tundra need not be involved. The process can take place anywhere at any time. While walking on a New York avenue one windy spring day, for example, wearing "a sweater given me by the wife/of a genial Manchurian" ("The Sweater of Vladimir Ussachevsky"), the speaker is suddenly transported to "Siberia or Mongolia" as a result of the life of the animal who gave the wool and the weaver who wove it into shape. Those "dream" elements are in the "real" sweater, yet we seldom note them. Haines feels them, and at once "the buildings were mountains." Poetry had been made.

If dream and reality are equally real and accessible, and humans, animals, plants, and stones are equal partners in the full complex of life, then there is a reciprocity between human and nonhuman just as there is a reciprocity between dream and reality. No one takes dominion; all are equal partners in the world. This reciprocal, respectful relationship extends to the predator and prey but also beyond, to the poet and subject, who are in a relationship analogous to that between the hunter and the moose, or between the lynx and the field mouse. A good illustration of this is "The Girl Who Buried Snakes in a Jar," which narrates a tale of a girl who buried snakes in her back yard to see if, when she dug them up a year later, "sunlight/still glinted in those eyes," and "to ask if a single tongue,/ one forked flicker in the dark,/had found any heat in death." The answer to both questions, as we could predict, is "no." The girl who had "walked in the canyon early" and been so impressed by "the living snake, coiled/and mottled by a bitter pool," discovered that when she "unearthed her jar in the spring," "the snake spirit" was gone, replaced by "only a little green water standing,/some dust, or a smell." Capture the snake, try to keep it, try to arrest its life and preserve it for your pleasure, curiosity, or other selfish ends, and you kill the spirit, which is a far different and less respectful action than tracking the animal and killing it properly and quickly as part of the ongoing life and death process. The implication is that one whose vocation is capturing in verse the spirit of the snake has a pretty difficult task, accomplished only by identifying with the subject and moving into the realm in order to bring it back spiritually intact. Stevens' jar in Tennessee may take dominion, but Haines is not interested in dominion. The best way to write a snake poem is analogous to the proper way to hunt: feel with the snake from the inside-out, get inside the snake spirit, and enter into "the original mystery of things" (*Country* 9). Identifying is his method of merging "life and dream," which have been "scattered/through the flung constellations" and now "each" is "seeking the other" ("Victoria"). His poetry wants to put the universe back together and in the process answer in the affirmative his own question, "Will we ever again be at home/on earth?"

"Rain Country" is a good example of the poet simultaneously living in a dream world and in actual life, in one of those

moments when he is clearly "at home/on earth." The result of
being at home is the poem itself, a manifestation of the align-
ment of dream and actuality, earth and imagination. The poem
is set in the present act of writing as the poet remembers the
past, a long hunt into the woods he took thirty-one years ago
with two friends (Peg and Campbell, an old homesteader now
dead) who are no longer part of his life. The season is autumn,
"the woods are sodden,/and the last leaves/tarnish and fall," a
foreshadowing in the opening stanza of the losses he is about to
narrate. The mood, however, is more joyful than mournful, as
the three friends, though "bone-chilled," have "singing hearts."
As they sit around the campfire drinking coffee, Campbell tells
tales of the old days and thus releases his voice into the still air,
where it falls like the leaves and Haines retrieves it for his song.
In section III, the whole earth seems to speak to the poet:

> Shadows blur in the rain,
> they are whispering straw
> and talking leaves.
>
> I see what does not exist,
> hear voices that cannot speak
> through the packed
> earth that fills them.

In the twilight of a camp, listening to a friend's words, the
poet hears the earth speak to him, in the blur where actual life
and dream life complement each other, in the whispering interstices where the imagination finds its perfect counterpart in
the external forms. Suddenly, various other friends he knew,
"shadows" in his imagination, come to him and speak as the
"shadows" of the fading light surround him and he embraces

them. Even the "stammering folly/aimed toward us" by "fox-eyed men/who align the earth/to a tax-bitten dream" is muted by the "silence/to which we turned." Those jarring noises fade from the poet's ears and are made powerless because he has aligned himself to a different dream and has heard the woods call of "an ancient love." Since the time of the hunt, "much rain has fallen" and everyone has left, except the poet who, true to his obligation, keeps alive the songs of "the singing heart/driven to darkness" by "remembering, fitting names/to a rain-soaked map." He aligns himself with the earth, recalls the past, hears the earth match his internal voices, and then composes his poem, which is a kind of map of the route between the dream world and actual life, written "in the brown ink of leaves," that is, written with nature and the imagination squeezed together through the pen's nib. One is reminded of Whitman's declaration, in the 1855 "Preface," that the poet "indicate[s] the path between reality and [the readers'] souls."

The paradox here is that discovering the inarticulate enables articulation just as discovering the darkness enables true enlightenment. In "Hunger," from *News from the Glacier,* Haines declares that he has finally learned "to read the soil" and to gather "such wordless images/the earth gives up." Having entered imaginatively into his own past, the archetypal ancestry he feels while in the wilderness, he understands that part of him is "an animal, stripped/of all comfort,/not able to speak my name." This inarticulate animal component is also the source of his very human and articulate poetry. His poetic project is to be still, listen, and notice while pressing himself deeper and deeper into those elusive original mysteries:

> We will not look back
> but press on, deeper

than the source of water,
to the straw-filled cave
of beginnings.
   "Harvest"

An obligation burdens one who has rediscovered the ability "to see as once I saw" ("In the Sleep of Reason"), for no matter where you are, in Missoula (as in "Alive in the World") or "any crossroad in the west," while you stand there "alive in this place" the world around you is slowly vanishing, like leaves falling, and the present facts are simply "things that are smoke tomorrow." The seer's task is to "go into the surge of it," live it and write it, make the familiar unfamiliar and get the reader to see the dream in the reality that he or she takes for granted. This is to make poetry of the world, to show the side of the actual that the poet sees but that too many of the rest of us have forgotten how to see. This is to reinvigorate reality with its dream side, to flesh out the dream with the actual and to create a poetry of living:

> When the two [dream and actual life] are brought together by an act of imagination there occur those sometimes brief moments of compelling clarity and completeness. And these moments are, or ought to be, part of the real life of humankind: place and image, reality and dream made one (*Country* 40).

The sadness, of course, is that most of us simply "pass through,/going blindly into our houses." The hope is that we can, as Haines does, "strike a match, kindling/the cold, untraveled sun" ("Harvest"), and then we will be able to say as we move on that "we have kept faith/with ourselves." To keep faith with ourselves is to keep faith simultaneously with the earth and our imagination and to create out of that faith—never cynicism, never alienation—ourselves and our song. The "harvest," then, the end of life to which all animals come, can be a joyful rather than a mournful arrival, can be poetry that nourishes as well as death that perpetuates life.

Haines depicts death frequently (Carolyn Allen, professor of English at the University of Washington, refers to his "continuing preoccupation with death," 33), especially in his early, Alaskan poems where he must have faced death daily, but hardly ever meditates upon his own mortality. The most extended discussion of humanity's ends, in which we hear the poet looking at himself, is "Meditation on a Skull Carved in Crystal" from *New Poems.* In notes Haines provided for his volume of collected poems, he tells the reader that, "This long poem resulted from a visit to a branch of the British Museum in London in the spring of 1977. One of the primary objects on display is a larger than life-size human skull carved in pure rock crystal, and said to be of Aztec or Maya origin." He worked on the poem for years, developing it from a brief affair into a nine-section meditation. He begins by staring at the oversized skull, some earlier artist's homage to humanity's power perhaps, impressed but wondering how anyone can imagine that the creature whose cranium is thusly shaped can be the center and end of all existence:

> To think that the world
> lies wholly within the mind;

> that this frozen water,
> this clarity of quartz,
> this ice, is all.

He has seen too many rotting carcasses and scattered bone piles to believe that one species is significantly superior to any other. In our "glass house/of wit" we may believe that what we see of the world through our narrow eyes, "the inch of sky/ in the well of windows," is "all," but Haines' skeptical tone in section I suggests that he knows differently. The large crystal skull suggests hubris to the poet, a monument to an anthropocentric vision of the world.

Yet not quite, for the poet does not simply judge, he also mourns the passing of a human, the transformation in a moment's time of a shape, the skull, from a place "where intelligence/kept its station" into nothing more than "a small, green hollow/holding rain." He dwells in section II on images of loss, noting the "ear-ports catching wind" and "the long porch of the nostrils" from which "predatory" flies and beetles have "long since gnawed the solitude/and eaten the silence." Man the hunter becomes man the prey, as every hunter does. The poet observes with the eye of a human but writes with the indifferent tone of nature herself. A man was here. He was, as all humans are, a repository of intelligence and memory. He died, and the insects devoured him. Perhaps, he fears, "nothing but death is here." Perhaps death is death and nothing remains afterwards. Perhaps after life all that remains is emptiness, "windless and calm—sheer/absolution in the slow/cementing of sand grains." With this thought, the poem reaches its emotional nadir at the conclusion of section III. The words themselves—"drop by drop, the fate/of water in a sealed jar"—drip slowly to dissolution.

Haines creates a silence that so thoroughly mimics the mute crystal head's silence that the reader has difficulty beginning section IV. Can there be a way up out of here? All effort seems pointless, and loss is just loss. But then Haines looks again and realizes he has been seeing only the actual life and not the dream, only the physical facts and not the shadow world. He has seen only the doomed movement forward of a human life and been so caught in its futility that the circularity of life in which all parts connect and all journeys reach their opposites has been overlooked. "Go now," he says in IV, return to your water and mist.

> You of the fireborn, go back to rain,
> be what in the beginning you were:
> seed of ice and brother to grain.

The crystal skull looks so isolated when set apart from its context and placed onto a pedestal, as if humanity really lived that way. One life is unimportant in the scheme of things. Seeing a single life in isolation not only kicks us loose of our earthly context but silences us, as Wendell Berry explains: "[Haines] opposes the shrinkage of the world to the limits of the isolated, displaced, desiring and despairing self, the self that ultimately knows nothing and can say nothing" (110). This is the silence that strikes us as we conclude section III, the ultimate silence of any merely physical existence.

Haines is seeing beyond the physical now, and the occasional religious tone ("Go now, . . ." "this is the way of winter,/ on earth as in heaven") suggests his focus has shifted from the absence of the skull's flesh to the presence of a spirit more permanent. "Nothing of beast or man/remains," he says (V), except an oxymoronic smile "of ferocious peace." The skull becomes a mirror, "that/which sees if looked upon," in which Haines sees the story of a life that, while mysterious, no longer seems despairing. The crystal skull now seems less like the remnant of a lost life and more like the reminder of a life everlasting, not in any narrowly orthodox religious way, but in the larger sense that all animals fall in order to contribute to the momentum that keeps the earth moving. The epigraph to the poem, by Martin Buber, reads in part, *"After is the wrong word. It is an entirely different dimension."* The afterlife, as commonly understood, suggests that life splits into halves—a now, then an after. Haines sees a long, single flow. Just as dream and actual life are one, as prey and predator are one, as inner and outer are one, so life and its continuation in death are one.[10] The dead flesh provides silent testament to the rightness of this process, as we hear in section VI:

> Swear by the fallen blood
> and burnt savor of the flesh
> that the sun will rise,
> that the wheel of the calendar,
> carved with its lunar faces,
> will never stop turning.

Seeing beyond the actual into the dream, the poet is able to reconstitute the living being from his crystal death mask and then, in the terms learned on the hunting trail, strip the flesh away once again to see the place of all life in the cycle of life and death, in which death, as a positive fact, does not really exist:

> Put death aside,
> there is nothing to fear

> from the sleep-walk of spirits
> in this darkness
> not wholly of night.

Darkness is "not wholly of night" because it carries its opposites, day and light within it, just as we occasionally lament that light and life, even in our prime, carry their opposites within them. We remember that the fallen moose's bones feed the field mice.

He reconsiders the skull, this time seeing its glory, not its fallen glory, noting the magnificence of the hinged jaw and "glassy brow" (VII). Hollow but "never empty," the skull now seems the "completion" of "all suns, all moons, all days." This assertion, reached at the end of seven sections, seems now not at all like the hubris of section I. It is not one man asserting his centrality in the universe but one man understanding his role as part of a thriving organism—all earth and the universe beyond—that includes him. Perhaps we want to deny the darkness and the shadow, a trait Haines has learned to abandon. Perhaps we need to see only the actual life (and mourn its passing) or the dream (and deny the flesh of the actual). But, he says, both are real, and all our "pain of thought," even if we use it to administer "repeated blows" to the universe's logic, will never enable us safely to conclude that there is "nothing but light in the end," a pleasant afterlife of lighted, endless tunnels leading to bliss. Darkness, the darkness of a sixty-below winter day waiting on a game trail or checking one's traps, constitutes the universe as much as light. We take our rationality like a weapon and try to badger the world into allowing us to reside comfortably in our hierarchies, divisions, and classifications (for example, "life" versus "afterlife"), but in the presence of this skull the poet sees these devices as merely "names/that vanish among/the catalogues that vanish" (VIII). He knows that death is the phenomenon that challenges all our assumptions about divisions and separated realms, that makes us confront our egotism and belief in our specialness but that also enables us to feel special and alienated because we believe we understand something about death that animals do not. He calls death "the last confusion," mildly chiding himself for allowing himself to be confused earlier.

Again and finally, in section IX, he calls the skull a mirror, one with "holes for its eyes." We can use those holes, as he has in the poem, for our eyes in order to see through them from the inside of death out to the world. That way, Haines suggests, we may be able "to see/what the dead see dying" and come to terms with our lives while living, just as he sees what the prey sees when dying and thereby comes to terms with his role as predator. And what do the dead see?

> a grain of ice in the stellar
> blackness, lighted
> by a sun, distant within.

The sun within is the same as the sun distant. The myth of our alienation is held up as a lie. We are part of the cosmic dust of the universe, one mote in "the debris of dying stars" ("Little Cosmic Dust Poem"). In these final words, he fulfills the promise of the remainder of Buber's epigraph: *"Time and space are crystalizations out of God. At the last hour all will be revealed."*

Adrian C. Louis
1946–

CHAPTER FOUR

Dispossessed: The Poetic Inferno of Adrian C. Louis

*A*drian C. Louis, an enrolled member of the Lovelock (Nevada) Paiute tribe who now lives on the Lakota Sioux reservation, writes disturbing poetry.[1] The cumulative effect of his repeated tales and images of barroom brawls, drunks sprawled in corners of rooms, profane and misogynic exchanges heralding the end of love, cars crashed into frozen roadside ditches, and the perpetual tumescence of Louis or one of his personae cruising the world in search of the unwary or the simply indifferent weighs on one. The reader feels as masochistic as one of the author's characters for picking up the book for another round of abuse. The white reader, especially the white academic, who enjoys and returns to Louis' work must wonder if he is consumed by self-loathing, for Louis has little love for cultural exploiters and a great talent for expressing distaste. At some point, many readers of Louis must stop, throw up their arms and say, with A. E. Housman's fictional interlocutor, Terence, this is stupid stuff:

> You eat your victuals fast enough;
> There can't be much amiss, 'tis clear,
> To see the rate you drink your beer.
> But oh, good Lord, the verse you make,
> It gives a chap the belly-ache.

Louis is both perverse and wise enough to want precisely this effect.[2] He knows, with Housman, that "Luck's a chance, but trouble's sure," especially if you are a Native American in modern America, a nation of thieves, in Louis' opinion, who are the more irksome because they have never had any intention of making retribution for their larceny and have by now grown weary of being reminded of the debt. Louis has to speak a bit more loudly in the land of the deaf, show a more vivid scene of horror in the land of the blind. The pity and tragedy is that he shows us scenes from his own hellish life, realistic pictures from the Inferno that is Indian reservation existence. Yet there is more method to his apparent madness than simply the desire to rub white folks' noses in the dirt they have created. Housman defends Terence's bitter and unappetizing poetry from several angles, but concludes with his best defense in the form of a tale of King Mithridates, a Persian potentate. Mithridates lived surrounded by those who would foist upon him "poisoned meat and poisoned drink." So he gathered to him all the venomous plants of the world and sampled each, building up his immunity. When he had "sampled all [earth's] killing store," he sat down to dine. His loyal retainers were amazed and "stared aghast to watch him eat," for they had poisoned the food, yet Mithridates ate heartily and survived. "Mithridates," Housman tells us, "he died old." Survival in a poisonous world: that is Louis' real agenda, and he pursues it paradoxically by immersing himself in the muck and insisting that any reader who wants the truth must follow him in hip-deep.[3]

The usual interpretation of Louis' brutally honest portrayal of contemporary Indian life, inasmuch as there is a usual interpretation given the small body of current critical response, is that Louis "writes to dispel the romantic notion, so dear to New Agers and others, that Native Americans are the wise and innately spiritual children of nature" (Hadella 285-86).[4] This romantic notion is often phrased in terms similar to essayist and writer Paula Gunn Allen's when she says, "The American Indian sees all creatures as relatives (and in tribal systems relationship is central), as offspring of the Great Mystery, as cocreators, as children of our mother, and as necessary parts of an ordered, balanced, and living whole" ("Sacred Hoop" 7). A similar point is made by Kenneth Lincoln in his *Native American Renaissance* the poetics of Native American literatures is founded on a belief in "a poetic kinship that unites the people, other earthly creatures, the gods, and nature in one great tribe" (45). The fact that Louis eschews just this sort of "romantic lyricism" (Bruchac n.p.) that normally would result in poetic expressions of one's ties to Mother Earth, incorporation of lyrical landscape imagery into one's poetry, or something similar, means that absent in most of his work—except for an occasional reference to the sacredness of Devil's Tower—is any acknowledgment of the land's importance or his understanding of himself and his identity as grounded in the earth. Of all the Native American poets one might choose to include in a study of the western poet's relationship to the land, Louis seems the least likely to produce anything fruitful.

Yet, just as Louis' morbidity functions paradoxically as a survival technique, so the absence of explicit references to the importance of the land suggests the centrality of that land to Louis' poetic and personal predicament. The land's absence is the central wound in the poet's psyche, and the land's absence from the surface of the poems is the clearest indication of its presence behind the poems. His poetry is a poetry of loss, and the primary item lost—to the white invaders—is the land. Therefore, while Louis may avoid the expected portrayal of the sacred landscape, that does not mean that he is indifferent to the land's loss, for with that larceny he has lost his identity. Louis' collected work is like a Native American novel in which the main character searches for his identity, realizes it can only be found with his people and on his people's land, and then returns home (often to the reservation from the city) to find the missing pieces (tribalism, a place in a community) that make him whole. Whether Louis' poetry has yet reached that happy conclusion, and whether it ever will, is debatable, but wherever it does conclude, pain is the only clear current reality as long as Indians are deprived of their land: "The Hell Bus Station is the life of Indians living on this stolen land" ("The Blood Thirst of Verdell Ten Bears"). The repeated references in Louis' work to stolen land are, oddly enough, easily over-looked, especially, one assumes, by the white reader used to similar indictments. But for Louis, these statements are more than simple reflex reactions or formulas. They are his sincerest statement of the source of loss that is at the center of his pained universe. Louis is lost, as are his brothers and sisters, because the land on which his traditional identity would have been formed is lost.

The absence that the poet feels is so poignant, Louis sometimes simply blurts it out, as in "The Bloodwine Epigrams":

> In the smoothing of warm and ageless sand
> an arrowhead found and pierced my hand
> O how can the white man own our land?

At other times, more rare, Louis gives the reader a history and context for the depth of his pain at being that oxymoron, an Indian with no homeland. "A Post Card from Devils Tower" gives the big picture, beginning as Louis drives aimlessly, "Zipping past Rapid Creek in the vicinity/of where Crazy Horse was born." He wanders a lot, as if never sure where to go, what direction to take, waiting for inspiration or a bar to appear. Even when he decides to spend the night in Rapid City and leave to see Mt. Rushmore—for the first time—the next morning, his actions seem peculiarly volitionless:

> At six in the morning the car heads for McDonald's.
> At seven it takes off for Mt. Rushmore.

The faces of Mt. Rushmore ("those massive stone idols of Indian killers") are as beloved a symbol of America and Americanness as exists in the country, flocked to by bikers in leathers as well as families in pressed shorts and tennis shoes, which means to Louis the faces are his "demons" who cannot be escaped. Halfway to the monument, however, "the car," which seems to be making all the decisions, "turns back to Rapid." There seems to be enough pain in his life: why ask for more by going to see massive images of the ones he holds responsible for his alienation? Driving west through Rapid City on I-90, again aimlessly, Louis notes the tourist and gambling towns of Lead and Deadwood, South Dakota (not actually visible from the Interstate): "minuscule festering scab[s]" he calls them. Suddenly, somewhere on the highway as he drives, he sees what he has been driving at: "The intruders' diseases plague these sacred hills." Immediately, he is in control: "I blink at the map/and decide to drive to Devils Tower," over the border in northeastern Wyoming.

The journey is typical: rootless and roaming, observing, letting the impressions flow into his brain, wandering passively, until the individual images coalesce and form a direction. Crazy Horse juxtaposed with Washington, Jefferson, Lincoln, and Roosevelt; casinos juxtaposed with the sacred Black Hills through which Washington's heirs have poured wide scars of concrete; a highway loaded with tourists determinedly heading to their next destination juxtaposed with his wandering, over the same road Crazy Horse must also have ridden. Suddenly he realizes he must make his own journey of homage, not to the sacred sites of middle-class, white America—neon lights or KOA campgrounds—but to what should be a sacred site for him. The direction he chooses is usually a momentary one, and as often as not, it is toward the nearest bar or former lover for more abuse. This time, however, he seeks something else. He usually resists such homage as too romantic, too melodramatic, or perhaps too threatening: the Tower first appears to him "like a slap in the face." As he comes nearer, "words cringe/and refuse to seek air." His words are his armor and his warrior's spear. Now they desert him in the presence of true sacredness, something he cannot shrug off ironically:

The Tower assaults my soul.
This is the eternal cathedral
of the great Spirit.

Too much for him, he distances the Tower with the words that now have apparently regained their power:

Were I to awake one morning and find
the prize between my thighs
had doubled in length
I would have been less impressed
than this first visit to the Tower. . . .

As vulgar as it is, and as resistant as it is to the seriousness of the moment, the comparison sounds sincere.[5] Louis is proud of "the prize between my thighs," and so often chooses lust as an escape or retreat that sex becomes an alternative to vision in many of his poems. Sex becomes one more component of Adrian Louis' self-destructive life so that here, saying that the Tower is more impressive than a doubling of his sexual capacity, is saying a lot. He knows that the Tower, as a sacred place suggesting hope, and his "prize," as a profane place suggesting flight, are opposed, representing two opposing roads, as it were, in this road poem.

Why, then, does he so rarely allow himself these moments in the shadow of his people's sacred places? Because, as he says immediately following the last-quoted section,

but brothers, the Government owns it.
The Government owns it,
just like it owns our Indian asses.

The most important single fact in all of Louis' poetry is that the government owns the land and therefore owns us. Everything else depends upon that. Take away that fact, and Adrian Louis is unimaginable, because he takes as his poetic vocation the task of imagining just exactly what that fact means, that the government now owns the Indians' land. As usual, that realization concludes the poem and this day's journey. Louis can never, it seems, end in hope. He always forces himself to turn to the pain and face it. He begins a journey with a sense of loss, makes a loop away from that loss, seeks compensation or succor, and then returns again to the wound, his one constant.

All losses stem from that first loss of the land, without which, or so the logic of Louis' poetry suggests, the Indian problems as they are seen today—alcoholism, poverty, early death, spouse abuse, self-destruction—would not exist. Louis' relationship to the land is the paradigm for all his other relationships, just as surely as Peggy Church's understanding of her relationship to the land establishes the model for her understanding of all her other relations. Therefore, Louis has an oddly fluid and unstable sense of self, specifically his identity as an Indian, because that identity is traditionally based upon one's relationship with the land. He tries unsuccessfully to fill the emptiness and compensate for the insecurity with women, booze, and brawling, but nothing satisfies him for long because none of the substitutes is an adequate replacement for one's sense of self. In this, he reminds one of Leslie Marmon Silko's characters in *Ceremony*:

> Every day they had to look at the land, from horizon to horizon, and every day the loss was with them; it was the dead unburied, and the mourning of the lost going on forever. So they tried to sink the loss in booze . . . (*Ceremony* 169).

The problem is that the identity Louis seeks and believes is necessary for his wholeness can only, as he suggests, be achieved as a warrior on the land, a life irretrievably lost, which makes his quest for selfhood frustrating if not doomed. He writes so angrily because, as long as his people's lands are held by whites, he can see no way to become Louis the Indian he wants to be or could have been.

Similarly, his relationship to other humans is almost always tainted by loss. Comrades, friends, lovers, relatives, heroes (usually Crazy Horse or the poet's grandfather) are all lost to him through death or disappearance directly or indirectly caused by the white man's seizure of the land and the consequent displacement and desperation of the Indians. No one we meet remains visible for long. Characters enter, it seems, as raw material for future elegies. The poems are littered with suicides, rolled cars, stabbing victims, and bitter, romantic break-ups. To compensate partially for this loss, Louis writes elegies and what he calls "tombstones" to his departed acquaintances. In addition, the poet feels intense ambivalence about his vocation, his relation to his words. Educated in white schools as he was, he has lost his native tongue and now employs the white man's language, the traditional vehicle for dissemination of the rhetoric that justifies and rationalizes the taking of Indian land. How can one use the enemy's tongue to reveal the lies told by that tongue, he asks himself throughout his career, and, as partial but inadequate amendment for his loss of a language more suitable to his political agenda, he sprinkles Indian words and phrases throughout the poems.

As a man whose relationship to himself, others, and his vocation is by definition insecure, he inevitably has only the most tenuous sense of his relationship to the cosmos around him. In addition to the losses already noted, which would have been enough to make his sense of his place in the universe shaky, Louis also believes he has lost his native religion, traditionally the explanation of one's place with respect to the cosmos, because that religion was at first suppressed and later appropriated by whites as a faddish addition to their spiritually moribund culture. And, as a displaced person, he has difficulty committing himself to his people's religion knowing that tomorrow he may doubt or want to dump everything, including his Indian-ness. Louis' periodic flirtations with both the Lakota sweat lodge ceremony and Christianity (the occasional plaintive calls for Jesus to reveal Himself), however, make clear his need for some sort of religious truth.

The various losses and their interrelationships come together in "Song of the Messiah," about the prophecy among some tribes in the 1890s of the coming of a new Indian Messiah. Section One reports the words of a Sioux who had met the Messiah at His camp. In the messenger's tale, the Messiah talks:

"Each red spirit now dead
shall return and walk this earth,"
He said in a language
we had never heard
but understood so clearly
that we might have been born
to those rabbit-robed People.
Then, to those of many tribes assembled there,
he uttered more strange words that changed
in mid-air to those of all listeners.
He said, "The white man will vanish
like snowflakes in summer."
He told us to rise.
We did and joined hands.

In a spiritual language that transcends dialectal differences between individual tribes, the Messiah returns the land and those lost on it while simultaneously banishing the white man forever. The listeners are returned to their dignity as Indians and join hands to signify their common identity on the land that has been returned to them. All aspects of Louis' loss—of personal identity, friends and brothers, language, spirituality—are here addressed and redressed. The poet makes it clear in the conclusion of Section Two, a 1990s updating of the story, that at the heart of all those losses is the loss of land:

> The white man will vanish
> like snowflakes in summer.
> The earth will open
> and swallow them all.
> Our mother will belch and be ours once again.

The loss of mother Earth began the Indians' long period of indigestion, and when the mother is returned to her original inhabitants, with a satisfying belch after ingesting the insignificant and temporary aberration known as white people, all intervening losses will be wiped out and the rightful residents will march arm-in-arm back to their places on the Plains. Such is the diagnosis of the problem and the imagined cure. The reader cannot tell whether Louis, elsewhere the unflinching realist, believes in the prophecy or if the telling of the prophecy in a poem is his construction of a more pleasing, surrogate reality. Whatever his hope, Louis and the reader know full well that such a vision is not likely to be realized soon.

In the meantime, Louis' job is to keep alive his pain, describe his dispiriting world, and seek compensation where he can find it. To lose one's hatred for white America is to become evil:

> During the second week of jets
> dive-bombing Iraq on CNN,
> Jake Red Horse said he stumbled
> to shave the face of a middle-aged drunk
> whose boyhood contempt of America
> had eroded, cracked, and fallen away
> like an old man's teeth.
> His evil twin smiled back at him
> from the bathroom mirror.
>   "Last Song of the Dove"

The "evil twin" who has failed to nurture his bitterness ironically finds himself rooting for the white war and propaganda machine as it conducts a twentieth-century version of the taking of Indian land. Jake has let the difficulty of maintaining his hatred erode his memory of how he got to be a middle-aged drunk with no land to call his own. Louis' task is not to forget and to help others not to forget. A desperation lurks: to give in to the desire for peace with the white man starts one down the slippery slope that ends with listening to people like Dan Quayle "saying comforting, cheerleading war words/to a group of flag-waving yahoos," and becoming a yahoo oneself. If Louis' primary identity as an Indian has been robbed along with the land, he at least does not want to lose his secondary identity as an angry rebel to conformity. So he keeps the wounds open as the only hope of ever moving beyond them honestly.

But one needs some succor while living with the pain, and the most consistent sources of nurturing in Louis' poetry are beer and women. "Whiteclay, Nebraska" describes a significant part of the poet's world, the road between the "dry" Pine Ridge reservation and the small Nebraska border town that sells more beer, Louis tells us, than the state's two largest cities combined. This road, he reminds himself, is "where our fathers died," when they should have died on the warriors' road, yet this road is also "where our children died/on their way to getting born." The drinking that temporarily soothes him and his comrades also results in bad health, suicidal depressions, and fatal, late-night car crashes that, combined, rob the reservation residents of their future. At least the fathers had died in battle. Not even spring lightens the poem's mood:

> Green in purity. Green in spring,
> wine bottles and cans wrap the dying road
> and eighteen crosses mark departure spots
> on the two-mile jaunt from Pine Ridge.

The heroic deaths of the fathers, the drunken deaths of the sons; the green of spring, the green of broken wine bottles—Louis consistently focuses on the demeaning juxtapositions that comprise his life.

The small, daily contrasts between reality and desire, present and past, are summed up in the large contrast between solid, stable white culture and the disintegrating Indian culture he sees all around him. A perfect image presents itself in "Another Indian Murder":

> Beneath Mt. Rushmore's
> heightened air, drunk redskins

were stumbling everywhere
dead but for the deed of dying.

The icons of the culture that tried to eradicate the Indians
stare impassively as the Indians themselves take over the task of
their destruction, and Louis, unwilling to let juxtaposition imply
what he wants to be explicit, chooses the verbs to make clear
how the past of conquest and displacement continues to poison
the present:

> . . . that bitter December night, the granite shadows
> of Lincoln and Washington descended the slopes
> and infected all that was good below.
> Two Oglala boys with baseball bats
> scrambled the brains of a drinking buddy. . . .

One more reason to keep alive the hatred that Jake Red
Horse's evil twin has allowed to dissipate. The boys, infected by
the long shadow of the past that has robbed them of a future,
get drunk and kill their buddy without even being conscious of
the act. Like disembodied doubles of themselves, they look at
the product of their drunken, misdirected rage and try ineffectually, always ineffectually, to "plug the brain-seeping/holes
with Kleenex."

Alcohol is such a versatile aid: it not only causes or allows
violence against each other that, in the drug-induced stupor,
can seem like vengeance against the white man, but alcohol
also provides a haven when one is the victim of that misdirected
violence. "Her Wake," for example, finds us at a funeral, complete with the requisite greasy foods and grief. Something,
however, is out of place: "That man over there," Louis tells us,

"shouldn't be here," because when the deceased had rejected his advances, "he raped her/and she had his daughter/and never, not once, did she go to the cops." Where did she go? "She just ran to the warmth, flash,/and flames of the fire water world." Cause of pain, refuge against pain: alcohol can serve many functions for Louis and his friends, but can never do the one thing that is needed, which is cure the pain. When bad things keep happening to you, you cannot help thinking that perhaps you are the cause, a point Nietzsche makes more eloquently in a statement Louis has appropriated for an epigraph to "Summer Solstice at Taos": "Terrible experiences make one wonder whether he who experiences them is not something terrible." The poet wants to avoid that conclusion, wants to be the voice that will remind his people who their real enemies are. Unfortunately, like those to whom he speaks, he cannot always avoid the lure of alcohol that provides relief but that also releases the self-hatred and self-destructiveness that are the real infections spread by the granite sculptures on Mt. Rushmore.

The lure and beauty of beer is that it is always there, more faithful than any lover and easier to come by than the warrior life. In "The Hemingway Syndrome," the poet sits late at night, depressed in a "bleached board shack," alienated from that "unquestioning night" that serenely mocks with his own compulsively questioning mood. Soon, "My rifle becomes a black snake/desperately trying to kiss me." The tool of the warrior's trade tempts the poet, but tempts him to what we are not yet sure. He certainly has no real use for it, and that perhaps is what annoys him. "Bored," he works himself into a self-destructive mood: he remembers the past of the Ghost Dances, feels ashamed of his own history (from which the snake image arises, apparently unbidden, as a habit of thinking acquired in white schools), and gives thanks that tonight "there is no one here to question my past." "So," he says, suggesting some causal link between the above ruminations and his next action,

> I gouge the barrel to my mouth
> and tease the trigger like a very cheap whore
> and sweet pain explodes into starlight.
> I throw the air rifle to the floor,
> spit out the b.b. and head out the door
> to the cooler of iced beer that beckons.

The beer cooler is his icon, his grail, his church, his diminished equivalent of Devils Tower, a spot on the landscape where he is always welcome, the contents are always cool, and his doubts about his past and his potency are always soothed. Of course, it is also simply a tastier version of self-destruction than a bullet in the mouth. The past—of the Ghost Dance and of warriors who used real bullets—can neither be escaped nor lived up to, "so" he runs to the cooler. Hemingway at least was serious: he used a shotgun and got the job finished. Louis invites the reader's disgust. He tempts us to hate him as much as the poems suggest he hates himself. He may even feed off the revulsion he assumes he creates in his readers. Does he perhaps, somewhere in his subconscious, imagine a white reader? Would that make his shame more complete and temporarily cathartic?

The end of the road is assured for him, he knows that, as long as he listens to the beckoning song of the cooler. He begins "Fire Water World," the title poem from his 1989 book, with a portrait of his uncle, a victim of alcohol, "coughing blood/and thinking of thirty years past." Louis sees his own future portrait, and notes the drug's effects:

Your words would flow in endless meaning
if you were whole
but in the stillness of your shrunken soul
you rub your manhood with uneasy breath
and whisper sweet nothings at the jester death.

Words, soul, and manhood: alcohol attacks one's vocation, spirit, and temporal identity. Despite his bravado ("Who is not afraid?/My feathered answer is only me"), he clearly is frightened:

My balls click deftly in my drawers and I bow
to the endless liquor stores
who have given us courage and death.

With a bow, he respectfully acknowledges the power of the enemy that has taken his uncle. "Who" makes the liquor stores almost human, letting them participate as warrior enemies in this twentieth century version of a would-be warrior's fight for his life.

One suspects that, in the chronicle of his on-again-off-again relationship with the wagon that takes place primarily in his early volumes, the battle with alcohol is a battle Louis is willing to lose, if he can figure out a way to do so honorably, as a warrior falling to a stronger enemy. Too many images of death and self-destruction litter the poems to be there accidentally. Behind them is a deep guilt that Louis battles to remain sober and alive. In "Blame It on the Dog, He's Dead," for example, he recounts taking his dog to the vet's to be euthanised:

Several dollars buys release
and I fake no maudlin tears.
I think of the strength

of your quick parade
down the partial path of my years.

It is a dog's life, but at least a pooch can get put to sleep
and find "release." Yet a tenacious sense of self-preservation
remains beneath the almost equally strong sense of guilt and its
calls for self-destruction, because Louis refuses to use the
dog's symbolic death as an opportunity to reenter the fire-
water world:

and I fake no maudlin tears
but an hour later, I almost wipe
the slate clean
of the chalked days
of four thirsty years.

That internal battle manifests itself in the external battle
between Louis and beer. One would think that if the white man
is responsible for stealing the land then all we would see in the
poetry is the ample amount of invective aimed at whites, not
the equal dose of self-loathing. For what, after all, are we supposed to "blame" on the dog, Louis' fall-guy and double, in the
poem? The answer is that Louis feels implicated in the white
man's victory. He looks into his poetic mirror and sees a fifth-
columnist. At an early age, he ran from his Nevada home, tried
to enter the "white bread" world ("I prayed one day I'd live a
life/as white as store-bought bread," he says in "White Bread
Blues") and pass as Caucasian. He went to white schools, lived
in white cities, and was tempted by teaching jobs in white col-
leges (where, he suspects, he helps satisfy some EEOC or
Affirmative Action guidelines). He is the talented child who
feels guilty for being lured away from the family, lured above

the family, succeeding in a world where his loved ones still live a dog's life. A common enough guilt-producing scenario, here aggravated by the historical fact that Louis' family is the victim of the racism of white America, where Louis has found patronage and success.

The Scylla of his friends' destructive ways on one side of his path is balanced by the Charibda of the tempting white ways on the other. "Stoned to the Bone" finds him being conned into driving Jake and Verdell to Whiteclay just in time to beat the liquor stores' closing hour. He is sober now but mightily tempted to join his friends, out of love and loyalty and guilt, in their ritualistic self-destruction:

> We walked to my car
> and I mind-plugged my ears.
> I refused to listen
> to their deathsongs
> even though for many years
> those same sad sounds
> squeaked past my own lips.

On the other hand, there are the dangers of believing oneself capable of being at home in the white world. In "Fish Fry at a Panhandle Bar," for example, "a sleek green mermaid with emerald nipples" somehow finds her way into a Nebraska bar where Jake and Verdell are drinking. "'But there ain't no ocean near Nebraska,'" one local chimes in, as if an ocean would make sense of the mermaid. No, this is a dream to Jake and Verdell, enjoying a quiet afternoon at the bar, this clean, well-lighted place, lulled into believing that perhaps they might be welcome there. The boys from the reservation are like their Indian ancestors on the Plains, not noticing that they are slowly being surrounded by hostile whites because their eyes are focused on the green prize, an image of their ancestors' green lives, explicitly contrasted in the poem as more real than the lives of the cowboys' ancestors (she is "not mere illusion/like the Texas longhorns upon the walls," representing "decades of insatiable American dreams").

We hear Louis trying to shout to Jake and Verdell to watch out, to warn them that they are surrounded, but they listen no better than he does at other times:

> A quaint white mob approached:
> old sunbaked women with knives and linen.
> One carried a bowlful of lemons. The boys
> made no words to fend off white blood lust.
> Their mouths were too busy drooling.

Louis, too, drools at what white America can offer, but knows, sometimes, that his job is to resist its call and steer his route between the destructions offered him on one side by his Indian peers and on the other by the knife-edged smiles of welcome beamed his way by his enemies masquerading as friends in white America and cowboy bars (which seem to be Louis' synecdoche for all America). In the poem, Louis says Jake and Verdell "made no words" to protect themselves, not "made no move" to protect themselves. Only his words, his poems, his songs will drown out the lies of the siren calls and save him, if anything will. The only way he can fail is if, like "the boys," he drools so much at what white America offers that he is unable to form his words of protest.

Nevertheless, forming those words is best done while sober, and whatever the horrors of alcohol abuse may be, being sober on the reservation is no treat. While drunk, Louis can at least forget temporarily that he will eventually have to wake up, but while sober he is painfully aware and sometimes prays for unconsciousness: "This is only a prayer for black, dreamless sleep," he says soberly in "Tangled Up in Lilac." The rewards of sobriety are small: the reservation world does not become a paradise when he is on the wagon ("The sobriety does not come in sweet softness/but in the mechanical clutches of remembered desires"). Weighing the costs and benefits of drinking, however, is just too dry and reasonable a way to understand the lure of the bottle. Louis' compulsion runs deeper than that and goes beyond the personal calculus of sobriety. There is a deeper and more dangerous reason to stay drunk:

> Maybe I am as strong as I ever have been.
> Maybe I am as weak as my drunken neighbors
> fighting and puking, chaotic and angry,
> in the invisible stalag their minds
> have designed.

Finally, there is the rub: if I am strong, and if this is a prison house I have to some extent created myself, then I am obligated to do something more than remain in a blind haze. The statements are carefully qualified to avoid commitment, but who can doubt that in the poet's heart, those "maybes" do not exist. He knows there is something for the warrior to do, something very frightening. Better and easier to tell himself that he is powerless than to admit that one's songs are sung in the key of self-pity. Nothing very heroic about that realization. What is heroic, however, is the poet's passionate dedication to investigating and bringing to light all the nooks and crannies of his and his people's psyche. He huffs and puffs and backslides a lot, but he never does become "as weak as [his] drunken neighbors." He guiltily sends his emissaries Jake and Verdell into the world to take the punches he wants to avoid so that he can remain a "hard punching son of a bitch" ("In the Little Waldorf Saloon at the End of the 20th Century") and a poetic battler. Somebody has to stay sober, he seems to say, to keep the songs alive, to face the fears, and always to hope "for beauty,/that great, wingless bird" ("That Great Wingless Bird").

Beauty, that elusive and perhaps extinct bird, brings us to the second of Louis' two favorite compensations for the life of loss he has inherited: the endless pursuit of women, or lust, or love, depending on the poem. Louis' relationship to women is as ambivalent and complex as his love-hate affair with liquor. On the one hand, women are the nurturers who provide psychological and physical sustenance. A relationship with a woman, no matter how temporary, provides the antidote to the alienation fostered by dependence on alcohol:

> Explosive you bloomed before me
> warm radiance sheathed in silk.
> Attempting to quell my liver
> I drained your white breasts of milk.
> "Recurring Nightmare"

Milk as palliative to liquor: the breast as alternative to the bottle; a life-sustaining fluid is substituted for the life-destroying one. The women he sees on the reservation are models of strength, good examples for him to learn from. He also appreciates the female form on a physical and aesthetic level—there is something pleasing to him about being in a female's presence.

And yet, and yet: women's strength threatens him; as a man whose possibility for heroic warrior action has been taken from him, women's quiet strength diminishes him. If the breast symbolically replaces the bottle, as in "Recurring Nightmare," Louis is turned into an infant, no comfort for the would-be warrior. Plus, nurturers can also be betrayers: women leave him, throw him out (albeit usually with good cause), and generally give him a taste of the tenuousness of any relationship, the insecurity of relying on another for succor. Women's acceptance and love occasionally appear to him, one raised to keep his guard up, as suffocation or even as castration. He will be eaten alive, he fears, if he gives in to his need:

> White witch on my throne of winter
> don't just tease dry leaves with ice.
> Hurry, conjure your favorite dinner:
> Indian cock with wine and rice.

We see the ambivalent dynamics of the relationship: he gets to play the invader (or conqueror) taking back, in symbolic terms, a portion of what the white world has taken from him. He has no land to call his own, but he has his white woman, a small piece of white territory who prefers him to the less colorful competition. In the act itself, though, he suspects he is the one who has been had, who has given himself away to the enemy, or who has denied his Indianness by too close an association with the white world. His very manhood is caught in the dilemma: the "white witch" becomes a castrater and consumer of his genitals, just as her white brothers have figuratively castrated and consumed the manhood of his ancestors. Sex, it turns out, is as dangerous as beer. Beauty is as threatening as the bottle.

Loving an Indian woman is no less complicated than falling for a white one, for the Indian woman reminds him of lost opportunities:

> South Dakota woman. I remember winter.
> Prurient recollection is gravity
> debasing my jaded continuum.
> In your flanks I saw the blood drive
> of brood mares.
> In your flanks I saw my warrior sons.
> "South Dakota Woman"

He should be with an Indian woman, not a white one, and she should be the mother of his warrior sons. Except he knows he will have no warrior sons, that all the warrior sons that ever will be born have been born and died already with the passing of Indian land to the whites. Lust, then, can never develop into real love, for its hope can never last that long, and its movements are pointless:

> How mean and meaningless
> our perfunctory thrashing
> done in the name of desire's death.

A pervading distrust of relationships underlies all the poetry. Having been cheated before he was born, Louis is not about to be hoodwinked into trusting again, no matter how great his need. In part I of "Urban Indian Suite," he wanders alone in a city far from the reservation, needing companionship: "and I need to talk to other skins/and to touch a brown-skin girl." In part II, he finds his brown-skinned girl and, through connection with her as some sort of flesh-and-blood embodiment of his lost past and heritage, the brown Earth Mother, he is temporarily brought back to his sense of himself as Indian:

> Her skin is brown and we both grew up
> using outhouses.
> She smokes the same cigarettes I do:
> Whatever's free and available.
> We are both Indian
> and not, never, God-damned Americans!

Predictably, the euphoria and sense of self pass, as they must if based upon nothing more than a brief physical union. Part III is strewn with images of decay. The words surround the reader with images of loss—spook, gone, shabby, dust, dimmed, discarded, poison, weakest, bloat, gray, angst, and lies, all within ten lines—until Louis' victory cry of part II is forgotten and replaced by another image of castration, suffocation, and disempowerment:

> I was trapped by a rapacious groin and
> cuddled between the passing seasons
> like a huge, hairless rodent
> allowing any mousetrap of feminine mirth
> to refine and define my dirt birthright.
> I did not know that woman gives man strength
> and then takes it back to double her own.

Indian women, it seems, dine on Indian men, too. The problem is that loving implies commitment, and commitment requires strength, and the poet doubts his power. Historical and personal reasons related to the loss of Indian land and his

consequent loss of his identity dictate his sense of place as a
man in the world. Better to be free (or unattached), an alien
without commitment than to have anyone else make demands
on him that he may not be able to satisfy. Therefore, he concludes the poem (part IV) with a rant both phlegmatic and
juvenile, reminding us that dependence on "breasts of milk"
is no less infantile than the fear of the commitment those
breasts imply:

> So, the hell with all of you.
> This place is good enough for me
> and I live here under an alias.
> I have come, now will go
> when I damn well please.

The final fear of giving up alcohol is that to do so would
make one face one's own responsibility for this hellish life,
which recognition would obligate one to change that life, which
obligation would threaten one's sense of potency and compe-
tency. The same dynamic holds for love: giving in to love commits one to someone else's expectations, which in Louis' case
are also the expectations he holds in himself of what it means to
be an Indian and what he would have to do to earn that name.
The prospect so frightens him that he is content to wander the
streets of a vast city and hurl petulant cries at anyone who
would dare love him rather than accept the challenge of his
own Indianness, which he feels is irretrievably lost to him or
beyond his powers.

To make matters worse, he suspects that women are
stronger than he is. During a powwow at Pine Ridge ("Relapse:
Blue Spring at Pine Ridge"), women dance:

Wild Indians were everywhere
and still the women sang.
They mouthed the very sounds of survival
outside the circle of men singing stronger.
The whole world was held in their tawny arms
and the sweetness of brown embrace.
Those siren women softened the impending
demise of that long-dying race
until the raging drum drowned
their elkskin voices.

For a sane moment, the women's voices emerge from the background of despair and sing of hope and survival. Here Louis admires that female strength (although the use of "siren" carries a suggestion of the women's potential for betrayal) that elsewhere he feels diminished by and distrusts. Women hold the power, he suspects, almost to transcend the loss of land that is so important to his loss of identity. In a similar vein, in "Elvis Presley in Pine Ridge," a hung-over Verdell attends a powwow:

Sweating, he watches a ravishing
young lady fancy dancer
kick up the clay dust
that clings to his wine sweat.
She spins like she owns the land!

The dancer for the moment or in the imagination makes the loss of the land irrelevant or untrue. At fourteen (to Verdell's forty-one) she has not yet lost her joy and dignity. By contrast, Verdell "can't remember what honor/means these days." But her femininity is more important than her youth.

The female seems to hold the power to remain strong, which the men lose. The men try to regain that strength by drinking and then beating the women whose image of strength mocks and shames them. Verdell's desire here is less hateful:

> Her spinning binds his heart
> with desperate longing
> and he sways into the recognition
> of the fact that if he could have her,
> his whole life would change,
> things would be good,
> he'd be young again
> and his future would stand before him.

If he could have her—the one who can make the loss of the land disappear—he would be young and potent again, with a future.

The men in Louis' poetry need but powerfully distrust and fear the strength of women, who are typically associated with the land, the very absence of which has robbed the males of their virility, which they try to recapture in sexual exploits and spousal abuse. In some moments of clarity, however, even a wobbly Verdell can see something pure in the female energy that would perhaps be a source of the power needed to overcome the loss. Here Verdell is saved from having to make a choice about accepting that energy or fleeing it (she is, after all, only fourteen) and can content himself to remember fondly his past, when "at her age, fourteen/he wore an Elvis pompadour." The lost land seems historical—get over it, we hear unsympathetic voices tell Indians—but the past is present for Louis and his comrades. The poet is kept awake one night (in "Pine Ridge Lullaby") by violence in the alley outside his window:

Sitting upright in bed it's impossible
not to hear the dull thuds of pistols
popping in the sharp autumn air.

The woman in his bed can tell him, "Go back to sleep . . .
It's no one you know and none of my family!" but Louis hears
more than the present screams: "Almost feminine, his voice carries the ghosts/of the men and women massacred at Wounded
Knee." To him, born to be a warrior, the massacre at Wounded
Knee, even though he was not there, marks him with a legacy
of the one defeated in battle. The woman can sleep; Louis
reaches for his gun. Her voice is wise, of course, but to him it is
the siren call of passivity. He has failed to protect his people.
His dream that night says it all:

In my mind's frayed corral
a gelding circles mares and cries.

He fears he has abandoned women as much as the women
he loved have abandoned him ("'Please, Mom,' I sang, weary
from memory,/'Don't drink no more here now tonight.'"
["Muted War Drums"]). His loss of territory is his failure;
women's failure to nurture is theirs. And both failures are
couched in similar images of the nurturing breast that is both
salvation and betrayal. "I am beside her," he says, "like a baby at
a dry breast" ("Muted War Drums"), where "her" can be any of
the women he meets who suffer the burden of saving him
through their embrace but whose embraces are feared as deadly. And the land, the source of salvation, imaged in female
terms, that has been stolen and by which the poet feels abandoned, is itself a dry breast, that cruel joke to the needy infant:

> In '68 I ran from a fish hook nation
> haunted by the dead, dutiful sons
> scorned by the dry breast of their motherland.
> "For Wonder Bread Danny Quayle"

Is mutual disappointment the only relationship between men and women in Louis' poetry? No, as evidenced by *Ceremonies of the Dead,* a 1997 sequence of poems, but even in an earlier poem, "Fullblood Girl on a Blue Horse," Louis renders the possibilities for males and females to serve as mutually inspiring and fertilizing agents. The poem finds Louis in a redneck border town, probably Rushville, Nebraska, where he takes up temporary residence before returning to Pine Ridge. He is in enemy territory and the local whites are whooping it up:

> One cowpoke chucks a beer
> bottle and it explodes
> on the street bordering
> the back edge of my yard.

It is a symbolic invasion of his territory and Louis wants to make a warrior's stand:

> I want to go get my pistol
> and make that heifer-humper
> crawl up the street
> and pick up the glass shards
> with his teeth and tongue.

His manhood wants to respond. His reason and sanity, however, convince him to try another afternoon activity than reenacting Wounded Knee. He goes to the post office to mail some poems. Poems, not guns: he has chosen a life-affirming form of potency over a self-destructive form, just as he had hoped the breast would wean him from the bottle. But here, the poems are powers he controls himself. He will beat back the invaders with words over which they do not have command rather than guns over which they do. The words he writes are his power, and he knows it. They are his power against both whites and his own people's more self-destructive tendencies:

> The mailbox outside the Post Office
> on Main Street is my thought temple.
> It stands alone in defiance
> of nature and winos.

As he mails his poems, he must wonder if posting his words is truly an effective statement. Sometimes he feels that "Those sacred words" are nothing more than "useless bits/of wounded pride."

But today, his manhood and his choice of vocation are validated, almost magically, by a "long-legged fullblood/girl with teenaged thighs" who "sit[s] astride the cold blue/box like it is a wild stallion flying/her over this prairie town. . . ." Inserting his poems into the mail chute between her thighs is of course sexually symbolic and brings us back to the theme of love. His muse and sexual fantasy, who importantly is fullblood, a true representative of the true life (Louis is only, much to his regret, halfblood), accepts his offerings and blesses his efforts as he sends them out into the vast mystery of life. His poems are his warrior sons, the only ones he will ever have, and she is their symbolic mother, for they emerge into the mailbox more or less from between her thighs. His present-day weapons—his poems—are validated as proper replacements for the warrior's stallion, the symbol of a glorious past represented here by the fullblood girl. Together—muse, lover, poet, and the U. S. Post Office mail box, some sort of blue steel surrogate sweat lodge and warrior pony all in one—his words fly over and transcend the yahoo thieves of the land. Such hopeful transcendence is temporary—when he gets back home he is still tempted to "shoot me/some rednecks today"—but it does exist, and the poem gives us an image of how Louis can battle the forces that plague him, with the help of the empowering but not castrating woman, with the weapons he has at his disposal.[6]

As is true for alcohol and women, Louis is by turns attracted to and repulsed by his own words. As the tools of his battles but also the products of a white culture, his words work for his freedom while reinforcing his servitude. He curses the "polysyllabic lunacy" of his expensive schooling as a "perverse perpetuation/of the white man's paternalism" ("After Long Silence Marilyn Returns"). Every word of English he speaks, informed by his Ivy-League education, is a debt to the white culture. He devalues his education ("crosstown in the sane precincts/of Brown University . . . I added rage/to Cliff Notes and got two degrees") to minimize its effect on his thinking, to pretend that going to a white university has really had less effect on him than it has, but deep down he knows and powerfully resents the range of that education's influence: "I'm in the dry hills with a Winchester/waiting to shoot the lean, learned fools/who taught me to live-think in English" ("Elegy for the Forgotten Oldsmobile"). The manner of his speaking reveals his debt to Western European literary history and how much he has learned to "live-think in English." His work is more informed by the Romantic, Modernist, and Confessional modes than by any tribal traditions. Occasionally the reader is moved by the inconsistency of this voice praising Indian ways and excoriating white while speaking within the poetic traditions dearest to the invaders' culture. The problem of how to speak authentically is a major dilemma for Louis. In fact, critic Craig Womack calls "the [characters'] failure to find expressive language to carry forward the culture into contemporary existence" "the heart of the problem" (Review 107).

As always, at the center of Louis' attitude toward his poetry and his poetic vocation is the experience of loss and guilt: loss of his Indian tongue to history, loss of his Indian ways to his white education, and guilt at being a voluntary participant in the white man's paternalism. He fears he has lost not only the land but his brain and tongue as well. When he writes in this mood, he creates only self-pity, which he acknowledges in more lucid moments, is fruitless. In "Among the Dog-Eaters," for example, he battles the siren song of self-pity but seems armed with little more than the urge to resist. As usual, Louis works circuitously, beginning the poem with a rant against "squawmen," that is, white men who have fathered children by Indian women. Louis' unnamed friend in the poem (perhaps Verdell?) reminds him of his own guilt in the matter by noting that these "Indians by insertion" are responsible for "more breeds like you." What really irritates the poet, however, is that he overhears a couple of squawmen in Big Bat's Conoco "whining" about the Indians' refusal to accept their help. Louis ironically notes that the two seem unable to "fathom/ such limited response to salvation." The men's presumption and condescension anger the poet, of course, but, again, what really bothers him is guilt: here are these fake Indians worrying about the future of "the people" when the people themselves seem completely unconcerned and willing to be defined by white attitudes. "The real bite of Louis's bitterness," as Leslie Ullman says, "settles on the red man for his complicity in his own demise" ("Betrayals and Boundaries" 191)[7]:

> By his naming us *victims*, we become victims.
> When he says we are *oppressed*,
> we learn to oppress each other.
> But is he why we must accept welfare?
> Is he why we drink and beat our wives?
> Is he why we molest our children?
> And is he why we are programmed to fail?

He knows that the words spoken by the white culture at large and this morning by two squawmen in Big Bat's take the power to define themselves out of Indian hands. Words are powerful weapons, as powerful as the Winchesters of his dreams.

Once again, however, the would-be warrior feels powerless because his words inspire no greater "response to salvation" than the squawmen's:

> In Big Bat's Conoco I wanted to scream:
> Wake up, you damn *people*, wake up!
> America does not owe you a living.
> America does not owe you your souls.
> You've got to grab your balls
> and fill them with fire
> and stop whining
> and drinking like bums,
> but all I did was murder
> an ant.

The urge to use his words to drive from the field of battle the white words that define his people as oppressed victims is there, but he remains silent, knowing—perhaps only fearing—that his screaming will be ineffective. The apparently unrelated killing of the ant is more than a pointless projection of his anger. Earlier in the poem Louis had watched the ant circling around the Sweet n' Low spilled near his coffee: "The ant danced in circles around spilled sugar/imitating our Indian nations." So the ant he crushes is a symbol for the Indian nations' futile circling and circling around the "sugar" promised by white culture, the false promise (a sugar substitute) of materialism and government support. By crushing the ant, he symbolically continues the self-loathing that he denounces when decrying the acceptance of welfare, the drinking, and the abuse of spouses and children, all manifestations of the same sort of self-hatred symbolized by the crushing of the poor insect, "intoxicated upon the largess/of some alien God." He despairs of his words' ability to save him and his people, but he shows us in a powerfully casual image that he knows his silence will only fuel the fires of self-hatred and self-destructive violence that have almost consumed modern Indians.

He captures the self-destructive cycle in a different image in "Degrees of Hydrophobia," which finds him driving home "from the Indian college" (Oglala Lakota College in South Dakota), where he has spent all day teaching English, or, as he says, where he has endured an "eight hour siege/of the language of the enemy." Siege suggests a battle: fighting off the enemy's language today is similar to his ancestors' fighting off the enemy's military attack. The metaphor makes Louis a frontline warrior in the war for the word, a poet battling for his potency and his tribe's future with his words, while, of course, teaching those very words to other Indians. The poem begins with an epigraph from Sherman Alexie: "It's the same old story. How can we imagine a new language when the language of the enemy keeps our dismembered tongues tied to its belt?" The dismemberment image connects with Louis' castration imagery in other poems. Losing one's tongue is losing one's potency.

The background of the poem is the writer's struggle with the tools of his trade. In the foreground, he is simply driving home with a "lone can of Bud" in his lap, hurrying and "hoping to make/halftime of Monday Night Football," when a "dumb-shit coyote skitters/in front of my T-Bird/carrying a quivering jackrabbit." The coyote emerges out of the dark and disappears back into it (after Louis brakes and avoids the collision), like some messenger from the other world. All we see at the moment, however, is that the coyote made the driver spill his beer. Later, at home, he makes the connection: the coyote is a wild hunter, the same animal it always has been. His people were once wild hunters, living off this land that others now control. The coyote can survive the intrusion of highways (that is, if the driver is willing to brake and spill his beer) and really does not care if white or Indian owns the road. It continues to kill jackrabbits and live off the land as it always has. The coyote feels no identity crisis. But Louis and his fellow Indians are now more like domesticated coyotes, like the dogs that the poet shifts his attention to after the near-miss on the highway. His own dogs are still "ball-biters on command," but most canines on the reservation get abandoned "and hang around Sioux Nation Shopping Center/with two-leggeds who were abandoned/as children." Dogs and Indians become "kindred spirits," both abandoned, and the Indians now perpetuate that abandonment (as Louis elsewhere shows us they perpetuate the violence done to them) by letting their dogs run free. The cycle seems doomed to go on and on.

Perhaps, however, if he can make the move to accept the responsibility, then being a poet can be his compensation for not being a warrior, can give him a dignified role, and can help others break the cycle by example or inspiration. Louis makes it clear that he wants his verse to serve just such a communal purpose, something as grand as saving his people, but he fears that poetry, especially his, makes nothing happen. In "A Prayer for the Lost" he makes a nighttime run outside with the trash:

> To escape marauding in-laws
> whose kids slosh Kool-Aid
> against the walls of my heart
> and moisten the dry-dirt memories
> of my own childhood,
> I slink outside carrying garbage. . . .

Inside, the next generation, so young and alive, raises hopes in his heart that he knows are doomed. The in-laws' kids remind him of his youth, but even as they play, Louis knows that the future will hold no more meaningful roles for them than the present does for him. He refuses to let himself get too attached to them or to his dreams for them, just as he will not let himself attach to the women in his poems or make a poetic commitment to writing his people's saving words, for that is the road to more painful loss. "Life/as I know it is dying" he says, so why commit his emotions to a bunch of rowdy kids who simply are not old enough to see the futility of it all?

Escape, however, is not so easy. The sky is clear, and under the stars he begins to feel Indian again and imagine what it must have been like to live as part of this "laundered April air." He talks to his grandfather, a full-blood who, other than Crazy Horse, is the only consistently positive male role model Louis allows himself:

> In the purity of starlight, I ask Grandfather
> to salvage this battered Indian nation
> because my words may be no help.

What can his words do to save the children inside or the child next door, visible suckling the "cantaloupe breasts" of "a dope-dealer's wife"? Clearly he wants his words to be of help but fears they cannot, just as he fears his power in so many other respects. We discover he is carrying his own poems to the trash bins:

> Should the coyotes burst the cold
> steel, drums, pale white flowers would bloom.
> Upon countless crumpled pages
> variants of this prayer for the lost
> would be found.

His poems are prayers for his lost people, and this poem is a prayer for those other lost poems. Perhaps if the coyote, a representative of the non-human natural world, would make the effort to release and somehow sacralize his poems, they would truly blossom. Louis seems to distrust his own power and authority to bring to life the words that are required. His people's need is great: with "no words of pride for our past" ("Without Words") and only "our song of self-pity" ("Pabst Blue Ribbon at Wounded Knee") to sustain them, Indians need someone like Louis to speak pride in the present and reject fatalism. He wants his poems to be nothing less than the voice of his grandfather salvaging this Indian nation ("Let me speak in the spirit,/in the voice of the warrior," he says in "Postscript: Devils Tower," in a rare moment of unironic emotion), but he fears his verses are so powerless that he crumples and discards them as waste.

Of course he does not discard them all. He preserves and publishes enough for us to see and understand the knife edge he walks. Being silent is self-destructive. Speaking in the enemy's language seems futile. Being silent emasculates him. Speaking places him in a position of failing and being emotionally castrated, as he fears in the presence of women. There would be no need for a saving poetry if not for the loss of his and his people's identities through the loss of their homeland. It all seems so futile. And, anyway, what would a poem that would "salvage this battered Indian nation" sound like? Perhaps if he can define the terms of living from the Indians' perspective rather than from the whites', that would be a start. With this in mind, in several poems he "rewrites" history—he supplies an Indian version of cherished American myths—or provides an alternate voice to the mainstream song. In "Statue of Liberty," for example, first he cuts the icon down to size by describing it in decidedly unheroic and antimythic terms:

> Cold, worn gears whine inside
> your bronzed vulva and dark bodies
> are dropped to the tired sea.

As he imagines the "dark bodies" swimming toward the "cruel illusion" of freedom, he hears "the awkward gaps/in their prayers of thanks." Those gaps are the voices of Native Americans who never needed to enter the country through Ellis

Island, and whose prayers were simply prayers to be left alone to live peacefully where they were. The reference to prayers introduces the auditory element, and Louis concludes with it:

> When I listen closely I don't hear
> the midnight ride of Paul Revere
> but ghosts of dead tribes
> bonesinging under concrete.

He rewrites, or rehears, history, substituting his own sub-text for the text represented by the Statue of Liberty (America as land of opportunity) and literally represented on her bronze ("Give me your tired, etc."). Louis hears the words that preceded this overlay of white myth and that were drowned out by white history. The poet becomes the archeologist of the auditory and releases the Indian bonesongs from beneath the Statue's foundations.

In another example of the poet accepting his responsibility to construct or resurrect an alternate red history, we find him in "Corral of Flame Horses" mimicking the form of a student paper on western history with his own revisionist interpretation substituted as the thesis statement:

> THESIS STATEMENT: The romantic American West, that purple-saged cowboy stage where upright and rugged individualists of European descent carved out their God-given empires with six-guns blazing, never existed.

In his SECOND ATTEMPT: THESIS STATEMENT, he makes it clear that the Wild West as romantic frontier has never meant anything to the Indians and has in fact been promulgated in denial of the Indians' understanding of the same place and period:

> In a nutshell and beyond any conversation of quaint mani-
> fest destiny, primitivism, or cultural colonialism, for the
> Indian the West was simply home and not the new fron-
> tier, not the European model for a new hope.

The white story of the West not only differs from but also replaces and supplants the Indian story, and in the process paves the way for the replacing and supplanting of the Indians themselves and their culture. Louis wants to get his version on record before it is too late. The exam-answer format of the poem reminds us that Louis wants to re-educate himself and learn how not to "live-think in English." The format also suggests that both whites and Indians have been educated to believe a history of the West that makes Indians either savages or oppressed victims, both characterizations the poet rejects. If words are as powerful as Louis elsewhere says they are ("By his naming us *victims,* we become victims"), then he will appropriate some of that power to write his own story to drown out, or at least compete with, the voices that have entered his mind. Taking back the words will compensate, if only to a small extent, for not being able to take back the land.

But how to take back the words while writing in the "language of the enemy"? He seems not to mean that he must actually speak and write in a native tongue, which he does not know—although he sprinkles a few native words throughout his volumes—but to mean somehow speaking English with a tongue not "dismembered," in a manner that would provide a substitute for the habit Indians have developed of thinking of themselves in the terms provided to them by the words of the white majority. Perhaps if he can reacquaint the domesticated dogs with the words of that coyote he spilled his beer for in "Degrees of Hydrophobia":

> Beneath Sirius I dream of ghost dogs
> reinventing the bark.
> Hounded and clawed by the lost bones
> of life, they yip and nip
> in folly and foam
> at the hovering bitch moon
> and its dancing moans of a time long ago
> when words had meaning
> when language had value
> when both men and dogs
> were strong silent hunters.

The key is to reinvent the bark. To speak in the language of the enemy without sending the message that "We are victims" or "We are oppressed." But what is that bark?

First, the bark is definitely not silence. It keeps alive the anger and pain, which, if they disappear, emasculate the poet/warrior by their absence. Having moved again to Rushville, Nebraska, for example, away from reservation land, Louis says,

> I have murdered all inner conflict.
> I have no anger, no remorse
> and the white world

can just sit on my face
if it wants to.
                    "Breakfast at Big Bat's Conoco
                    Convenience Store in Pine Ridge"

To murder the anger and conflict is to become silent and passive. The bark must keep alive that venom. To do that, it must be fed by reservation noise and Indian land:

Verdell once said:
If an Indian does not live on Indian land
then he is not an Indian.
And I shit you not, the boy is right.
We're moving back to the reservation
soon when we grow weary of sanity.
                    "Small Town Noise"

To reinvent the bark is, first, to keep the protest alive, not to escape the insanity by moving to a quiet small town, not to drown the insanity with liquor, not to lose one's pain in sexual conquests. To reinvent the bark is to feed off that pain while not mistaking the pain for one's identity. To feed off pain and anger need not be the same as to be their victims. You need not be what you eat.

Second, the bark must be unrepentant and defiant. It must not hide from, accommodate, or placate white sensibilities. It will not be mystical, spiritual or transcendental, those traits that attract and comfort white readers to some Native American poetry. Louis understands that game. A particularly good example of his refusal to become a New Agers' favorite is "Petroglyphs of Serena," a poem from his 1997 volume,

Ceremonies of the Damned. It is a poem of several hundred lines and begins like many Louis poems: while in the middle of a simple daily activity (visiting Yellowbird's Store), he finds himself "thinking of the wondrous/and drool-making beauty of my student Serena." By the fifth unnumbered section, the poet has caught her in a fairly conventional (for Louis) conquest scene:

> We were naked, biting each other hard
> and the air, oh, the air was good
> and I drank it in without
> the slightest cough of guilt.

Just as we wonder where this is going, we learn in the next section that "she's drunk-rolled/a car and is dead, just like that—dead. . . ." The poet attends the funeral, standing on the periphery, and soon has a vision of Serena. But that is not the point. He refuses to let that be the point, refuses to be the stereotypical mystical-lyrical Indian poet showing us the secrets hidden from uptight white culture. In fact, his vision of Serena is all Louis:

> She was with some strange-looking Skins,
> drove a different car, and looked puzzled,
> half-angry when I waved at her.
> Acted like she didn't know me.
> Kind of gave me a kiss-my-butt look
> and then flipped me the bird.

Louis barks his own bark, the defiant and unrepentant snarl that is his personal style. But then we notice that this bark expands beyond personal lust and simple iconoclasm into the realm of the communal.

The focus shifts from Serena's ability to comfort the poet to the loss of Serena and others like her, young reservation Indians who seem born into a lottery world: some will end in prison, some dead in a car wreck, some in a lousy job, some with six kids by six different men. The children seem to find the quickest route to destruction, while the elders lament the loss of the past. At the funeral, Serena's mother lists all the modern problems that did not happen "in the old days." Louis recognizes that neither solution—early death or middle-aged nostalgia—is adequate. The real need is to bridge the gap between elders and children, between past and future:

> We are all hiding from the truth.
> Our children have no respect
> because their parents cannot connect
> the values of the ancient chiefs
> to the deadly grief that welfare brings.
> We're reaping the womb's reward of mutant
> generations who stumbled toward dismembering
> the long and sometimes senile span between you,
> Great Spirit, and your artwork, man.

Now the defiant bark is given a third characteristic and a program beyond simple defiance. Realistically, to be defiant is still to be dependent on the person or party being defied. Hating or cursing whites and going no farther keeps Louis tied to the white perception of the Indian and in an ironic way is the true emasculation because it is just a futile noise. To get past simple hatred, of which he has an ample supply ("Underneath all . . . is that simple urge to scalp a white man"), is to make progress. Resisting but not ignoring the pain and anger he ingests daily, resisting but using the education he has earlier been fed, and then rewriting history to suit his perspective becomes the poetic task of connecting the past to the present— in order to keep both past and present alive. To connect the wisdom of the past to the vulgar world of today, and thereby to connect the sacred to the profane, to illuminate the present with the light of the spiritual, to connect, as he says in another long poem, the earth bone to the spirit bone: that is a poetic task worthy of his talent. (This does not mean, of course, abandoning the earth bone entirely or sounding like some tame coyote: Louis ends the poem in bed with Thalia, Serena's younger sister, "in the snug, smug darkness/of lust.")

What if no one listens or no one responds? What if you stick out your neck to retrieve the spirit bone, drag it into the earth bone light, bark to your heart's content, and nobody cares? What if you give up self-pity, try to write your people's war song, and your readers would rather not hear your efforts? Then you feel like a fool, shouting to the world with no one listening or even whispering back. How do you offer that kind of love anyway? This, I take it, is the significance of *Ceremonies of the Damned* (in which both "Petroglyphs for Serena" and "Earth Bone Connected to the Spirit Bone" appear), a book in which Louis wrestles with his wife's Alzheimer's disease. The topic may seem unconnected, but it is not. On a personal level, the poet finds himself forced to offer love that he cannot hope to have returned. His wife often does not recognize him. She responds to none of his words. His efforts are unappreciated and apparently unending. He is forced to extend his love because she needs and demands it, yet he never knows if that love is accepted, acknowledged, or noted. His actions require warrior courage and a leap of faith, which he has been resisting and retreating from, always retreating from seriousness and commitment, always undercutting his motives with self-pity, irony, verbal wit, and cleverness.

On the communal level that Louis' poetry now reaches toward, that relationship has all the emotional and philosophical markers of the Indian poet's relationship to his culture. People would rather not hear him. Verdell still comes by to bum money to get drunk on. Louis has to offer his poems anyway, even if they show no hope of doing what he wants them to do, that is, forging the consciousness of his culture. He has to admit what he wants them to do. He cannot hide from the fact that he is trying to keep his wife alive; he cannot hide from the fact that he wants his poems to be taken as articulations of Indian pride and constructive anger. The world—wife and Verdell—refuses to say it cares. In both cases, personal and poetic, the poet can only persist, keep throwing out his words as if they matter.

That is love, which Louis admits he has often abused but love now stalks him. He doubts his qualifications to be part of a positive program rather than simply an articulator of the negative: "But then what do I know?/I can only set up situations and point my finger" ("Earth Bone Connected to the Spirit Bone"). He would like to give up the ghost but cannot help wanting to be of cosmic assistance:

> And I pray that I could take all man's
> infirmities of flesh, all the little cancers,
> the tooth cavities, the blackheads,
> the failing kidneys, the wrinkling skin,
> the allergies, the clogged arteries, the aphasias,
> take all those bad things from one's body, suck
> them out by cosmic means, compress all those
> negatives into a cosmic ball of black star mass

and hurl it into the sun.
Then I would pray that the molten-golden
dew of love would cover this land.
"Earth Bone Connected to the Spirit Bone"

Unrealistic, he knows, but he keeps trying, just as he keeps talking to his wife. The fact that she cannot respond to his words is particularly significant. As a poet with large hopes, he needs response to his utterances, or so one would think, if he is to keep offering them. But in "To Bill in Minneapolis, Minnesota," he writes a dialogue with his wife that could be his dialogue with his people:

Don't say I don't know, I said to her.
Howcome you say that, I said.
I don't know, she said.
No, really, howcome you're saying
I don't know to all my questions?
I don't know, she said.

Louis has to know for both—for himself and his wife, for himself and his people—and that is a trying task, speaking into the void. No easy solution is forthcoming, but even the poet's doubts now contain a seed of hope, as in the conclusion to "Black Crow Dreams," in which he recounts a dream:

A flock of crows landed on me
and carried me across town.
They dropped me down
inside her bedroom.
I sat on her bed and watched her undress
and then I fell deep asleep.

I awoke fourteen years later,
my morning mouth full
of black feathers,
eternal fear,
forlorn hope, and restless love.

Are our wings broken, darling?
Or have we simply forgotten
how-the-Christ to fly?

It will take all the poet's eternal fear, forlorn hope, and restless love to teach himself and his people how-the-Christ to fly again. But he believes in that love and that mission, and his wife's need has brought out in his poetry the naked hope, that he has often dressed in irony and obscenity, that love is indeed possible and necessary. These are the last words in *Ceremonies of the Damned:*

Skin memories fading.
Skin memories being created.
Love impossible. Love still possible?
        "This Is the Rez"

Of course, love is possible. It just takes the nerve of the warrior-poet to announce that this world of loss need not be a lost world.

Richard Hugo
1923–1982

CHAPTER FIVE

Surf, Rivers, and Salmon: The Northwest in the Poetry of Richard Hugo

"Stark abundance," a term Richard Hugo uses in one poem, succinctly summarizes his understanding of the world, influenced by his early life in the Pacific Northwest where the poet was born and raised and whose landscape left an indelible impression on him the rest of his adult life.[1] When the salmon run in the rivers, when the jacks and the kings, their names appropriately reminiscent of a card hand in the gamble that is life, make their way back upstream to spawn, then life is full and the universe is characterized by plenitude. The rivers are alive with roiling, vivid life, and the shops in the towns at river's edge are packed with tourists whose pockets are packed with dollars. The salmon are new life insisting upon returning to its root waters in a wombward charge, as Hugo struggles throughout his work to find some "home" where he can believe he belongs.[2] The salmon run is a return to origins and a reminder that origins exist, a river red with wild critters intent upon certifying for the fishers on the bank that life returns, stability persists despite appearances to the contrary, and our true home is out there somewhere, a place where we may all potentially find fulfillment.[3] True, the fish die, but so do we all, and how many modern Americans, living out the lives of quiet desperation Thoreau predicted, would not be content to perish knowing that they had returned home after successfully fulfilling their life's work? Abundance reigns in Hugo's world when the salmon run.

But stark is the world when the run is over, when the kings and jacks die on the free-stone river bottoms and sand banks of Northwest rivers with mysterious names, the Duwamish, Skagit, and Hoh. When the salmon leave, tourists leave, stores close, streets empty—in a Hugo poem you can hear the rot advance and see the mold thicken on floor boards. The landscape goes bare and we notice the detritus of our lives, as we notice on a beach at low tide the refuse that had been so benevolently concealed by the high water. Angry men, scraggly dogs, women who slam doors in your face—the stark other side of life comes out of the woodwork. So much for stability, fertility, abundance, and, yes, love, the hope that the world or at least someone in it or perhaps someone in charge of it might love us enough to offer up a river of life. Understanding that the world moves to this back-and-forth rhythm between starkness and abundance keeps the poet on his toes, or, more precisely, keeps him a horribly insecure mess throughout most of his life and work.[4] The highs and lows of Hugo's verse—whether he writes about Washington, Montana, Italy, or Scotland—

reflect the realities that he saw in the rivers of his youth, a bipolar reality of mania and depression that dogged him all his years, runs in his veins like river water, and makes reading any large chunk of his poetry an experience in emotional whiplash.

The human response to such natural insecurity, Hugo suggests, is to try to tame nature, to enclose it and impose our will on it, not just for our material benefit but for our psychological and emotional security. While Hugo's poetic world is dominated by his personal vocabulary of rivers and boundaries and enclosures of various kinds, the central conflict in this world of "stark abundance" is familiar, because it is perhaps the most persistent theme in the poetry of the last two centuries: the battle, internal as well as external, between the competing demands and allegiances of civilization, on the one hand, and, on the other, the demands and allegiances of nature.[5] The war in Hugo's Northwest pits a culturally approved imposition of the human will upon the outside world for the sake of what we call progress and security against the silent source of all our lives. In this battle, images of human constructions find themselves opposed to images of rivers and oceans. Images of enclosure and containment, associated with the imposition of human will, are juxtaposed with images of openness and flow, associated with loving acceptance and reception of nature and life, including its vicissitudes. Moreover, the enclosure-imposition-will-civilization group of ideas is linked to the power and practice of human reason and contrasted with a group of images and characters associated with poetic inspiration, creativity, and an innocence that is sometimes akin to feeble-mindedness and allied with the openness-receptivity-nature cluster of ideas. Or, as the poet says in "Duwamish Head" in his *Making Certain It Goes On* (1984): "To know is to be alien to rivers." (*Making Certain* 68)

For example, we encounter many maps (Hugo is fascinated by maps) that purport to depict the true course of a living
river but that become images of a human prescription of how
the river should flow rather than a description of how it does.
Or we walk through houses—usually dilapidated or on the
verge of being torn down for a new freeway—whose rooms rep-
resent in their angularity a rigid mental dividing into small
compartments of otherwise vital human life. At other times we
see a painter's canvas upon which the artist arrogantly believes
he can capture a living fish's image. And we come across fences
doing what fences do: separating the flowing land into pieces
constructed to fit the human residents' needs. Any image suggesting a set of rules dictating the course of human or natural
energy and action eventually becomes suspect. Hugo shows us
our persistent quest to create some large gradient upon which
to plot our lives and draw a fake stability, as when we make
those maps whose designs pretend to contain nature within
hard edges of many colors, only to discover our neat edges
overrun when a river refuses its traditional channel and sweeps
away our structures, or an ocean recalls a beach upon which we
had counted and arrogantly named after ourselves.

Hugo is no "mad poet," however, who thinks he can really
live like a wild hermit or the salmon. He worked first for Boe-
ing Aircraft and then in the academy, so he understands and
has benefited from the way of life associated with the imposition of human will and discipline. As much as he fears and suspects that way of life, however, he does not fall for the trap of
primitivism. What he does believe is that he is duty-bound to
question the effects of humanity's presence on the natural
world. The images that finally come to suggest the proper balance between human and world, imposition and reception, will

and flow, are, when we notice them and see what they are doing, fairly predictable given the poet's history: fishing and writing are for Hugo vocations and avocations that employ human skill to create a respectful relationship between the human and natural world, a balance that can reveal the true stability that Hugo insists informs this world.[6]

The term that best describes the balance he seeks is taken from one of his last books: "the right madness." Not simply "madness," but the "right" madness.[7] No simple formula for such a tenuous state exists. In fact, the tenuousness connects us to the other major theme in Hugo, the "stark abundance" that is associated with cosmic insecurity. People and things always seem on the edge of imbalance, much like those sinners Jonathan Edwards addressed, in "Sinners in the Hands of an Angry God," as he warned them that at any moment their foot could slip and they could be well on their way to hell before even realizing they had fallen. The battle for such balance, a temporary sure footing in the world between the demands of nature and civilization, reason and flow, a balance that allows one to survive the wrenching changes from abundance to starkness and back, is never won but must be continually fought. As minister Edwards knew in the eighteenth century, we humans are always at war with the internal and external weather of our souls tempting us to fall to one side or the other. We walk a muddy road one step at a time, always one small slide from damnation that we fear we will not recognize until we have fallen so far that the climb back up the slope to the relative safety of the perilous road is well beyond our powers. And throughout his career Hugo conducts this battle for stability in images impressed upon his mind during his formative years in the Pacific Northwest. He does incorporate important imagery from his later travels and his years of residency in Montana, but his work would have been altogether different had he been born and raised in a different landscape.

Hugo's early poems are like verbal abstract paintings. He juxtaposes one obsessional word or image next to another, refusing the reader any logical or narrative connection.[8] As we struggle with some of his work, we do well to recall that he is the poet who proclaims, "It is impossible to write meaningless sequences" (*Town* 5). We rely upon the tone of the whole poem and the connotations we have come to associate with repeated words to grasp an overall effect or theme. The poems are really more like hard stones, like the rocks the poet shows us that ring against and polish the metal of the shovels employed to dig them out. The rocks resist the shovel, but sometimes the jarring notes of the resistance produce a chord we recognize from past diggings, and we approach clarity. The image in most poems, however, is not rock but water, through which flows the notion of the relationship between the natural world in which we live and the human world in which we make our living. Sometimes the water enters as an unnamed, out-of-sight river on the edge of the poem as it runs by the edge of town, affecting everything. We see instead the effects of the river, specifically the effects of the seasonal economy based upon fishing the salmon run. When the fish are gone, as in "West Marginal Way," the town is a dark, violent, mossy world, a world resentful of being abandoned:

> One tug pounds to haul an afternoon
> of logs up river. The shade
> of Pigeon Hill across the bulges

in the concrete crawls on reeds
in a short field, cools a pier
and the violence of young men
after cod. The crackpot chapel,
with a sign erased by rain, returned
before to calm and a mossed roof.

But all will revert to relative affluence when the fish return: "These names on boxes will return/with salmon money in the fall. . . ." This instability is the background color for all Hugo's poetry, an emotional hue that keeps in front of the reader's eyes the poet's need for something stable but not stultifying. One season, everyone is flush:

Whites pay well to motor up the river,
harvest blackmouth, humpbacks, silvers,
jacks and sea run cuts.
    "Tahola"

The next, everyone is busted: "When whites drive off and the money's gone/a hundred mongrels bark." A warm-water bass lake makes the same point. When we first see Kapowsin Lake, in "Kapowsin,"⁹ from *A Run of Jacks*, (1960) Hugo's first book, it supports a shore economy that is alive though barely hanging on:

The town beside it died in 1908
and these remain: a man gone dim—
a girl is swimming in his dead Tokay—
a woman who gets pregnant from a song,
the tavern always filled but never loud.
    (*Making Certain* 34)

The lake is already depleted ("To count/the ducks divide the guns by five."), but by his 1965 book, *Death of the Kapowsin Tavern,* and its title poem, the tavern is burned ("Not one board left. Only ash a cat explores/and shattered glass smoked black . . . "), and the lake is as dead as the local scene it once sustained: "most homes abandoned to the rocks/of passing boys."

Repeatedly, whether the image is of rivers, lakes, or oceans, we see humans experience the slow or rapid loss of what had sustained them, a nurturing power on the periphery of their consciousness that diminishes and then disappears. The anonymous characters—indeed, in early poems few humans are seen close-up—kill the nature that had kept them afloat psychologically. The spawning run of the salmon provides Hugo such a serviceable image because it accelerates the process of loss: the fish are here one day and gone the next. But the slow death of Kapowsin Lake or the decades' long deterioration of a neighborhood reminds us equally well of our human vulnerability in this world and our self-destructiveness. Nature quietly sustains us while we ignore or abuse it, but most of Hugo's characters feel so powerless that it never occurs to them that they have any role in destroying the lake or themselves. They ask so little: "Now . . . where can the troller go for bad wine/washed down frantically with beer?" They stand before the world passively, assuming all power lies elsewhere, which it usually does in a Hugo poem.[10]

While salmon, rivers, and the Pacific dominate and initiate this starkness/abundance theme, the losses Hugo depicts go beyond the rivers' banks. Mines shut down, gold peters out, mills close and lay off their unskilled laborers, even breweries fail, despite the author's single-handed efforts to keep them in business. The result of all such loss is a raw awareness of the thin line between security and insecurity, sanity and madness.

In "Helena, Where Homes Go Mad," (*The Lady in Kicking Horse Reservoir*, 1973), we are told that "the brewery failed" taking with it the veneer of suburban bliss: "Helena/insane with babies and the lines of homes (*Making Certain* 176)." As Hugo says, "The world discards the world" in a continuing process of sloughing-off that alternates with the high times of full rivers and full employment. The one stable center or still point in Hugo's early work is often the corner bar: "past hotels/that didn't last, bars that did" ("Degrees of Gray in Philipsburg"). The bar is not only a stable institution, it is a supportive refuge where one's pain is understood: "If you weep/deer heads weep" ("The Milltown Union Bar"). To the poet, the bar is a double-edged sword: it serves his need for stability, but it allows his self-destructive tendencies to flourish.

"Here today, gone tomorrow" runs throughout the poetry, the starkness and the abundance chasing each other around like a dog after its tail. But we would be hasty to assume that the good times, for Hugo, are really that much better than the bad. He distrusts his own or others' success. On the one hand, he refuses to believe, until his later poems, that he deserves success, the burden he carries from a childhood in which he was abandoned first by his father and then, at twenty months, left by his mother (who was only seventeen at the time [Holden 6]) to be raised by strict maternal grandparents, creating in the child what one author calls, in what must be understatement, "a strong sense of marginality" (Gertsenberger 5-6). He often looks at a drunk on a bar stool, then looks at himself—now the respected poet and creative writing professor—and launches into a "There but for the grace of God" meditation. On the other hand, the success of others is usually associated with ideas loosely clustered around the concept of civilization—humans taming the wilderness, making their money, and advancing their culture's claims—and, in one of his dominant moods, Hugo indicts civilization as a destructive force set loose in the world. This mood gives rise to the many images of enclosure and constraint, mentioned above, that illustrate humans' domination of nature in the name of civilization and progress, resulting in destruction, a maiming or draining away of something vital and living in the nature that humans enclose, and in turn an enervation of those humans left to live in the scarred land that reflects their own psyches.

From the beginning of Hugo's career, humans' desire to curtail nature in the name of progress emerges as a theme, as in "A Map of the Peninsula," from his first book. He starts by telling us that "This map is right," but the rest of the poem calls into question the early assertion:

> And there is drama in the annual run
> of kings, though recently some bones
> were left to testify they spawned
> while we were tracing glaciers on the map.
> (*Making Certain* 24)

We missed the spawning of the kings because we diverted our eyes to our maps and away from the real life of nature that the maps supposedly captured. The map is described as if it were a painting rather than a conventional chart, but the image of a painted canvas that attempts to capture the reality beyond the canvas and serves the same theme:

> Paint it grand with mountains, but the scrub
> some gypo left, the one-o-one in ruts
> from constant rain, shabby meadows

> elk create, fog that fakes the ocean's
> outer rim will smear your canvas. . . .

The "grand" painted map misses most of the life lived in the area it depicts. The sharp lines demanded by a map cannot do justice to the wildness of real life, which, if it were incorporated into the picture, would "smear" the canvas and blur the hard edges the artist wants to create between nature's realms of grandeur over here, and detritus over there. Maps are impositions of human will and mind in the interest of civilization, marking a path for settlement or exploration, dragging one more unspoiled landscape within the ken of humankind.

It is not surprising to see Hugo sympathize with the trout who finds itself enclosed within a lake—"his-stream-toned heart/locked in the lake, his poise and nerve disgraced," "Underwater Autumn." We are perhaps a bit surprised to see the extent of the poet's distrust of enclosure: seemingly innocuous constructions like the edges of a snapshot are exposed as deadening framers of experience. "A Snapshot of the Auxiliary" finds the speaker examining the 1934 photograph of the St. James Lutheran Women's Auxiliary. In the first stanza, the women seem sad ("the sadness of the Dakotas/in their sullen mouths"), and in the second, gray, but only in the final stanza do we get the sense that something is truly amiss. The poem ends as Hugo turns the album page: "The next one in the album/ is our annual picnic. We are all having fun." The snapshot has lied; they were not having fun at the picnic, which he knows because he was there.[11] They posed as if they were having fun, in response to the pressure of the snapshot-moment, and the technology that saved the image is guilty of memorializing a lie that distances viewers from their own lives. The snapshot takes over the lives of the picnickers and compels them, when the shutter snaps, to pretend to an emotion not felt and to pass that lie onto every generation that views the photo before it decays, long after the subjects themselves have gone. The technology not only allows deceit, its use almost demands it—would the supposed revelers dare to let their official picnic snapshot be ruined (for "ruined" is the way we would describe a photograph that reveals unhappiness when we expect gaiety)? Knowing that the photo of the picnic is a lie, can he trust any snapshot? And thus are our emotions and lives forced into inauthentic poses, all in service of progress, here represented by the camera.

Life is truer outside the frame and beyond the bindings of the album. One of the women in the picture of the Women's Auxiliary, Mrs. Noraine, is described simply as "Mrs. Noraine, Russian, kind. She saved me once/from a certain whipping." In a subsequent poem devoted to her, "Saying Goodbye to Mrs. Noraine," Hugo returns for a visit after forty years and fills in some blanks. He finds himself standing on her front porch, wondering if she will think it strange that he has come. (He has not yet told the reader why he is there, so Mrs. Noraine would not be alone in her curiosity.) He is outside, as he was when viewing the snapshot. Only after being allowed into Mrs. Noraine's house, stepping as it were inside the frame to places the camera cannot take the viewer who must reside on the surface of the print, does the speaker truly understand his subject: "When I walked in her door/I knew more secrets than ever about time." Somehow, while inside her house, Hugo learns the true version of town gossip he had heard ("It turned out I remembered most things wrong.") and, going further, learns about the woman's secret life, a depth of experience not possibly communicable in a snapshot:

The rest was detail I had missed. Her husband's
agonizing prolonged death. Her plan to live
her last years in another city south.

The details revealed to him about the life beyond the
enclosures we place around it create a temporary readjustment
of the poet's perspective. He sheds his years of adult wisdom
and finds himself responding to the world with the freshness of
a youth:

> . . . everywhere the dandelions adult years
> had taught me to ignore told me what I knew
> when I was ten. Their greens are excellent
> in salad. Their yellow flowers
> make good wine and play off like a tune
> against salal I love remembering to hum.
> (*Making Certain* 222–223)

Joy, respect, and wonder replace judgment, which is the
frame through which the elder Hugo had learned to see the
world, the distrust of the world that the "adult years" had
taught him. The snapshot vision that allows one to weed out the
undesirable elements of the world here is obliterated by the
simple meeting in a vulnerable moment of two humans who
took the chance to step beyond the frame.

As an artist, he finds himself tempted by the unity that
enclosures allow and has to remind himself occasionally to be
faithful to the diffuse. In "A History of the Sketch," from
What Thou Loves Well Remains American (1975), Hugo tells
us that "Now" he is more open to randomness and less con-
strained by his dedication to a kind of realism that murders
to dissect:

> . . . Now, when I sketch
> a perch and get the wrong green on his rib
> no preacher hounds me to correct the color.

The preacher is his internalized cartographer, the encloser in us all who demands the "right" color, which may be justified as an attempt to capture the perch artistically. But it is also a sin against the poet's or painter's imaginative freedom, a sin that is connected logically in Hugo's work to the vital, living freedom of the natural world, the perch, and the way humans ought to live. Stop molesting the perch ("the perch/slips off the sketch-pad into the lake/and darts for sedge"), and the imagination will still have plenty of raw material from which to create: "Bubbles of his going/bloom along the surface." The bubbles bursting, or blooming, release the essence of the fish ("They give off/definite odors") without trapping the living being, and the good poet will make do with those. Note that the true artist who can write of the perch with no more definite evidence of the fish's existence than its bursting bubbles is identified with the social outsider: "They give off/definite odors hermits remember well."

But life is risky, and there is the rub. Enclosures make life seem less a mortal battle, even though we know we are all cursed. Mortality is the ultimate reminder of life's final "starkness," so it is understandable that we would want and need to keep all reminders of our frailty fenced off at a safe distance from our lives. In "Graves at Elkhorn" the fence around the cemetery, more than the grave stones themselves, is the symbol and image of humankind's need to fence in nature, to keep the influence of its more chaotic elements carefully circumscribed within our constructed barriers: "The yard and nearly every grave are fenced./Something in this space must be defined."

We define the cemetery as the realm of the dead and the town as the realm of the living, to keep the phenomena separate ("The yard should have a limit like the town."), but Hugo will challenge that effort. We read of our need to define a limit beyond which "the body must not slide," and we recall the earlier use of "slide" to suggest the impossibility of creating hard edges in a world of overlapping boundaries, life pouring into death, abundance sliding into starkness.

The fence around the graveyard is like the embossed ridge in a paper dinner plate that separates the gravy from the peas: an innovation in the service of the ethos of enclosure and containment. Our need for these enclosures is testified to by the energy and time we spend constructing them, while nature's refusal to respect our efforts is testified to by its insistence on tearing down the same barriers: "The fence around the yard is barbed, maintained/by men, around the graves, torn down/by pines." We think of Frost's famous New England fence, torn down by nature's freezing and thawing, patiently rebuilt by "good neighbors" who believe that if they make a show of taming the wildness of nature they can also tame the savage inside them. Fear of that savage is a good reason to pretend we have enclosed him and that we live in a part of town where no such anti-social residents are allowed, but an equally important reason to fence off the darker sides of life is self-delusion. If we were always aware of the impossibility of anything lasting, would we not be tempted to chuck it in, give up now, and get out of this doomed affair before we are inevitably dragged out? The lie of enclosures keeps the world going:

> The yard is this far from the town because
> when children die the mother should repeat

some form of labor, and a casual glance
would tell you there could be no silver here.

A constant reminder of starkness would make it impossible for us to pursue abundance: bad for business and bad for
the psyche.

Despite the dangers of openness, however, one solution
Hugo offers to our enclosing, snapshooting, grave-marking,
and map-making needs is simply to wipe the canvas clean and
start over:

> . . . Soak the map
> in rain and when this cheap dye runs
> only glaciers and the river names remain.
> "A Map of the Peninsula"

Just erase the map altogether if you want to see what really lives
here. The map that began so "right" is soaked clean by the end
of the poem. A similar solution is offered in "Goose-prairie,"
but in a different image:

> Let the log jam break and run
> and the latest maps are obsolete.

The log jam, a product of humans' harvesting of nature in the
name of progress, neatly symbolizes the imposition of human
will: it stops the flow of the otherwise free river and stops the
flow of nature's energy. Break it up and let the river run, Hugo
urges. Later in the same poem, he says,

> and now our throats are stinging
> from those ninety years of looking for hard lines:

and all that time
the secret of the world was slide.

Hard lines versus slide, log jam versus flow: the world's dynamic data flow around our static structures, and Hugo wryly
celebrates when any human markers—more gravestones, for
example, in "Graves at Mukilteo"—slip loose from their appointed task of keeping tabs on a disorderly world:

> The town has plans to put the stones in order,
> cut the grass, reinforce the mortar;
> but the offspring of the dead are scattered
> and their O.K. hard to get.

Another image of the chaotic world Hugo likes to believe
in but understands the dangers of is an abandoned house,
memorialized in "1614 Boren," an abandoned apartment house
in Seattle, "room on room" of "debris." This house-microcosm
does more than suggest humans' ultimate inability to carve neat
parcels of living spaces from wild matter. The house on Boren
shows the limits of humans' reason, the limits of our ability to
know and understand our world. "What does this picture mean,
hung where it is," Hugo asks of a landscape painting in one
room. "Why could room 5 cook and 7 not?" he wonders in
another place. The house is flawed (Dave Smith calls the poem
"a guided tour through failure" [108]), and not merely as a
result of its age. The flaws seem part of the design: "These dirty
rooms were dirty even then,/the toilets ancient when installed,/
and light was always weak and flat." The world is a bit of a joke
on us, and we are a bit of a joke on ourselves, pretending with
our structures and maps that we know more and have more
control than we do. When, later in the poem, Hugo looks again

at the painting that had earlier puzzled him, he still cannot make it out. Perhaps, he says, "It's just a Sketcher's whim." Yes, perhaps the world is simply some great Sketcher's whim, a cosmic joke on us all. Hugo resents human impositions on the natural world in part because he feels those enclosures violate nature's vitality, but he also fears the opposite, the chaos and debris, the shifting gravestones that he champions. They make him small, as undeserving as he feels inside. Sometimes, then, his role as exponent of wildness stems from a humble recognition of his cosmic smallness, and sometimes that voice is the adult remnant of the small voice of the frightened, abandoned child who feels himself unworthy and fears he will never understand or find his real home.

The theme of borders and enclosures persists in his later books. As he says in "Spinning the Sava," from his third volume *Good Luck in Cracked Italian* (1969), "all borders" are "silly as a map." The book returns Hugo to Italy, where he flew thirty-five missions as a bombardier during World War II (M. Allen, Human 115). "I was home in ruin," he says ("Sailing from Naples"), and we think he must mean he learned to adapt to the chaos of war, but from earlier poems we get the impression that he has always mistrusted too much order, as well as rejected it on a philosophical basis. He is more attuned to ruin than prosperity (which makes him feel like a faker in his successful years later), abundance, or even love: "When twelve I ran from love, afraid . . ." ("Sailing from Naples"). The psychological and philosophical merge as his sincere distrust of civilization's effect on nature (and, at least until the development of atomic weapons, there was no better example of civilization's destruction of nature than a heavy bomber) fits so well with his personal belief that he merits nothing better than debris, instability, and confusion. The rational, as it replaces

the wild, turns us against each other as an extension of our project to dominate nature and each other: "We need a name," he
says, "not Jew or man but something not so old/formed wild
downstream" ("Morning in Padova"). At some "wild" substra-
tum of our existence, we connect as simple humans living as
parts of simple nature. Undifferentiated being—the image of
humans "formed wild downstream," before personal and cultural distinctions emerged—suggests to him human harmony
as well as harmony between human and nature, obviating the
need for bombers and maps.

It is difficult to achieve a vision of such harmony, he suggests, especially in the United States, a nation of emotion-enclosers
("I'm so American, embarrassed by their tears," "Maratea Porto:
Saying Good-bye to the Vitolos"), but the book builds hope that
perhaps here among Italians, stereotypically portrayed as emotional people in an emotional land, Hugo will be able to unbur-
den himself of his war guilt and allow whatever is in him to
come forth. Something like that must have happened, for in
"Spinazzola: Quella Cantina Là," Hugo is able to remember a
wartime experience of one rare moment of undifferentiated
existence and openness to life during the war.[12] Hitchhiking
back to his base one day late in 1943, he told the man who
picked him up to take him to Cerignola, only to discover after
a long drive in the wrong direction that he had been dropped
off at Spinazzola, a town with which he was unfamiliar. He
walked out of town for about an hour and then sat down beside
a field of grass. The poem recounts the epiphany that Hugo
experienced:

> A field of wind gave license for defeat.
> I can't explain. The grass bent. The wind
> seemed full of men without hate or fame.

The persistent Italian wind blows away all war-related thoughts and returns Hugo to a mode of apprehending the world not tainted by "hate or fame," those attitudes learned in life but manifested so extremely in warfare. Hugo had been in a rut, on a track that let him see the world only through a warrior's eyes. He had been imposing his hard-edged vision on a world that perhaps could be bombed into submission but that would never conform to his war-will. Losing his way in a strange land ironically returns him to the truth: "Here, by accident,/the wrong truck, I came back to the world."

After the initial stanza, Hugo repeats the phrase "I can't explain" once in every subsequent stanza, a total of seven times. He has lost all sense of mission, direction, goal, even knowledge, and in this stripped-bare state, the innocent in the world of wind and wheat and sun, he sees through the imposed ideas he has been carrying around in his head and his plane. The land is no longer a grid upon which to drop bombs. His uniform no longer identifies the truth of his identity ("My uniform/turned foreign"). He cannot explain but he also need not explain: the "crude bench and rough table," the wine, the clouds are all enumerated in a mode of acceptance that confirms that the things of the world exist wholly without—and prior to—humans' explanations of them. As Hugo notes, the moment is "a moment of surrender, when my system could no longer take the fear and pressure and I gave up" (*Town* 84).[13] For some reason, it is tempting to imagine the field surrounded by a rock wall upon which Hugo sits in the poem, but he never mentions a wall, either in his prose reminiscence or his poem, because a wall, even a picturesque, crumbling rock wall, would be another human enclosure and would be out of place in the verse. The field is instead completely open and becomes a character in the poem, a friend or an alter-ego that reveals the

poet to himself: "Don't honest fields/reveal us in their winds?"
Such a moment of surrender and self-revelation, of course, is
rare, but Hugo, after finally returning to town, suggests that,
rare or not, the field and its possibilities are always there: "Outside, on the road/that leaves the town reluctantly,/way out the
road's a field of wind."[14]

The abundant times, therefore, are good but are not a pure
good—inasmuch as affluence encourages destruction of nature
and those who dare stand in the way of progress—and the stark
times are bad but are not a pure bad. Thus, paring away the
accumulations of the culture's pandemic materialism may leave
us open to the winds that blow news of our deepest, most
frightening and frightened selves. Hugo nonetheless is more
seriously tempted by failure and celebrates several primitivist
characters who have missed the salmon run of affluence and
who are celebrated precisely because they fail.[15] As a collection of "the old and odd," the outcast and the marginalized,
Hugo's poetry is a lot like a threatened market he celebrates
in "Pike Place Market":

> Who plans to tear this market down?
> Erect a park? Those militants who hate
> the old and odd, and dream of homes where lawns
> are uniformly green.[16]

The market is a refuge for derelicts—not necessarily of the
human variety, but all those items deemed valueless in the
name of the uniformity that fuels progress.[17] The market is an
example of "slide" that some want to replace with another

image of enclosure—those neatly platted and manicured lawns. Resisting the appetites of civilization, this bum of a market becomes an anti-cultural hero in the verse, "a metaphor for the authentic, idiosyncratic inner life that is threatened with extinction" (Holden 65).

Other hermit or derelict characters are actual humans, including one hapless panner for gold in "The Gold Man on the Beckler." Hugo makes it clear early that the man will never be threatened by affluence, for the only gold in the river is the river itself:

> Here, the gold is river, coiling gold
> around gold stones or bouncing gold down
> flat runs where the riffles split the light.

The man takes only what nature offers and what is easily replenished. Despite his poverty, he seems both well fed ("how could he get so fat?") and happy ("Why so cheerful, with a flimsy roof,/no money and that crude hair in his ears"?) while living divorced from the rest of the world ("What put him this far from the world?"). Hugo imagines freely exchanging his life for this simpler, ascetic existence: "If I could live like him, my skin stained gold/from this gold stream, I'd change my name." He idealizes the man, surely, but his point is clear: "Failures retain their identities as people" (Bellamy 111), and Hugo feels that his current identity is the product of "always playing somebody else's game" (Bellamy 111). Changing his name (which he actually did, from Hogan to Hugo) would be a way of returning to the real Hugo identity that he trusts or hopes persists beneath his successes. This is a different process from that idealized by the notion of the self-made man, a staple of the American Dream, in which, by sheer power of will, the individual effects a systemic change. For Hugo, taking a new identity is really rediscovering his old, true identity.

The gold man at the Beckler is not the first fat man beside a river in Hugo's work. "From the Rain Forest Down," from his second book, features a fat man playing a "vicious clarinet" next to a river, initially laboring under the delusion that "his music makes the current/permanent and warm." He learns, however, that this too typical human delusion of control over nature disguises his real effect on the world. When the fat man "lives to learn his music only drove/trout upstream," he feels the tide turn: "Now the river slams him with its noise." Humbled by the river's resistance, the man confesses ("To the river/he admits he came to stop the flow," a human version of the earlier log jam) and loses his clarinet, which had been his chosen weapon of fantasized control ("His clarinet is floating past Marseilles"). The fat man is the image of one of the dreaded enclosers, dammers, and grid-makers reformed, the bad artist or poet who first thought to turn his subject's dynamism into some static testament to his own power who then sees the light. The river always has the last laugh ("The river laughs his feet away") and refuses to be captured or understood (it "keeps the fat man guessing"). Hugo celebrates the world of freedom in which nature changes course, overflows our constructed banks, and overwhelms our noisy self-celebrations. Even the foolish— perhaps only the foolish—realize that the world will not be man-handled:

> The town drunk knows
> the world blurs, drunk or sober, and the world
>   moves on
> out of reach against the wind or with.
>   "Late Summer, Drummond"

Far from puzzled, Hugo identifies with the fat man and the town drunk,[18] and we can read these poems as self-correcting cautionary tales, his recognition of the "flow-stopping" urges that are so much a part of the poet's vocation.

Whatever the spiritual rewards of material starkness, however, being a hermit has its down side. Because the poet's or hermit's gaze sees through to the truth of things ("When lovers pass me/on their way to love I know they'll end up hating," "Why I Think of Dumar Sally"), the seer is offensive to others ("The nerve I ask forgiveness for is in my gaze"). The poet/hermit consequently often finds himself alone ("Me on foot alone, asking what I do wrong"), an *isolato* in this world that does not want to know or hear the truth. Hugo thus piles ambivalence upon ambivalence. Abundance is bad and good; starkness is bad and good; the good side of starkness is itself bad and good; and on and on. Readers have noted that Hugo's work never "progresses" in the sense that his subjects remain constant throughout his career, a charge to which the poet pled guilty.[19] There is no simple movement toward clarity and away from ambiguity. Instead, Hugo feels the attraction and the danger of all set positions, and that helps explain why he has found so many responsive readers for his work: he is as ambivalent as the rest of us, standing like Frost's character where the road in the woods splits, unable even to lie to himself, as Frost's walker does, that one road really is more deserving than the other. The result is a complexity of emotional response to the modern existential condition that continues to draw readers to Hugo's work.

Complexity and ambiguity, however, are not the same as indecisiveness. While Hugo gives no easy answers, he does point some directions. Despite a loveless childhood, battles with alcohol and depression, a failed marriage, various types of self-destructive behavior, and a general disgust with the rats' alley world our materialistic culture has created, Hugo survived to find love, write poetry, and, perhaps his greatest achievement, accept Richard Hugo. He is a survivor who shows us the way but shares his readers' tentativeness about taking the first step to salvation. In his "Canto 81," Ezra Pound refers to "the diffidence that faltered," which is a fairly typical modern condition. To move beyond that diffidence requires courage, not the macho chest-thumping of which Hugo is occasionally guilty when he assumes a tough-guy persona,[20] but a true courage to move beyond one's self-imposed enclosures. The first step is to face the grayness of one's life:

> . . . You conquer loss
> by going to the place it happened
> and replaying it, saying the name
> of the face in the open casket right.
> "Montgomery Hollow"

In "A Snapshot of 15th S. W.,"[21] he examines a photograph and refuses to sugar-coat the despair in the image:

> . . . That gray is what it is.
> Gray gravel in the street and gray hearts
> tired of trying love.
> . . . .
> The empty lot is where a house burned down.
> Shriek of siren. Red on cloud. Suicide.

The point is that hope remains, the field of wheat persists just beyond the camera range. The sun shines beyond the limits

that we normally impose upon our perception and our estima-
tion of our possibility, the limits imposed by "the diffidence that
faltered":

> Deep back, out of camera range
> the sun pulses on fields you still might run to,
> wind a girl's hand on your ear.

You can run to the sun by accepting the untamed ("The
way out can be wild") and stepping out of the gray enclosure.
One caveat: the longer you stay in the shade, the harder it is to
escape. Or, as Hugo says, "The longer the gray heart took to
teach/the heavier the thicket," the more formidable and
entrenched become the obstacles between oneself and the sun-
drenched fields, because, in time, one becomes accommodated
to the limits imposed by the camera, map, or other enclosure.

Openness is a component of the courage that leads to
rehabilitation, and Hugo associates the openness that allows
mental health and enables artistic creation with nature, not as a
friend but as an inspiration: as the free-flowing rivers and
sprawling lakes of his youth find their place in his work, so the
grassy plains of his adopted Montana become an image of the
necessary openness.[22] In "Open Country" he begins with a line
("It is much like the ocean the way it opens/and rolls.") that
could easily have been written, and probably was by someone, a
century earlier. Hugo is not deterred by knowing that comparing western prairies to the ocean is old-hat, because he takes
the hackneyed image and invigorates it with his obsessions:

> Let me guess:
> when you repair the damaged brain

> of a beaten child or bring to a patient
> news that will never improve, you need
> a window not a wall to turn to.

The window is an image of openness and the wall one of enclosure, and suddenly the cliché grass ocean that could have been written by any Great Plains adolescent has become Hugo's pet. The beaten child reminds us of the young Hugo, as the terminal patient recalls the poet's years of wandering from bar to bar trying to erase himself. Recovery requires openness, not more control, a fact that he tells the prairie or the prairie tells him.

To incorporate the prairie even more solidly into his emotional and poetic world, Hugo concludes:

> And you come back here
> where land has ways of going on
> and the shadow of a cloud
> crawls like a freighter, no port in mind,
> no captain, and the charts dead wrong.

The prairie provides solace because it is beyond control, a wandering hermit that denies enclosure and proves the inadequacy of maps to chart a course. Given Hugo's early life and adult mistakes, the "charts" would have predicted he would end in some "port" well beyond hope's latitude. He shows us, through the prairie image and many earlier images, the conditions required for personal renovation: you somehow gain the courage—from experience, despair, and nature's model—to chart your own course internally; all you require externally is an open field upon which to play out your life.

⟡

Nature, although rarely warm and cuddly or basked in the sunny glow that concludes "A Snapshot of 15th S. W.," can point us beyond the camera range, even if it does not welcome us with open arms. "Turtle Lake" opens with Hugo hopping into his car and leaving an unwelcoming Dog Lake: "The wind at Dog Lake whispered 'stranger' 'stranger'/and we drove away." So Hugo gets out quickly, and whatever "thickets" may obtrude between him and his escape, they are no match today for his Buick: "My Buick hit a note too high/for dogs at 85 and cattails bowed like subjects. . . ." Nearby Turtle Lake is more hospitable. It welcomes the odd, as Pike Place Market and Hugo do ("Turtle is a lake the odd can own.") and, like any good rebel, it is unbounded and refuses to acknowledge its limits: "It spreads/mercurial around those pastoral knolls." Hugo is freed by the freeness of the lake and detects the promise of rejuvenation: "This is where," he says,

> we change our names. Five clouds cross
> the sun: the lake has been six colors,
> counting that dejected gray our lives brought in.

The lake refuses to be enclosed or to take on the speaker's mood. Therefore, its colors drive away the grayness of the speaker's life and in doing so provide, at least temporarily, a new identity and hope. The Turtle Lake experience creates a paradoxical response: the poet feels empowered ("Whatever color water wants, we grant it with a wave.") but also indebted ("We believe this luxury of bondage, the warm way/mountains call us citizens in debt."), suggesting a mutuality between nature and human, not a blending or merging but a mutually respectful face-off—Hugo on the shore, the lake opposite, neither imposing itself on the other, both gaining from the other's presence. The solidity of Turtle Lake, defiant in the mercurial spreading of its colored waters, returns the poet to what is true and stable. While nature in Hugo is closer to Stephen Crane's coldly indifferent universe than it is to Wordsworth's benign bank of daffodils, that very indifference and insistence upon its right to live here, regardless of human violations, makes nature one of the few stable phenomena in Hugo's experience.

Change, progress, growth—all the mantras of modern culture—are anathema to Hugo. The title of one of his books, *What Thou Lovest Well Remains American,* alludes to Pound's lines in "Canto 81":

> What thou lovest well remains,
> the rest is dross
> What thou lov'st well shall not be reft from thee
> What thou lovest well is thy true heritage. . . .

The title and its source suggest the value of the stable that is not the result of human imposition of order.[23] Love does not change (as another poet says, it is an "ever-fixèd mark"), nor is love deterred by change. It attaches to the essential and the permanent and weathers the storms of progress. Novelty has nothing to do with truth, at least in Hugo's poetry. The beauty of stability, of the permanent, is that it is capable of accepting every manner of chaos without a blush or a need to control. Hugo chooses natural images for this stability, a persistent habit that begins in "Triangle for Green Men," from his first book:

> He knew a secret of ground,
> how it assembles into sand or clay,
> and is, even under floods.

Dirt, the "ground" of our being, "is," even when temporarily overwhelmed by the "floods" of the world, including any number of personal, natural, psychological, or other disasters. The ground remains, as an image of what remains within the poet to brace him against the world's onslaught that comes in forms as diverse as new freeway construction displacing lonely men or a poet's writer's block.

A mountain, in the same poem, illustrates:

> A mountain is also ground
> where it is not rock or rock
> becoming ground beneath snow
> feeding roots at timberline,
> never succumbs to a wind bigger
> than mountains, faster than rivers
> fall when earth falls sharply below
> what had been sedate current.
> Even when wind caves the ribs of a fawn
> the mountain, braced by blueness, is not stunned.

The stable ground of the world and our being resists the ubiquitous Montana winds, and will not be "stunned" by adversity, even the destruction of an innocent life, perhaps an image of the poet's self, the fawn crushed by the world's ill winds. And stability need not be, though it may sound so at first, allied with enclosure and limitation or an enemy of vitality. It is simply a still point and therefore a source of hope amidst human—not natural—destruction that masquerades as progress. Contemplating the changes wrought by Montana Fish and Game to one of his lakes, in "Changes at Meridian," the poet explains:

> One poet said it is enough to live perpetually
>   in change.
> He didn't believe it. I say we want everything static
> including farms we lose and rebuild. That way,
> when the fish start feeding and the first chill of day
> reminds us we haven't come far, home is a mild
>   row back,
> we love the old man repeating over and over,
>   "Keep your line in the water."
>   (*Making Certain* 357)

Not stasis or rigidity but stability: keep fishing, keep hoping, and do not be deluded that "this rehabilitated water" surrounded by "clustered dull homes" represents real progress.

Progress is an illusion. Vision is what Hugo seeks, and vision is a constant that does not rise and fall with the tides or the salmon run. Not surprisingly, Hugo's vision begins on a river: "My vision started at this river mouth" ("Duwamish Head" in *Making Certain It Goes On* 65–68). Vision enables poetry and a good life by allowing one to see inside the river, not to know it (as mentioned earlier, "To know is to be alien to rivers"), domesticate it, or impose one's needs on it, but to see its life and in the process be reminded of one's own, that one is probably in the process of wasting:

> If I say love
> was here, along the river, show me bones
> of cod, scales and blood, faces in the clouds
> so thick they jam the sky with laughter.

Rather than try to impose one's need or will on the world, Hugo gives us an image, in fishing, of the supplicant offering to the world what few talents he has to give, drifting the offering on the world's current (rather than under one's own power) past the place where we hope hope resides, and waiting for acceptance, validation, or acknowledgment. Throw your burden onto the water:

> A good cast is loss of mills, of women
> knocking five days following the burial,
> words that never heal, silk organs droning while
> the sermon crawls down empty pews, a plea
> for money for electric bills.

The offering comes with no guarantees of a nibble, and certainly with no quick-fix promises ("Nylon takes a life to reach the lunker caves"), but, unlike a sermon ("All sermons warp with one slight knock"), a netted fish is the real thing: "a mottled monster ages down the net,/brighter than answer, big enough to see." In Hugo, the lunkers, the big fish every fisher pursues, hide out in deep water, as they do also in Hemingway's "Big Two-Hearted River," and one may take a lifetime working up the courage to pursue them. The secret of the pursuit is not control of one's craft, as in Hemingway, whose Nick Adams carefully opens his cans of beans and spaghetti and ritually baits his hook, but release of one's control, casting one's offering, which is one's life, upon the water and letting it drift. Hence, Hugo's chosen method is worm fishing, in which one has little control, rather than fly fishing in which one does, for in worm fishing, the fisher makes the offer and then hangs on waiting for the world to respond: "The worm spins/warm to German Brown." Not the most noble of sports (the worm does all the work) but the best image for Hugo's ideal of right living. The worms are clearly sacramental offerings (he calls them "hymns"), and Hugo, although he claimed no specific Christian affiliation, would not mind the association in our predominantly Christian culture of fish with holiness,[24] the inexplicable and awesome (a "monster") mystery of the deep, which, when hooked, changes a life: "Nylon sings and reassembles day. . . ."

Fishing and poetry are both processes of "slide," in Hugo's lexicon, products of "the energy that unifies and brings together disparate elements" (M. Allen, *Human* 10), and are often spoken of as if interchangeable activities. In "Langaig," for example, he recalls getting fired for sneaking off from work after hearing about the death of a favorite singer. Music, or art in general, conflicts with work ("I heard music and lost my job."), for work encloses the creative spirit in daily obedience to material profit. Hugo's memorial service for the singer consists of going fishing. Since that day, he claims to have given up the world of work entirely in favor of the world of poetry, associated with fishing:

> I've not worked hard since
> on anything but words, though I fish all waters
> devoted and hum old songs when I fish alone.

His "ideal" method of being-in-the world works as well for writing as for fishing:

> To relax, to slide with, ride the forces of whatever
> sweeps us along, jokes well timed, phrasing under
>   control—
> that was my ideal.

The ideal is not passivity. Control of a sort is present, but it is the control that follows relaxation and submission to the life around and within one, rather than the control of enclosure that enforces its will on the slide. He admits not being able to realize the ideal ("I didn't come close in real life"), because he is still plagued by impatience, trying to force or control the result rather than relax and slide ("I set my line/too soon and lose the black brown."). Nature reminds him of the ideal ("The eagle yells/from the Quirang, 'Go easy. Give him time to take it.'"), and, educable poet that he is, he succeeds by not trying too hard. The result is not just a fish; it is a poem: "I've got a brown on. My line is writing a song." Success gained ("I'm fishing. I'm singing."), he recapitulates what he has learned:

> . . . to locate by game
> some word like "brown" in black water, to cast
> hard for that word, then wait a long time to set.

Locate, cast, wait: Hugo's recipe for fishing, writing, and living.
    While he admits being able to follow his own advice but rarely, the goal is not success as conventionally understood. Hugo, rather dramatically, claims, "All art is failure" (*Town* 72). Perhaps it would be more reasonable to say that poetry is beyond success and failure, words and attitudes Hugo would associate with the world of "work." Poetry is failure ("I will write some more forever/though only poetry and therefore always failure," "Letter to Reed from Lolo"), but failure properly understood, as the antithesis of progress, to which Hugo explicitly contrasts art in this poem about "this nation,/dying from faith in progress," specifically the destruction of Chief Joseph. Hugo echoes Chief Joseph's words ("I will fight no more forever") because they exemplify the victory of failure, the victory of remaining true to a stable "resolve" even if you, as Joseph, are doomed to fall "a few miles short of your imagined

goal." Poetry, then, is a heroic way of living, though it is also failure, because, ultimately, the merely "victorious," all those cavalry soldiers, foremen, preachers, and purveyors of the new and progressive, are "bent and forgotten," while the words of the poet remain, blessed with the stability of truth and therefore potent, "erect in surrender." The failures in our culture are ironic successes, because they do not sell their selves for success but retain their stable, true identities.

Although Hugo is admittedly a bit macho at times, this vision of noble failure is not one of those moments. To him, poetry is more than a test of his manly courage. It is sincerely a way to connect to others on the level of humanness that transcends success and failure. Success and failure are the ephemeral judgments of one season's taste, lasting no longer than a salmon run. Poetry is longer than that, and it is deeper, connecting failures to each other. (And we are all failures, all subject to the "degraded human condition"—some simply try to cover the failure by a temporary pretense to victory.) In "Letter to Annick from Boulder," he writes to a woman who has lost her husband a year earlier. As consolation, Hugo offers the thought that, "The beautiful never go far," by which he does not mean that the beautiful (including the letter recipient's husband) are not successful, but that they, being ones we love, being truth, remain: "They wait beside roads when we come back/from petty fresh triumph, holding our trophy. . . ." Losing is life's constant; trophies are fresh, but doomed to fade. Religion offers consolation to some, but none that Hugo can embrace: "This is the bad time, Christmas, and the myths are honed fine./I don't believe in them. . . ." What he does believe in is the power of the heart "to absorb and reject and still pound/like an Indian drum or the ocean, to reach/by sound or in person the other. . . ." The sound that reaches the other is poetry, and, "the moment success and failure/make no matter," poetry is produced that persists, remains, and connects:

> We touch each other
> and ourselves no special day, no designated season,
> just now and then, in a just poem under an unjust sky.

According to Hugo, poetry can make something happen. It can provide an image of a life lived well, and its model can help us—especially the poet who discovers the model—live that life. If this is true, then Hugo, after a successful life and a long struggle to come to terms with his past and his art, should be able to go back home and apply the fruits of his poetic and personal labor. His penultimate book, *White Center* (1980), attempts just that.[25] White Center is a section of Seattle where Hugo was born on December 21, 1923. The town could not have a better name, suggesting as it does a coldness at the core, a fearsome and empty place at one's heart, the very loneliness and lovelessness that Hugo carries around with him for years as a legacy of his youth in White Center. Recall Melville's discussion of the color white: when allied with something noble, whiteness elevates the object's nobility, but when combined with something ignoble, whiteness increases the object's horror and terror. Hugo's home of White Center, when encountered after reading his first six books of poems, accumulates a chill comparable only to the frozen center of Dante's hell. We enter the book as we would enter a deep-freeze, wary of encountering raw slabs of meat, humans frozen to the bone. We are not disappointed with the first poem, "Museum of Cruel Days," in which the speaker finds himself contemplating a bad mural, "Serbs tearing Turk horsemen down, Turk swords/flashing . . ." an opening image of the "dead long moan from the past" that will be the book's subject.

The museum of cruel days, in reality a museum in Belgrade (Holden 160), becomes in the poem an externalization of Hugo's memory, filled with images of "gratuitous blows," the world's "indifferent tune" playing in the background, a veritable "volume of grief" making "dissonant" demands upon those who have become so inured to stories of horror ("One village nearby, the Germans/shot every male dead in front of mothers and wives./The count: 7,000.") that they are in danger of "feel[ing] nothing in time." This museum is Hugo's past that threatened to turn him into the man indifferently watching terror as if it were mere spectacle, or the man casually wielding mace and chain. But he resisted, and he resists still, concluding with an admonition to himself:

> And if inside you
> a fist waits to beat back the bad man you are
> that hand opens in hunger. The market opens
> and peasants start eating. Not well. Just staying alive.
> You're armed with local coin. Buy whatever hunger
> looks good on the stand.

Turn the hand of anger into the hand of acceptance. Use your past, your "local coin," that knowledge of coldness and experience of indifference, to buy whatever you need to survive, whatever is offered in today's market. "Don't come back" to this museum of horrors, he says, as if warning himself, upon entering this hell of his past, not to abandon hope. We feel

Hugo wrestling to spit out the words that will move him beyond this dead space in his past into a present and future that less resemble a wax museum of horrors.

But the past is seductive. It is, after all, his past, and simply walking away is not an option. The past lives within him, and, even if he could abandon it and rise Adamic, a new man, that American construction, would he want to? Would not that be abandoning part of his identity, a kind of self-mutilation? And, no matter how rationally we see that our past bad habits were self-destructive, we also believe in their power. They kept us well for a while, until carrying them was a greater burden than dropping them, and they still tempt us by the power they gave us when we needed them to stay alive. This approach/ avoidance conflict with one's history is documented in "Doing the House," in which the speaker returns to his childhood home and discovers its current and last occupant, his "face the color of snow," "the man I would have become." Haunting is the word to describe the encounter, which Hugo manages to control, or keep at bay, for much of the first stanza by describing the house's external appearance. He is then drawn back to the man:

> [I] want to tell him
> he's me, menial job at the door plant,
> table set just barely for one.

Of course, the man is not Hugo. The poet, at the time of the publication of *White Center*, was successful. So why does Hugo say, "he's me," rather than repeat what he says earlier, he is "the man I would have become?" Because the poet at some level still associates the man's dereliction with creative power: misery makes poems better, he is tempted to say. A good life and a good poem are not correlated here, despite the fact that we have seen his work moving toward just that theme. A bad life, that siren voice in his head keeps telling him, is the true spring of good poetry:[26]

> I've been writing poems
> the long time I've been away and need
> to compare them with poems
> I left here, never to be written, never
> to be found in the attic where hornets
> starve and there's no flooring.
> Are they wild? Do they ring sad and real
> as the years here would have become. . . ?

Are his poems, he asks, as good as the poems he would have created had he stayed in this house and suffered the lonely, door-factory misery that this man has suffered?[27] Has he betrayed his craft, his creativity, and himself by becoming happy? By finding love? Note the identification of sad and real: has he created "unreal" poems by moving beyond sadness? Does he really need to believe, as he says in an interview, that "self-rejection is necessary to write the poem . . . up to a point?" Must he then choose between "perfection of the life" and "perfection of the work" (*Landscapes* 136)?

As much as he rejects, or wants to reject, this line of thought, he finds it difficult to escape the feeling. In "Second Chances," he lists his current assets: new wife,[28] new stepdaughter, poems that "appear everywhere," fan mail, "a profitable reading tour," even the occasional "young girl" who "offers herself" (and we can only imagine Hugo's joy at being able to reject rather than be rejected). Personal and professional happiness are his, yet,

> I can't let it go, the picture I keep of myself
> in ruin, living alone, some wretched town
> where friendship is based on just being around.

His head tells him to let it go, but his heart will not coop-
erate. Although his wife knows about the poetry groupies,
Hugo tells us that "she doesn't know" about the "vagabond
[who] knocks on the door" and whispers, "'Come back, baby.
You'll find/a million poems deep in your destitute soul.'" The
ghosts will not leave him alone. They break out of the museum
and pursue him to his front door. He banishes them ("And I
say, 'Go away. Don't ever come back.'"), but he then wistfully
watches them retreat down the front path. He is haunted by a
past that he knows he is lucky to have escaped but that he still
believes, with a strength and persistence that will never be
totally banished, is the source of his poetic power. If he had
never suffered, would he have ever become a poet? No, he
answers. Therefore, if he is no longer suffering, can he still be a
poet? The movement of his life away from the cold white center of loneliness and self-destruction, and the movement of his
poetry toward a life-affirming verse in which good living and
good writing are associated, is barely able to hold its own
against the weight of the past and the power of the ghosts who
live there.

These opening poems in *White Center* are a preparatory
incantation, a ritual putting-on of psychic armor, for his battle
with his past in the remainder of the volume. As critic Sanford
Pinsker phrases it, "*White Center* is an effort to 'take possession'—of one's past, of one's landscape, of one's life—by acts of
love that are inextricably connected to acts of language" (*Three
Pacific Northwest Poets* 93). As Hugo says, it is 'the internalized
town that has to die" before healing will occur (M. Allen,

"Because" 78). Fortunately for Hugo, White Center is not his only home. Returning to White Center, he also returns to the rivers of the Northwest and the Pacific shore, powerful, supportive images from his early poetry. The sea works as antidote to the house, the open sea nullifying the enclosed atmosphere of the oppressive home, in part because it antedates the structure, for the sea is our first home: "This is where we started, gill and fin and slow scan/of the ocean floor" ("Second Chances"). At the shore, there is, almost magically, "No sign of a home, no proof/we ever lived . . ." because the "Waves wiped out all traces/of our birth." The sea wipes out all traces of the house, not so much by allowing the poet to start over but by reminding him, in its wave action, that he existed before he ever resided in the house in White Center. Thus refreshed by the sea, he *feels* as if he is starting over: he is at the shore with his new step-daughter ("my sudden daughter"), significantly not alone, and allows himself to let go of his past failures, angry words, and shortcomings: "The sea is fond of saying that's nothing." He realizes that we all start in this gray ocean, all equal, all good, and that what follows—loving parents, hateful parents, prosperity, failure—is a function of chance that does not alter our initial state of grace: "What follows the first gray is luck."

He concludes the poem with a punning line that balances the cold white of White Center with a warmer white of shore-line ocean foam: "Foam glows in the dark, white with bones of dead sole." The waters that wipe clean have allowed him to shed his soul/sole at the shore, as a snake sheds its skin, and move away, with daughter Melissa, free and clean.

The sea welcomes and forgives as well as cleanses:

> On this dishonored, this perverted globe
> we go back to the sea and the sea opens for us.

> It spreads a comforting green we knew when
> children. . . .
> "Port Townsend, 1974"

Our sins become small, even laughable, next to the vastness of the ocean: "The sea makes fun of what we are/and we laugh beside our fire. . . ." The sea, in short, is a comforting constant, an image of stable fluidity, constancy without rigidity, and does all those things that the young Hugo's parents did not do: offers forgiveness, acceptance, and faith ("The sea believes us/when we sing"). Failing to find our way back to the sea, we are lost, a state of being that Hugo, consciously or unconsciously, depicts with the color white, connecting it with the town of White Center and the attendant theme of emotional coldness: ". . . lost men shred their clothes the last days/of delirium and die from white exposure." Again, we need to remember that the sea is not welcoming in any warm and cuddly way, but its very size and occasional unpredictable violence that shows no favors ("Logs fly over/the seawall and crush the homes of mean neighbors./Our home, too.") give the sea the power to obliterate our comparatively small errors and perversions. The message—that "We are absurd"—becomes oddly comforting and even non-judgmental.[29]

All of our wrong turns and animosities are exposed as temporary absurdities. Hugo sees the big picture where river empties into ocean in "The River Now." Standing next to one of his rivers and noting all that is gone (Slavs, Greeks, salmon, mills, even his imagination: "I can't dream anything. . . ."), he looks to the river for guidance: "The blood still begs direction home. This river points/the way north to the blood. . . ." He trusts this moral compass, walks north,[30] and what he finds, while not particularly spectacular, is stable, certain, and, as is

true in any good home, he recognizes his surroundings and
feels himself in place in them:

> I pass the backwash where
> the cattails still lean north, familiar grebes pop up,
> the windchill is the same.

Reconciliation, the word Whitman claimed as his own, is Hugo's
word as well,[31] learned on the shores of the ocean and the
banks of rivers. Whatever is missing, home remains, not White
Center but the rivers and ocean, because the base of life in general, and of his life in particular, is stable, as the river shows
him:

> No matter
> how this river fragments in the reeds, it rejoins
> the river and the bright bay north receives it all,
> new salmon on their way to the open ocean,
> the easy tub returned.

Whatever "fragments" his life may have splintered into over the
years, and whatever fragmenting of his psyche may have
occurred in his early years at White Center, he sees in the
river's reconciliation with itself and its entry into the sea an
image of wholeness that antedates and defies all efforts to tear
apart. The water will not be kept from its wholeness; the poet
sees this; he writes the poem; he then feels whole. His poetry
has made something happen.

This is not to suggest romantically that nature or the river
cares about the poet's fate. It is to suggest that Hugo sees in
nature, specifically in water's ways, an image of reconciliation
that encourages and inspires him. It is still his duty as poet to

do something with the inspiration, to make it valuable and visible in poems. For example, in "The Ballpark at Moiese," while remembering a home run of mythic length hit by his fourteen-year-old stepson in a tie game (Gertsenberger 43), Hugo knows "that the river doesn't care" about the hit or the score. In fact, the ball game seems to have had very few witnesses ("the only fans, bison/high above the park"). Nonetheless, as poet he has the power to retrieve this memory and make it significant in his life:

> And what you did that day, score tied,
> ignored by bison, the drive
> you sent beyond retrieve, you take home
> because it cannot mean. Because
> it is ignored and lost. Circle the bases again
> and claim they speak of it today in Dixon,
> the old men in the bar
> who were not there,
> who every afternoon
> take the train that does not run
> to Polson anymore.

The poet retrieves the lost, outcast, and ignored of the world and of his own psyche, those discarded "fragments," drunks in bars, ignored home runs, shameful desires, and gathers them to himself, playing the role of the river or poet or river-poet, embracing all its tributaries, even the muddy and silted ones, and returning them whole to the welcoming sea. The poet cannot expect nature or the river to do his work for him—nature will not care; nature will not tell Richard Hugo that Richard Hugo is okay—but the poet can take from the river and ocean permission to gather himself to himself, to return himself finally to his true home on his own words and poetic power, finally completing his long salmon-run home to a new White Center, taken possession of by the poet, its cold white heart now the color of forgiveness.

Jane Hirshfield
1953–

CHAPTER SIX

California as the World
in the Poetry of Jane Hirshfield

*P*oets are obsessive creatures. They return over and over
to their favorite images, themes, and motifs—Jane Hirshfield, a poet of northern California, would perhaps say
their heart's images, themes, and motifs. In one of the first
poems included in her early book, *Of Gravity and Angels*
(1988), the poet teaches the reader how to recognize one
of her poems. "In a Net of Blue and Gold" describes a
recurring poetic situation: something small but extraordi-
nary occurs in the ordinary world; the neighborhood flora
and fauna go about their business, accepting the extraor-
dinary as part of the ordinary or perhaps not noticing it;
the lone poet (almost always alone, except in certain love

245

poems in which the other is required) takes note, takes heart, and reflects. The net of the title is the world; the blue and gold are the world's omnipresent beauty, which should inspire humans' awe and compassion, but too often do not. We are trapped in the net, an unavoidable connotation, but more consistent with Hirshfield's imagery and tone elsewhere; we are one of the many strands in the net, not necessarily woven together by some higher power or grand net-maker but woven together by the simple fact that nets are woven. The event that catches her attention in this instance is when a "moored boat lifts, for its moment,/out of the water like a small cloud." The boat "floats there, defying the stillness to break," suspended for a moment, suspending for a moment the physical laws of the universe, "a minor miracle." The boat's hull is "doubled" on the water's surface and then redoubled in the poet's mind, a mirror image that occurs often, suggesting the complementary and interpenetrating relationship between inner and outer worlds, subjectivity and objectivity. "The bird on the bow line takes it in stride" and "the fish continue their placid, midday/truce with the world." The boat's lifting is the opening of a door to the beauty of the world—another recurring image—and allows the speaker to "catch [the] gleam" of the fishes' "jeweled, reflecting scales,/small dragons guarding common enough treasure." The oxymoronic "common enough treasure" is also typical of the poet's attitude: treasure surrounds us, almost casually, but only in certain miraculous moments are we allowed to see it, or are we able to apprehend it, or are we paying close enough attention to notice. The treasure, revealed to her so serendipitously, reminds her that we—fish, bird, water, humans—are "bound to each other," a buoyant moment to be sure, but also a moment that reminds Hirshfield of how far we are from what we could be. Why, she asks do "we fail so often, in such ordinary ways"?

A quite similar situation initiates "In Smooth Water the Mountains Suspend Themselves." The mountains are mirrored in the lake as a squirrel jumps from oak to pine and the poet takes in the scene. As the boat's lifting out of the water was "a minor miracle," the squirrel is taken as "one of the many possible angels/plucked from the blue of this lake." The squirrel, like the fish and bird of the previous poem, shows "no surprise" when he clambers up a tree trunk and climbs over the reflection of a trout, remaining as impassive as "one of those ancient creatures/found on cathedral walls." These angels, these common treasures of the natural world that we see often but take for granted, bear us along on their "folded wings," while we too often "do not feel" their presence. Grace is immanent in the world, and within us, for the inner and outer, objective and subjective, "double" one another insistently in Hirshfield's poetry. Her mission is to erase boundaries while keeping everything absolutely clear and vivid in its living, individual integrity. Our skin—spoken of often as an extension of our consciousness—is a semi-permeable membrane inside of which we reside comfortably most of the time. As she says in "Bees":

> In every instant, two gates.
> One opens to fragrant paradise, one to hell.
> Mostly we go through neither.

For the most part, "we nod to our neighbor" and go about our mundane business. Always in the background, the potential for heaven or hell resides, as a background music to life, a sort of white noise of our existence, just beyond our range of hearing:

> But the faint cries—ecstasy? Horror?
> Or did you think it the sound

Of distant bees,
Making only the thick honey of this good life?

How else could we survive? At times the heart just needs a rest
from this world, no matter how good life may be:

There are times
When the heart closes down,
The metal grates drawn
And padlocked,
The owner's footprints covered by snow.
"The New Silence"[1]

At times, however, we reach a level of what Hirshfield
calls "attentiveness," and the world breaks through: "Attentiveness is the only means by which we can know the nature
and qualities of our moment-by-moment existence—the entrance gate through which a person can not just 'be' his or her
life, but know it, taste it, consider it, work with it as a potter
works with clay" (Moore 2). In these moments of epiphany,
when the bees break through and the heart opens up, we
meet the world across that dissolved membrane of skin and
consciousness and look into the mirror of ourselves and at ourselves. These moments are rarely dramatic, grand, or even
beautiful in a traditional sense. A wonderful example is the
short poem "Floor":

The nails, once inset, rise to the surface—
or, more truly perhaps, over years
the boards sink down to meet what holds them.
Worn, yes, but not worn through:
the visible work reveals itself in iron,

to be pounded down again, for what we've declared
the beautiful to be.

The nails hold together the scene, but conventionally we notice
and call beautiful the wooden floor. The poor nails not only get
neglected but more, they get walked upon and even pounded
down, apparently repeatedly. Such neglect and ignominy do not
deter the poet, in this moment of insight, from calling the nails
beautiful. Nor does such ill treatment deter the beautiful nails,
which are worn but not worn through. Beauty, the blue and
gold of the world-net in whatever guise it appears to us,
remains despite all. Beauty holds, she shows, and perhaps
hopes Yeats hears, too.

 The boat, the boards, the squirrel: all show Hirshfield
paying attention to interstices, boundaries in the world that do
not stop, circumscribe, or limit perception and that do not separate phenomena but that instead open up a door to other realities, realities of interconnection, in the unattended gaps over
which our vision normally skips. The tone is always understated. Hirshfield is not surprised such moments occur. We
encounter small creatures, individual plants, domestic chores,
quiet walks. Neither Haines' charging bull moose nor Hugo's
lunker fish on a light line is required for a Hirshfield epiphany,
although a big fish lurks down there:

> A boat drifts far out
> On the river below the mountains,
> And below it
> The fish, the great fish
> That the one in the boat has come for,
> Swims in the shadow.
>   "Unnameable Heart"

The great fish is never hooked, of course, nor could it be reeled in if it were. For companions instead in a Hirshfield poem we have smaller fry: in "Unnameable Heart," a simple cricket. Her image of a day is consistent: "rutted lanes, too small for naming/that lead, one to another, through the day" ("This Ripeness"). Her vision requires a simple lane, not an Interstate.

The grand image is consciously eschewed. For example, what would we anticipate if we encountered a poem entitled "The Hawk Cry" in a volume by John Haines, and read these opening lines:

> I do not know
> What brought it to the middle
> Of the room made warm by the fire
> I had lit before breakfast.

We would expect—and would not be disappointed—that the antecedent for "it" was a bird of prey. In Hirshfield's poem, "it" is a mouse. As she says, "The gods/are not large,/outside us" ("The Gods Are not Large"). One is tempted by cultural stereotype to call this focus on the small and near (rather than the grand and panoramic) a "feminine" consciousness. Let us recall Peggy Church, whose moments of insight were more often than not inspired by the grand sweep of the New Mexico desert, the pounding of the Pacific surf, or the final step to the top of an imposing butte. Whatever one may label Hirshfield's vision, one can see that it clearly differs in detail from Haines' or Hugo's, but that it is still rooted in the earth of the poet's locale.

That locale, however, rarely includes a landscape panorama. We find no large-scale Moran or Bierstadt sunsets, but more often we are led to something right before our eyes or under our feet. The mouse, for example, in "The Hawk Cry" is simply discovered, literally at her feet. Sometimes the discovery requires a bit more effort, as in "The World." She enters a "half-shop, half-museum" and walks up a "half flight of steps" into a large room full of large items (painted cupolas, complete with copper roosters and weather vanes). Next, she goes into the "main room, huge," lined with crocks, a collection of Hummel, books, maps, everything calling for attention. She ignores the large, ornate, or gaudy and proceeds all the way to the back of the room, to a corner. There she finds what she seeks:

> A clutter of tiny white horses, sweating, their
>   heads held low;
> three ox-drawn carts; the fisherman heading off,
> his net slung empty as a blow on his tired left shoulder;
> a simple, sleeping cat; and a farmer whose feet
> assemble unseen furrows, the water bucket's weight
> minutely shifting as he goes.

Small, simple, humble in every way: Hirshfield's common treasures. "The World" is a rarity among the poems—a narrative—but its plot exists so the speaker can make her way past the grand to the small but paradoxically grand, for everything contains "worlds within worlds," and this collection of scrimshaw miniatures describes for the poet a life—a large, whole life in great detail. She reads the scene for us, and in another rare gesture, provides the reader with an explicit, emphatic theme:

> But these small figures, precise and homely,
>   carry a different gloss:
> a hard-won sorrow, a hard-won wonder is this world,
>   this life. . . .

The smallest of its parts carries the weight of the entire collection's wonder.

There is always something at least mildly elegiac in any nature writing (and there is no reason not to call this poet a nature writer), no matter how ultimately optimistic the poet may be. Hirshfield is no exception. But she knows that earth is all we have and, "with no invented God overhead," earth had better suffice. One consolation she finds, common enough among nature writers, is "a stubborn faith in rotting/that ripens into soil," a faith in the recurrence of natural life out of death and dirt. While "the old corm that rises steadily each spring" will not blossom into "symbols" of a transcendent, future bliss, it will produce the "reassurances" needed to send the poet each year to catalogues, seeking new seed ("November, Remembering Voltaire"). She finds more than simple reassurance, however. She finds positive glee. Her desire is to be so attentive to the pulse of the world that she enters into it and sees from its perspective. "All I want," she says is

> To hear as a sand crab hears the waves,
> loud as a second heart;
> to see as a green thing sees the sun,
> with the undividing attention of blind love,
>> "Rain in May"

She wants to receive the world as the grass unflinchingly receives the rain and sun:

> Still, in this rain soft as a fog
> that can only be known to be rain by the window's
>> streaming,
> surely all Being at bottom is happy:

soaked to the bone, sopped at the root,
fenny, seeped through, yielding as coffee grounds
yield to their percolation, blushing, completely
  seduced. . . .
        "Percolation"

Fenny, sopped, and soaked through: the world she wants to
receive is no symbolic or metaphorical world ("This garden is
no metaphor," "November, Remembering Voltaire"), no white
whale's forehead to strike through, no ornate guise for a spiritual reality neatly tucked behind the corporeal form, and no
barely sufficient rock upon which we are stranded. When she
says that Being is happy, she means it, without personification
or ornamentation. The frogs in the rain are happy. She would
be the same.

Underlying all of Hirshfield's poetry is her understanding of
her relationship to the world around her, the place where she
is at any moment. This understanding becomes the paradigm
for all other relationships: between poet and her work, between
poet and other people, between poet and society. In Hirshfield's case, her understanding of her relationship to place is not
really dependent on the particular locale in which she finds
herself but applies generally and equally to the entire earth.
While she clearly appreciates the beauty of her northern California locale, having consciously chosen her location, driving
her van from the east coast to San Francisco after graduating
from Princeton in 1973 and spending a year working on a
midwestern farm, place for Hirshfield is the entire earth. Continuum is perhaps the best word to describe the relationship

she establishes between herself and the natural world. In place of the traditional Western dualisms (inner/outer, human/non-human, subjective/objective, sacred/profane, soul/body, emotion/intellect, sensuality/spirituality), Hirshfield suggests that life is a series of continuums, based ultimately upon her understanding of the continuum between herself (and, by extension, all humans) and the non-human world, the total contents of the place around her. Her 1997 book of essays, *Nine Gates: Entering the Mind of Poetry,* repeatedly makes this point. Responding favorably to the statement by eighteenth-century German poet Novalis that "Perceptibility is a kind of attentiveness," Hirshfield says, "In this radical vision of vision, there is no difference between human and nonhuman, between sentient and nonsentient. All being becomes single, alive, available, and awake" (*Nine Gates* 118).

This sounds Oriental because from the age of twenty-one to twenty-nine, Hirshfield immersed herself in the practice of Buddhism in a Zen monastery in San Francisco, putting her writing career on hold. When she began, she says, she "knew almost nothing of what it meant to be a human being, to enter deeply a human life. I needed to learn how to pay attention, how to stay with my own experience, how to become more permeable to the real and also more grounded in it" (Mills n.p.). She did not reveal this part of her biography until 1994, in her editor's note to *Women in Praise of the Sacred,* believing that her religious practice was a private matter (*Atlantic* interview n.p.). She also contends that her Buddhist practice, which she continues, is "not the governing fact for a reader of my work" (*Atlantic* interview n.p.), and says elsewhere, "I hope my work is perfectly understandable to someone who has no idea that I ever practiced meditation; I would like it if whatever of 'Zen' is in it might be available without any labels or explanation" (Borders n.p.). To the work's credit, it is perfectly understandable without any Zen background. Even so, there are connections, and Hirshfield makes them more plainly than one unschooled in Oriental philosophy ever could. In "The Myriad Leaves of Words," for example, she notes, "The nonseparation of Buddhist understanding lies close to the ground of all poetry, western as well as eastern. Every metaphor, every description that moves its reader, every hymn-shout of praise, points to the shared existence of beings and things" (*Nine Gates* 99). What she calls the "shared existence of beings and things" is the equivalent of the continuum.

She sums up the thematic grounding of her poetry in Buddhism in a passage from another essay ("Two Secrets") in *Nine Gates:*

> Dogen addressed the relationship between self and other in the search for Buddhist understanding in a famous description: "To study the Way is to study the self, to study the self is to forget the self, to forget the self is to awaken into the ten thousand things." You cannot leap beyond human consciousness without first going through it; but if you gaze deeply enough into being, eventually you will awaken into the company of everything. The thought goes back to the Buddha, who stated at the moment of his enlightenment. . . . "Now everything and I awaken" (*Nine Gates* 140).

Her goal in her poetry, then, is to go through her consciousness to the shared ground of being of the world, of "everything." Human consciousness does not block or alienate one from non-human nature but is one of the gates through which one can pass to an understanding of that world, our world, the world.[2] A quotation from the famous Japanese haiku master Matsuo Basho might be appropriate:

> . . . all who have achieved real excellence in any art, pos-
> sess one thing in common, that is, a mind to obey nature,
> to be one with nature, throughout the four seasons of the
> year (*The Narrow Road* 71).

A metaphor used in one poem for the relationship between humans and the world, and between humans and each other, is a wedding, a ceremony in which one element is bound to its neighbor forever.[3] In Hirshfield's poetry, the relationship goes deeper than that, however, for we are not simply bound to one other, but to the world at large, in a state of interdependence. In the "wedded" state we metaphorically become each other, each other's essence, or, in Hirshfield's vocabulary, each other's mirror:

> How each thing meets the other as itself, the
>   luminous, changing
> mirror of itself—mercuric oxide tipped from flask
>   to flask,
> first two, then one, wedded for life in that vow.

For the poem "The Wedding," she chooses an epigraph from the scientist Antoine Laurent Lavoisier: "Nothing is lost, nothing created: everything is transformed" (*Elements of Chemistry,* 1789). This statement of the law of the conservation of matter, grounding the ancient Oriental idea in modern Occidental scientific thought, undermines any potential critical response that dismisses all talk of humankind's harmony and continuum with the world, especially in this skeptical contemporary age, as naïve romanticism. At death or dissolution, atoms are simply and eternally transformed, recombined, shared among and across species, making humans literal brothers and sisters to the surrounding world. The conservation principle welcomes death, for without it no new life or beginnings would be possible. Taking the idea all the way back to the hypothesized Big Bang, one can say that we all—rocks, fish, automobiles, presidents—are stardust rearranged. To suggest, as the poet does, that we actually meet our mirror is a metaphoric leap, but one that takes off from solid scientific ground and returns to it.

The wedding metaphor suggests gaiety and new beginnings, which may seem to expose Hirshfield to a different charge, that of sentimentality or optimism blind to the obvious pain and suffering that have always been a foundation of the world. Her poetry, however, again in the best tradition of both Buddhism and western empiricism, recognizes the inevitability of loss, pain, suffering, and grief and embraces them as parts of a continuum with joy and happiness. Ours is a "falling" as well as a fallen world ("To Hear the Falling World"), and the "small pains" keep one "from growing sure" and "perhaps forgetting." As Frost says, we need to be versed in country things. Moreover, we cannot avoid the knowledge of death, the ultimate indicator of our lapsed state and the suffering integral to human experience. When the daughter in "A Story" declares that the "small wild bird" on the windowsill, dead three days, is moving and therefore alive again, mother knows the double truth: yes, the bird is moving, but only because the carcass is being consumed by insect scavengers. In that sense, of course, the bird really is alive, with "true life," new life. The final lines

are interesting: the woman "turned her face/so her daughter
would not see, though she would see." "Would" is used first as a
synonym for "could," expressing the mother's intention, but
used next to express the intent or willingness of the daughter to
see and also the inevitability of her knowing the truth sooner or
later. Hirshfield manages to speak for the mother, the daughter,
and the world at once, while illustrating the continuum of life
and death. She knows what Stevens knows, that "Death is the
mother of beauty" (a line she quotes approvingly in "The Myriad Leaves of Words," *Nine Gates* 89): the wild bird truly is
"beautiful" in death, because its "emerald wing-feathers" shel-
ter writhing new life.

Despite the obvious beauty the poet finds on the earth,
she understands that, while her task is "to praise," she must
"not/be blinded by the praising" ("The Task").[4] It may even
seem to us that there are two earths, one beautiful and one
plain or even dangerous. When young,

> . . . we embrace trees.
> Lie with the swan, the bull, become stars.
> Blackbirds form bridges across the sky:
> We pass, lightly placing our feet.
> "The Other Earth"

The earth is magical, enchanted, always welcoming. The
revelation of the earth's opposite potential saddens but in
Hirshfield's poetry is accepted with something like resigned
equanimity:[5]

> When the plain world comes,
> with its explanations
> smooth and cool as a marble statue's skin,

we go, rising out of the dark.
Being careless and proud, we look back
towards the other earth:
how it wavers and goes out,
like a girl with an errand to do in another room.

What appeared to us as bliss had really been the "dark," and our exit from that state is a "rising," even though it is facilitated by a loss (of innocence, of youthful happiness, of security).

The compounded concluding metaphor is interesting: the other earth is like a candle with a definite life-span, now extinguished, or simply revealed as the dark that it always has been. And that other earth, the one that spoils our innocence, is a girl, perhaps off to accompany for a time some other immature visionary, but she is no thief, nor is there any hint of infidelity, characterizations that may have naturally occurred to a male poet. The girl is benevolent in her own way; her time with the speaker is simply over, nothing to be regretted or mourned.

There is only one earth, of course, an earth exemplifying the continuum of life and death, beauty and bareness, as Hirshfield makes clear in several poems about autumn, including the short "Autumn":

Again the wind
flakes gold-leaf from the trees
and the painting darkens—
as if a thousand penitents
kissed an icon
till it thinned
back to bare wood,
without diminishment.

A poem of praise, certainly, but one neither blind to the dark-
ening of autumn nor darkened by that starkness, the passing of
nature's gold, what Frost calls the "hardest hue to hold." In
eight short lines, she moves from nature to art to religion and
back to nature's wood, celebrating the way love wears out the
beloved. But nature gives us hope that here is extended
through simile to cosmic dimensions. The opening "again" and
the concluding "without diminishment" form an unbroken circle implying the cyclical permanence of nature's renewal, the
continuum of life and death, and the continuum of plenitude
(spring) and loss (autumn) for human and non-human nature.

The autumn leaves fall in response to the same force that
strips the apples from their branches in "A Sweetness All
Around Me as It Falls":

> . . . But the apples love earth and falling,
> lose themselves in it as much as they can at first touch
> and then, with time and rain, at last completely.

Nature's calling home of her offspring apples is an act of love,
the desire of the earth for your return, as the apples' falling to
earth (or "appling to earth," as Hirshfield says) is an expression
of their love, almost a wombward lunge, dissolving into the
original mother. Death is not only the mother of beauty, it is the
product of love, the force in Hirshfield's poetry that binds
together the terms of her various continuums and that engen-
ders beauty, whether the earth is displaying its "pendant gold
of/necklaced summer" or its "ice-cold mirroring starlight" of
autumn and winter. In autumn, the world is "still-wealthy": the
woods are merely "simplified" from their summer's "dazzle"
("The November Angels").

"It is not enough/to see only the beauty," she reminds us in "'Perceptibility Is a Kind of Attentiveness.'" Nature absorbs all, beauty and ugliness, and does so effortlessly but lovingly. In another bold poem, somewhat reminiscent of Whitman's "Lilacs," Hirshfield dares to conflate the blooming of the narcissus in San Francisco with the American bombing of Iraq in 1991 ("Narcissus: Tel Aviv, Baghdad, San Francisco; February 1991"). As the bombs are being dropped, the flowers bloom everywhere, but "after all in their own time," suggesting that their outburst of color and life is unconnected to the outburst of death thousands of miles away, the simultaneity being merely fortuitous. But Buddhism teaches her in its Doctrine of Mutual Arising,[6] and the world has taught her the same, that all is connected, and rather than take the easy course of contrasting the beauty with the horror, the life with the death, Hirshfield compares them with a series of similes and assertions, beginning with, "It seemed they [the flowers] were oblivious but they were not." The narcissi blooms are compared to the bombs' explosions and their green stems to the "green-flaring missiles." As the flowers had no choice to open, so the children at the target had no choice.

To this point, Hirshfield confines herself to comparing bombs and blooms, but she then goes one step farther and connects both to the earth. Just as "precise and in fact wholly peaceful the flowers opened," so the earth opened to the bombs, "precise and peaceful," "because it was asked." The earth could no more refuse to open for the bombs than the sea could refuse the seabirds passage through its "green surface," "that they may enter and eat." Both land and water open, always open, in an image wholly natural and clearly erotic as well, an image of loving acceptance of the other's entrance, just because that is what is asked and what is needed. The rain of bombs, connected through the imagery to the "dark mahogany rain" that enters the ocean, is a particularly horrible and condensed version of the flaws, imperfections, and disappointments that rain upon humans, non-humans, and the earth in general every day. We tend to decry the bombs, such clear examples of our potential for evil, while we ignore lesser, daily examples of that same potential—the road rage, the surly clerk, the colleague enjoying a "bad day," our own free-floating anger. The earth, however, takes all in stride because it is asked.

The poet repeatedly reminds us that this is a postlapsarian world, that everything, including us, falls, that this fact is natural and should encourage us to open up, like the earth, yet it seems not to. One unspecified morning, while drinking coffee, the speaker of "Needles of Pine, of Morning," watches pine needles falling outside her window and hears the newspaper falling against her door as it is delivered. She is tired of the falling needles, but they keep coming: "things do not stop simply because we have had enough." She turns newspaper pages, one story of tragedy after another, more metaphorical falling pine needles littering her "white table," her desire for some clean place away from reminders of the world's destructiveness. It is morning, the moment when people, at least according to Thoreau, should feel new hope if they are ever going to be capable of doing so. Yet needles and lives keep falling, and it is a hard world:

> And hard too to live in this place, where even the
>   best, the luckiest,
> lose everything if not today then tomorrow or
>   next year
> and still we have not found out how to be kind.

The inevitability of our mortality should make us sympathetic with all other mortal creatures, which is to say all other beings, even the rocks that eventually decompose, yet it does not. We flatter ourselves that compassion is a uniquely human trait, yet the earth, as we see, has been turning the other cheek to human abuse for millennia, while we continue to add cruelty to an already cruel world. Why? Because, for our psychological comfort, or perhaps simply so we can get the gumption to get up and go to work again, we delude ourselves into believing that what falls "is always on the other side/of the glass" (the needles, the newspaper) or "the other side of the world" (the stories in the newspaper, the bombs in Iraq) in order to hide from our "helplessness." Yet we are already as good as dead, she says, and "the black water rocks beneath us" and "the ferryman . . . holds out his hand," even as we refuse to hold out ours to others. The poet's job is to take the coins from her eyes, at least, to see clearly and show vividly the life/death, beauty/ugliness, human/non-human continuum, and, perhaps, in that way assert and confirm our connection with the earth through our human power of song or poetry.

The irony is that we all like to call ourselves realists. No one wants to be thought sentimental in this skeptical, tough era. We fancy that we have seen and understood that ferryman-shadow of ours and are sophisticated enough to go on with our lives. Is it possible, Hirshfield wonders, that our lack of compassion, including the rage, violence, and selfishness that accompany our enlightened age, is in some ways a product of that very enlightenment? As a culture we have steadily increased our power over the environment for the last few centuries, forcibly yanking vast chunks of the experience that had been for earlier people realms of darkness, mystery, and superstition into the light of scientific understanding and rational analysis. All the more galling, then, to discover that we are still, as Hirshfield says, helpless against our own mortality, which follows us around to remind us of the many other examples of our helplessness. More powerful than ever, yet still helpless in a fundamental and ultimate way: as much as we say we accept this fact, one could say that our coldness and rage, flip sides of the same coin, are the results of our desire to deny our vulnerability and to ridicule or denounce those who implicitly challenge our delusions by showing signs of their weakness. We dare not admit our kinship with the afflicted, for that would suggest what we do not want to acknowledge, that we are afflicted, too. As the poet says, "still we have not found out how to be kind." Hirshfield shows us that, while no amount of love, much less poetry, will ever stop loss or grief or pain or suffering, that is no reason not to offer the love anyway, to open like the earth. In fact, offering love in the face of acknowledged helplessness is one way to affirm our connection with other humans, the equally doomed.

Again, the world gives human consciousness a nudge and a model. While contemplating aging and mortality in general, in "Standing Deer," the poet looks at her life:

> Beloved, what can be, what was,
> will be taken from us.
> I have disappointed.
> I am sorry. I knew no better.

Transience, however, and suffering are no reasons not to offer what we can give, as she literally sees out her window: "This morning, out the window,/the deer stood like a blessing, then vanished." The blessing is short-lived, but it, like life, is still a blessing. In "The Pattern that Connects," a simple image, in a more immediately mortal context, makes this same point beautifully. While a friend's son, Gregory, is dying, his father shaves the boy's beard. The simple, loving gesture does not forestall loss ("The weight of his head for those moments/ held in your hand, and then not."), but the loss connects both across time and space, first, to each other, then to those somewhat removed ("you shaved him as your father had once shaved you"), and, finally, to all humans ("The melody that carries a children's rhyme/through centuries, though the meaning of the words is lost."). The actual words or touch disappear; the melody, the gift, remains. The actors disappear; the "pattern connects."

Suffering connects, as Hawthorne understands in *The Scarlet Letter:* Pearl is not part of the "magnetic" chain of humanity until she acquires her great grief in the final scaffold scene. Yet the tone is different. Hirshfield seems more optimistic by nature than Hawthorne, whom we always associate with the dour, gray Puritan citizens at the foot of the scaffold. Hirshfield can say, and one has difficulty imagining Hawthorne saying this, "So few grains of happiness/measured against all the dark/and still the scales balance" ("Weighing"). Observation of reality? Statement of faith? It sounds like either or both. The scales suggest a scientist's empiricism—we can actually go out, gather the world's sorrows in one tray, gather the world's joy in the other, and watch the beam balance. The "still" suggests an understated awe or wonder at the final result. The contrast between the "few" and the "all" suggests a process more supernatural than natural: some weighty finger must be on one side of the balance point. The poet's finger reveals the world's balance.

What, then, is a poet, and how is that definition related to the continuum theme? As expected, the first step in the poetic process is attentiveness, attending to the world. We spend most of our lives in what we might call a normal state of inattentiveness, for who could stand to function at the highest level of awareness twenty-four hours a day. But in certain moments of heightened attentiveness, the continuum becomes evident, and poetry breaks out as a collaborative effort between poet and world: "Through actively perceptive speech, outer world and inner experience collaborate in the creation of meaning" (*Gates* 129). The world and poet become co-authors: ". . . the poet becomes an intermediary, a medium through whom the world of objects and nature beyond human consciousness may speak" (*Gates* 131). The Buddhist roots of this opened consciousness have been mentioned already. The creative consciousness, as Hirshfield understands it, has also been explained in Western terms by Anton Ehrenzweig in *The Hidden Order of Art*:

> What, of course, is needed is an undifferentiated attention
> akin to syncretistic vision which does not focus on detail,
> but holds the total structure of the work of art in a single
> and undifferentiated view (*The Hidden Order of Art* 23).

Ehrenzweig calls this creative state the "'full' emptiness of unconscious scanning" (*The Hidden Order of Art* 25), by which he means the artist does not allow her rational mind to do what it wants to do, that is, to break up a perceived phenomenon into figure and ground, important and unimportant details. Instead, the poet or artist sees the whole picture at once, seeing right to its essence without applying the conscious or rational mind's categories of significant and insignificant. As Ehrenzweig says,

> The uncompromising democracy which refuses to make
> any Distinction between the significance of the elements
> building the work of art, belongs to the essence of artistic
> rigour (*The Hidden Order of Art* 29).

The creative artist is free to scan the entire field, to make her ego vulnerable to the chaos that results when the rational mind does not step in to order data, and hold herself in this dangerous position until creativity occurs. Ehrenzweig emphasizes this point: "Creativity is always linked with the happy moment when all conscious control can be forgotten" (*The Hidden Order of Art* 44). Ehrenzweig goes so far as to contend that, in certain extreme cases, the inability to engage in this temporary openness to reality is the sign of an unhealthy personality:

> This incapacity is due to a near-pathological dissociation
> of their ego functions. Because of this dissociation, the
> untoward breakthrough of undifferentiated modes of
> vision threatens their rigidly focused surface sensibilities
> with sudden disruption and disintegration (*The Hidden
> Order of Art* 24).

The unhealthy ego refuses to give up its control for even a second and see into the undifferentiated reality that surrounds it. The rational mind keeps that chaos at bay by creating a scale of value when encountering the world, assigning some phenomena in the perception field more or less importance than others and thereby reassuring the ego that everything is in its place and all is right with the world. In other words, in Ehrenzweig's words, "a rigid, uncreative personality" will not be able to "let go his hold on the surface functions" (*The Hidden Order of Art* 38). In Hirshfield's words, "Good poetry begins with seeing increasingly clearly, in increasingly various ways; but another part of poetry's true perception is found only in relinquishing more and more of the self to more and more of the world" (*Nine Gates* 151-52).

The premise, as translated into Hirshfield's poetry, is that, because humans and world are part of a continuum, the world's secrets and beauty are accessible to us—and rightfully part of us—if we clear our minds of our egotistical concerns and fears and actually listen to them. Listening too much to our ego is the only boundary between us and the world, and that boundary is of our own construction. Moments of insight may occur to all humans; the poet names and thereby preserves those moments. In "The House in Winter," the moment comes in stanza one:

> a corner cupboard suddenly wavers
> in low-flung sunlight,
> cupboard never quite visible before.

The cupboard suddenly stands out and stands up, revealing "jars/of last summer's peaches," now transformed into "their native gold." The poet translates the phenomenon into a word: "the mouth swallows peach, and says gold." Now things are beginning to happen: the world opens to the poet; the poet walks in; the body responds; the brain labels the response; a word is on the page. World and poet, body and mind, speak to each other, are each other—in these moments of attentiveness the harmony is manifest—and the preserved peaches of the world, although now eaten (they have to be tasted and removed from the physical world in order to be experienced) are preserved as gold, a poet's word. Then the cupboard is "swept back into shadow," and for now, "the deep shelves of systole and diastole empty." Back and forth rhythmically, like blood in veins, the world and the poet echo or mirror each other. Systole and diastole catch the connotations: one's very life blood, rhythmic, constant, interdependent, complementary, audible, a palpable experience, as poetry is for Hirshfield.

In her last stanza, however, the poet goes further, with a qualifier:

> Or perhaps it is
> that the house only constructs itself
> while we look—
> opens, room for room, because we look.

Now the poet's attention does more than notice: it contributes to the formation of the moment. By looking, by being attentive, she brings the gold to life. One could call this human-centered subjectivity, in which the ego forms the world, the world passively supplying the raw material for the use of our creative consciousness. Hirshfield means something else. The process is cooperative, not enforced from the outside by the seer onto the passive "house" or world: "The wood, the glass, the linen, flinging themselves/into form at the clap of our footsteps." "Flinging" suggests anything but passivity. It hints at motivation, an eagerness and desire on the part of the world to be attended to. Moving one step farther, Hirshfield connects the poetic process and product to nature's fertility:

> As the hard-dormant
> peach tree wades into blossom and leaf
> at the spring sun's knock: neither surprised
> nor expectant, but every cell awakened at the knock.

The poet, like the sun, awakens the dormant poetry in the world. And, again, "wades," while not as active as "flinging," suggests active cooperation on the world's part. Poet and world work together in a collaboration, each doing what it does best, the world blossoming, the poet writing. Art is a natural component of the world, a natural product of living in the world, as much as peach tree blossoms are, a fact that neither elevates nor devalues human creativity but simply acknowledges that human creativity is the same as nature's creativity, because, of course, humans are nature. Our highly developed power of language, related to our consciousness and self-consciousness, is ours alone, but it is merely a faculty that humans possess and non-humans do not. It is no badge of superiority or creator of an unbridgeable gulf between inner and outer.

In fact, speech is a natural extension of attention, which is the recognition of our intertwining with—not our separation from—non-human nature: "The world's effortless expression reaches outward and summons the only answer we have for its various music—a human song, a poem" (*Nine Gates* 84). The poem that results is less an individual creation than "an irresistible duet" (*Nine Gates* 84). If anything, then, our language, the result of attention and effort, is in some ways inferior to the "effortless expression" of non-human nature. And our poetry, our "only answer" to nature, is a weak response to the world's "various music." Poetry's devices allow us entry into this shared world: "The deepest of image's meanings is its recognition of our continuity with the rest of existence: within a good image, outer and subjective worlds illumine one another, break bread together, converse" (*Nine Gates* 17). Poetic images are not impositions of human will onto the world, nor are they simple devices for appropriating the world's raw material into a form called the poem. In short, ". . . images are no simplistic personification.

They are forms that let us inhabit abstraction as if from within, and so begin to know our kinship with the wide field of being" (*Nine Gates* 17). The poet's tools reveal rather than enforce a relationship: "Images, metaphors, similes, and stories are sliding doors, places of opening through which subjective and objective may penetrate and become each other" (*Nine Gates* 84). "Penetrate" may strike a wrong note in that sentence. It connotes a sort of masculine aggressiveness that is otherwise foreign to Hirshfield's work. Nonetheless, her point is clear: poetry is a way of opening the doors to a continuum that already exists.

The connection, when it bursts forth in beauty, is irresistible, like the Puritans' grace. The world touches us and we cannot refuse its call:

> And though the earth
> shuttles fearsome
> and everywhere cruel,
> the heart diamond flashed out
> once, twice, and once again
> the semaphore-reply
> it cannot help but make to beauty,
> before the bone-white cup
> is fully drained.
> "The Tea Light of Late September"

At times, the awe is overwhelming, and our only response is silence: ". . . before you,/words lie down in envy and silence . . ." ("Leaf"). Silence, however, seems to be a preparatory mode: "By removing the self from the landscape through silence and stillness . . . the watcher begins to perceive 'from the point of view of the animal,' as José Ortega y Gasset wrote in his *Meditations on Hunting* (*Nine Gates* 108). Silence is the cleansing

process that precedes the voice. Once inside the world and
filled with its plenitude ("O whirler of winds, boat-swallower,/
germinant seed,/O seasons that sing in our ears in the shape of
O"), we are compelled to sing:

> we name your colors muttonfat, kingfisher, jade,
> we name your colors anthracite, orca, growth-tip
>   of pine,
> we name them arpeggio, pond,
> we name them flickering helix within the cell,
>   burning coal tunnel,
> blossom of salt. . . .
>   "The Stone of Heaven"

The list goes on and seems spontaneous, an overflowing in
response to the awe (the "O") inspired by the world's beauty.
Like the woodthrush, the poet sings, "not to fill the world, but
because he is filled." The words pour out as if the body cannot
hold them and they fall out of the mouth. Then a human faculty
engages in all this spontaneous overflow:

> . . . we name them,
> and naming, begin to see,
> and seeing, begin to assemble the plain stones
>   of earth.

As we name, we begin to see: perception follows identification.
We begin to see the stones as part of the "pattern that connects," begin to "assemble" them into a shape.

So is this poem or song simply another modernist artifice
created by the imagination working its will on the lower world?
Note the definition of "assemble": "To collect into one place or

body; to bring or call together; to convoke; to congregate. . . . To collect and put together the parts of; as, to assemble an automobile, airplane, watch, or gun" (*Webster's New International Dictionary*, 2nd Edition, Unabridged). The poet calls together what belongs together. She puts together parts that are made to fit together. She intuits a pattern that she then assembles. Her opened imagination sees to the heart of the plain stones (sees from the stones' point of view) and arranges them as they need to be arranged. Awe leads to song that leads to perception that leads to revelation, for that is what the verb assemble most closely resembles here. World and poet again collaborate. The woodthrush is filled with the world and sings it back out, sings out the notes of the world to the world. The bird does not construct an artifact to fill the world because its soul needs refreshment. The bird sings because it is so full, and what it sings corresponds to the pattern that is the world. The poet, in like fashion, assembles the world. The poet's singing points to facts that she had not noticed before; though they were always there, and the more she points and sings, the more she notices, and the more she notices, the more the phenomena collect together, gaps fill in, and plain stones are assembled into a river bottom. Hirshfield shows how song opens the door to the vision that sees the connection, the continuum, even if a description and explication of that song gets bogged down quickly into fallacies of bifurcation, of inner/outer, human/non-human, revealing/imposing. Hirshfield carefully does what the poet can to step around those pitfalls, but, as Melville tells us, the world is full of man-traps (or woman-traps, in this case).

The difficult process begins by getting the ego out of the way, erasing the selfish concerns that shadow humans and block the light of the world and encourage us to think in dialectical terms. Hirshfield reveals her Buddhism training here. As D. T.

Suzuki says, in *An Introduction to Zen Buddhism*, "Zen takes us to an absolute realm wherein there are no antitheses of any sort" (68). Masao Abe, perhaps the best philosophical interpreter of Zen since Suzuki, echoes the point when he asserts that Zen at base is "liberation from the discriminating mind itself" (*An Introduction to Zen Buddhism* 115). Again, the premise is that the human/world dualism, like all dualisms, is a myth. The world's inspiration is always there, like the potential in a light switch, but only manifest when we complete the circuit by opening ourselves. Nathan Scott employs a western philosopher, Martin Heidegger to make a similar point:

> All things, of course, remain "silent" for as long as they are approached merely as things to be 'attacked' in the manner of a technological project, and, as Martin Heidegger often argued in the later phase of his career, they do not begin to "hail" us, to "salute" us, until they themselves are first "hailed." What is required, as Heidegger urged, is that we undertake to learn the discipline of "letting be" (*Visions of Presence* 6-7).

Scott explains Heidegger's concept of "letting be":

> . . . to let what-is be what it is is to confront it with such a piety as entails a grateful acquiescence in that plenitude of reality to which the particular existent belongs" (*Visions of Presence* 7).

In the poet's words: ". . . true concentration appears—paradoxically—at the moment willed effort drops away" (*Nine Gates* 4). "Inspiration" begins:

Think of those Chinese monks' tales:
years of struggling
in the zendo, then the clink,
while sweeping up, of stone on stone . . .
It's Emily's wisdom: Truth in Circuit lies.

"Struggling" leads only to frustration. Struggling is struggling for a goal, with a purpose, with a desire to satisfy the ego's demands for achievement. Struggling produces more struggling. Ceasing to struggle produces the "clink," almost the sound of a key turning, the music of recognition and entrance. The poem confirms what Hirshfield says elsewhere: her poetry is underlaid with Buddhist wisdom but is perfectly clear without any special knowledge of the Oriental tradition. Zen and Dickinson juxtaposed merge effortlessly.[7]

As the poet says, when your writing hits a block, stop, take a walk, and perhaps (no guarantees here) "a fox walks by," a "quite real" fox (again, her nature is never merely metaphorical or symbolic but is always itself), and that serendipitous encounter will be (may be) the inspiration you need. Inspiration and the creative process, traditionally thought of as uniquely human phenomena, are depicted in imagery from the external natural world, implying the continuity of human and non-human, and the world's active role in the human creative process. The key: "stopping all thinking," which may strike some as anti-intellectual and confirm the pejorative association of nature writing with mindless, awe-struck, regressive worshipping of innocent nature. Clearly Hirshfield has no illusions about nature's innocence or benevolence.

Even so, the anti-intellectual connotation should be addressed. To stop thinking is not to cease thinking or to be thoughtless or to be nature's passive amanuensis. It is to move aside from one's ego-driven vision temporarily, during the poem's formative stages, and to short-circuit the egotistical striving that is associated with thinking, the analytical parsing of the world that takes nature by pieces in order to accumulate enough data to then propound a truth. Hirshfield says take nature whole, which requires a mode of apprehension other than thinking. One stops thinking until the fox walks by. The mode of artistic production is simply a different form of apprehending experience. As she says, "Art-making begins when the mind enters a condition different from everyday, discursive thinking—the condition Mozart called being completely himself and I have called concentration" (*Nine Gates* 37). This is also the condition she elsewhere calls "the willingness to become transparent, to offer oneself to the Other" (*Nine Gates* 47). Thinking and intelligence are very much evident in all Hirshfield's work, however, and we need to remember that while the monk only hears the clink when he stops struggling, years of struggling had to precede the cessation of struggling. A quotation in the poem summarizes the idea much better than any explication can: "'Enlightenment,' wrote one master,/'is an accident, though certain efforts make you accident-prone.'"

Art, then, is a happy accident, difficult to seek consciously and impossible to anticipate, yet striking some more often than others. Why? The poet's honesty and attentiveness, as mentioned before, are lightning rods for the electric moment. The poet's orientation, also, or mode of being in the world, invites accidents to happen. One understands better now why Hirshfield felt it necessary to spend eight years in a Buddhist monastery before plunging into her writing career full-time. The point of that experience is not the philosophy so much as the orientation of openness learned during years of concentrated meditation. The monastery made her a poet. From then on, poetry found her. One implication for poetry— rather than for the poet—is that art is impractical, a god you can prepare yourself to encounter, and thereby increase the odds of meeting, but not a god you can count on in time of need, not one to turn to for solutions to your problems. The world is still fearsome and cruel, as she continually reminds us, and art does not cure that, because art belongs to a different realm than the useful:

> The useful part
> of things is elegance—
> in mathematics, bridges.
> . . . . . .
> elegance solves
> for the minimum possible,
> then dissolves.
>> "Orange Oil in Darkness"

Art is the "Not quite unplanned for,/more the unexpected, impractical gift": not quite unplanned for, suggesting the poet's active openness in anticipation of art's arrival; but unexpected, which suggests the poet's surprise and wonder when the god shows up on the scene and opens the gate to beauty; and a gift, not earned but a result of the world's plenitude, its overflowing, given to the poet in the same way that the world fills the woodthrush and compels him to sing. Oddly, one is again reminded of a Calvinist grace, absent the disdain for the average human sinner: grace unearned and delivered as an overflowing of love. "Art lives in a plenitude," Hirshfield says.

The poet's only responsibility, it seems, is to embrace the entire plenitude; her only possible sin, to refuse any part of the world. Refusal of the world is tantamount to self-refusal, given Hirshfield's continuum theme. Turning from the world's cruelties is like denying one's own demons, living inauthentically, and eventually poisoning oneself as the denied portions fester in one's soul. The poet's obligation to the world, then, as poet is the same as her obligation to herself, as person: live fully, be attentive, accept all, live and write from a posture of faith. She uses St. Francis as her model that "it is possible to cast yourself/on the earth's good mercy and live" ("Happiness"). She would be like the "actress from a Sanskrit poem" mentioned in "The Gift": her "greatness was showing two feelings at once:/ The mercies are boundless. Every country is death's." In her "Letter to Hugo from Later," a poetic epistle to the late writer, modeled on his collection of similar letters, *31 Letters and 13 Dreams* (1977), she notes the differences between the two poets' work:

> I envy the way you managed to pack so many parts of
> the world
> in such a little space, the way you'd go from pouring
> a glass
> of beer to something American and huge. I don't
> write much
> about America, or even people.

Despite their differences, they both know that the "one thing no poet does is look away." Her friend is dying ("Salt Heart"), apparently slowly and painfully ("even his wrists thinned with pain"). While she is understandably distraught and sympathetic with his suffering, she knows it is futile—even sinful—to look away or curse the night:

> The river Suffering would take what it
> wished of him, then go. And I would stay
> and drink on, as the living do, until the rest
> would enter into that water. . . .

From the Zen perspective, true suffering is produced by the effort to avoid the inevitable suffering. As Masao Abe says,

> The more we try to cling to pleasure and avoid suffering,
> the more entangled we become in the duality of pleasure
> and suffering. It is this whole process which constitutes
> Suffering (*An Introduction to Zen Buddhism* 206).

The ferryman walks always in our shadow. Only by being true to that vision can we write authentic poetry or live authentic lives: "I begin to believe the only sin is distance, refusal./All others stemming from this."

However, the poet must do more than simply acknowledge the river Suffering and not turn from it. She must greedily drink from that river:

> I want the place
> by the edge-flowers where
> the shallow sand is deceptive,
> where whatever
> steps in must plunge,
> and I want that plunging.
> I want the ones
> who come in secret to drink
> only in early darkness,
> and I want the ones

who are swallowed.
                    "Lake and Maple"

Hirshfield reminds us here of Whitman, consuming all, accepting all, embracing all, gulping down large chunks of experience, bitter and sweet indiscriminately. Refuse nothing in life,
refuse nothing in poetry: be, like the world itself, "without
judgment or comment." She understands Whitman's "procre-
ant urge."

   Desire, in fact, ultimately binds Hirshfield, as poet and
human, to the earth. Desire "pins us/to this world we thieve
and thieve from, want without pause . . ." ("The Thief"). Desire
is her gravity, a post-judgmental elemental force that swallows
and is swallowed. Desire is her muse and underlies her
repeated heart imagery and her general poetic technique of
immersion. She wants to get inside of everything, see from the
inside out, penetrate the heart of the world as she penetrates
her own heart, write visions of the interior. This is not the
"unpardonable sin" of Hawthorne, the dispassionate probing of
another's heart for its potential plunder. Hirshfield immerses
herself in the world's heart as a lover, giving her own heart
unselfishly and completely:

> I want to give myself
> utterly
> as this maple
> that burned and burned
> for three days without stinting
> and then in two more
> dropped off every leaf. . . .

   Desire starts in infancy, "from the first sound/of heartbeat
inconceivably there," and shifts its shape throughout life but

never disappears: "Always there is desire" ("Lullabye"). In perhaps her most Whitmanesque passage, Hirshfield catalogues what she loves, repeating "love of" seven times while focusing on images of aging and diminishing powers (for example, "the delicacy/that abandons the wrists" and "the strength/that is passing from the legs"). The goal of all this desire is connection, union with the world, making one's life a living continuum with the non-self, out of which will come poetry:

> And love of self that was once so clear
> grows suddenly simple, widens,
> as a mother's hand smoothing a sheet,
> as water that broadens and flattens,
> taking the shape of the darkened, still-reflecting
> world.

Poetry, then, is simply an extension of living, which is loving, based on an intense longing for connection and continuum. Hirshfield is no "transparent eyeball." Her favorite organ is the heart.

And the heart is very much a sensual as well as an emotional organ. Like Whitman, Hirshfield is a poet of the body and the soul, privileging neither, renouncing nothing, joining all in her vision of the continuum of life's processes. The sacred invests the profane as the profane joins hands with the sacred. Desire is physical and visceral. Desire is spiritual. The second section in *Of Gravity and Angels,* entitled "For What Binds Us," is devoted to love poems. In an interview, the poet comments on the section:

It's a section which basically tells the story of a relationship. And when I began putting *The October Palace*
together, I thought, where are the love poems? Then I
looked and I realized, they're everywhere, just not so
narrowly defined. To some extent it's a vocabulary choice.
One can say love, one can say gravity, one can say passion, and I feel there's not such a big distinction between
that emotion and the larger emotion that we feel in the
realm of the sacred or in the realm of the physical
(Hatcher n.p.).

The section begins at the surface of desire, moves inward, joins
two bodies and two hearts, and then moves seamlessly out into
the night air, all of humanity, the cosmos, and the sacred, never
abandoning or losing touch with the home base of physical
desire. The sacred and profane merge seamlessly, so naturally
that their identity does not require more than a passing
acknowledgment:

> . . . and I want
> all the unnamable, soft, and yielding places,
> belly & neck & the place wings would rise from
> if we were angels,
> and we are. . . .
> "Of Gravity & Angels"

"Desire," the first poem, describes a latent longing rekin-
dled by proximity, perhaps as the speaker reacquaints herself
with a former lover. Throughout the series, desire and sensuality are metaphorically linked to northern California flora and
fauna. Here, latent desire is like "manzanita/seed waiting a
fire." The desire, once reawakened, is overwhelming, irresistible

(again, like grace), and sweeps the speaker away on a tide of longing that begs to be compared to an ocean wave, and it is:

> desire,
> simple to say,
> and all the decision pours out of my life,
> leaving me buoyant, empty, to float
> towards your hand.

"Decision" and rationality are represented as weighty burdens, in this context deadly burdens that would bear the speaker to the bottom of the sea if not jettisoned first, thrown overboard by desire. The hand reaches out, almost god-like, to gather in the floating desirer without her ever seeming subservient or inferior to the bearer of the hand. "Empty" suggests the need to be filled, or at least the possibility of being filled, and the desire turns explicitly sexual and feminine. Looking back, we recall the manzanita seed, and note that the desire was already couched in female imagery.

The ability and willingness to abandon thought, choice, and decision in the presence of desire and to join oneself to another in love is analogous to the relinquishing of rational boundary-drawing and the willingness to join with the undifferentiated whole of one's perception that is required in the creative process. To have the courage and strength to abandon the ego's need for separation and self-protection in the act of love and in the act of creation are parallel processes. One gives oneself to the outside, lives temporarily without a skin. The reward is the filling back up that the other person's love does to us. As Hirshfield says in "Happiness" in *The October Palace*, "what else might happiness be/than to be porous, opened, rinsed through/by the beings and things?" Ehrenzweig makes a similar point:

> One can say that all good personal relationships contain
> an element of creativeness. This entails a measure of gen-
> erosity, humility and a lack of envy. We must not only be
> able to give away parts of our self to a loved person, but
> must be willing to take them back into ourselves enriched
> by the accretions stemming from the other's independent
> personality (*The Hidden Order of Art* 105).

We can never predict what we are going to get back from the
other, whether that other is a lover or the world we encounter
as we attempt a poem. However, we can neither give nor
receive unless we are open and get our ego out of the picture,
an act of courage. Or, again quoting Ehrenzweig, "If a neurotic
person has to dominate and control another person in order to
love him, he can only take back from him what he himself
deliberately put into him" (105). We see that both processes—
of desire and creativity—are a reflection of Hirshfield's basic
understanding of her relationship to place—the inside and the
outside are not sides at all but are ultimately pieces of a loving,
creative whole.

The speaker's hands do the gathering in the second poem,
"To Drink": "I want to gather your darkness/in my hands. . . ."
Desire continues to be represented through natural imagery:
her desire is like "a moth" at "the bedroom window," "beating
and beating its wings against cold glass"; it is also similar to "the
way a horse will lower/his long head to water, and drink. . . ."
Questions occur: what do those two metaphors have in common that allows them to describe the same phenomenon? And
what is "your darkness"? Both metaphors again suggest the
irresistibility of desire, for the moth is driven biologically to
hammer away at the window even if it kills itself in the process,

and the horse ignores its own fear—pausing to lift its head to look, but then going back to its water—to get what it needs. The metaphors balance in another way: the horse is being nourished, while the moth will probably be found dead on the ground outside the window the next morning. Both, however, suggest the overwhelming power of desire and need. The "darkness" of line one is apparently synonymous with the "everything" repeated twice in the last two lines: when the horse drinks, it takes "everything in with the water,/everything." As the poet, in Hirshfield's aesthetics, must turn away from nothing, so the lover takes everything of the lover's, even the "darkness," an ominous word suggesting shadow, perhaps even the shame with which our culture shrouds desire. Here the darkness is the mystery of the other, the other not yet known fully but only desired, only touched by the hand. The darkness is a feature of the other's internal geography that has not yet been revealed. One has to enter that geography with faith, the faith of the drinking horse, because as one takes in the water one must be willing to take in whatever enters with the water. One will have neither the time to reject nor the possibility of rejecting any of the water-borne elements before they are ingested, perhaps to contaminate as well as nourish the drinker. Once more, Ehrenzweig shows the connection to the creative process: "As it is, the creative thinker has to make a decision about his route without having the full information needed for the choice. This dilemma belongs to the essence of creativity" (*The Hidden Order of Art* 37).

The reader can hear the desire in the poems straining to move beyond the superficial touch of hands. In the third poem, "In Your Hands," the speaker enters the internal world of the lover, through the traditional gates of the eyes, but not without first linking her desire once again to the natural world: "I begin to grow extravagant,/like kudzu. . . ."[8] Physical touch soon leads to emotional and psychological union:

> Taking your peregrine tongue,
> your legs, your eyes,
> home to shuttered windows,
> to the cool rooms
> that invent themselves
> slowly into life.

The relationship between desire and creativity is affirmed as the union of lovers next becomes a poem, a song to the world, a separate entity that moves beyond the lovers out into the world, as the poet discovers,

> how what we begin we only think is ours,
> how quickly it passes from reach,
> some other life throating the air
> until it is utterly lovely and changed.
>   "The Music Like Water"

From a simple touch that breaks boundaries, love unites those broken elements and then moves beyond the union as naturally as bird song on a summer night. Plunging into the darkness of another's interior rooms, however, is always risky. The speaker of the poems is fearless yet patient, apparently content to wait while the lover's cool interior rooms emerge from their reticent darkness and clarify themselves to her vision. Again, the merging of bodies is parallel to the breaking of boundaries between inner and outer that takes place during the creation of poetry:

. . . I wonder then how is it
we even know which part we are,
even know the ground that lifts us, raucous,
out of ourselves. . . .
                    "Of Gravity & Angels"

Doubt persists, however, about how clear another's interior can ever become. Even while sleeping next to each other, all defenses down, all conscious reserve put to sleep, when "we are one geography,/every part of us inked on a map" where "continents' edges inexplicably match" ("Sleeping"), depths remain unexplored and perhaps unexplorable, provoking a rare note of frustration:

I move closer to you in the dark,
feel the slow heat
that embers you deeper into the night.
Where all fires descend a few hours
into their own slow-dreaming hearts.
Where the ravine hides in its own steepness
no matter how long, how fiercely we love.

The fire and light imagery, begun in "Desire," finds its complement in the darker imagery of shuttered windows and shadowed ravines that refuse to give up their deepest secrets, nestled in the angle the walls make on the far side of the room or in the impenetrable blackness at the foot of the cliff.

Hirshfield could not exclude the darker shades from her love poetry and be consistent with her vision. Like all phenomena, love has to make room for death and loss, grief and sadness, unfulfilled desire: "Even the language tells it: to satisfy and sadness rooted on one stock" ("Toward the Solstice"). The

end is always near. We are destined to awake one day and discover that the hills of our love "are a little less green than they
were." "Nothing lasts," she tells us, "only that desire/to which
you come as to a well." Pound tells us that "what thou lovest
well remains." Hirshfield tells us that nothing remains except
desire itself, and even desire is a kind of death. In "A Different
Rising," she explains:

> But mostly we are made
> of a heavier stuff,
> the slow descent of breast,
> foot-arches flattening towards earth,
> the hundred ways the body longs for home.

The movement of all matter toward home, toward death, aided
by gravity, is an act of love, both the love of the earth for the
return of its children and the love of the children for return to
their parent. Sex, love, death, physical descent, spiritual ascent,
physical rising, angels' wings on aroused flesh: the poet weaves
them all together, illustrates the union of all life's apparent
opposites, the connection of love to death, the underlying base
of desire that binds all things together, and shows us without
the least hint of a contrived effort the beauty of our need even
as it becomes death, perhaps makes itself a willing offering to
life's need for death:

> While in the water bird's throat,
> the white, visible pulse of a fish.
> Between being and becoming,
> turning wildly
> as it falls.

The fish is life ("pulse") seeking its home inside the bird's desire, as "the body longs for home." "Death," we are reminded, "is the mother of beauty."

The key to remember and the key Hirshfield saves for the final poem in the group ("For What Binds Us"), is that love binds us. Love is as elemental a force in the universe as gravity: "There are names for what binds us:/strong forces, weak forces." Love is a presence holding together the cosmos, not a weak-hearted poet's invention. One of love's offices is to wound us, as does gravity, but in the wounding to be taught and strengthened and made into fit residents of this universe:

> And see how the flesh grows back
> across a wound, with a great vehemence,
> more strong
> than the simple, untested surface before.

And like all elemental forces, love is eternal. We have seen how love may die, how love may even lead to death, but, true to the principle of conservation, love itself never disappears once it has come into the world:

> And when two people have loved each other
> see how it is like a
> scar between their bodies,
> stronger, darker, and proud;
> how the black cord makes of them a single fabric
> that nothing can tear or mend.

Thus is Hirshfield's concept of love and desire built upon her understanding of the relationship between the human and the place outside the human: the world itself is "a single fabric" of which we are all single threads attaining our identity within the whole, while our identity gives the whole its beauty, a fabric bound together by one element, love or desire, that shares the fabric's basic characteristic of inclusiveness without boundaries.

CONCLUSION

$\mathcal{T}$he poets discussed in this book are only a fragment of the poetic history of the American West. A sad fact of our region's literary history is that too many of our poets receive too little attention. The earliest writings of the West—diaries, journals, stories of settlement—were prose almost by necessity, but with settlement and population increase came a greater range of literary production. Readers, however, have been slow to catch on. Many good poets live and have lived in the West, and perhaps the literary world now could benefit from extended discussions of some of those neglected poets whose lives and work were formed west of the hundredth meridian. The poets discussed here have long understood how to treat the world around them, which in itself would be a good reason to study them, and have long understood what academics are now beginning to understand, that nature is neither a mystical other, nor fodder for progress, nor a blank slate upon which the imagination can freely project its products. The passion of the new lover, the indifference of the anthropocentric developer, and the egotism of the alienated are all inadequate responses to the world in their different ways.

Ironically, perhaps the western poets' ecologically mature vision is one hindrance to their greater acknowledgment. Most contemporary literary critics have been trained to accept as a given, in Robert Nelson's words, "that the human condition disallows any discovery of meaning or value because the human entity is fundamentally estranged from the world as 'Other'" (*Place and Vision* 3). This "Euroamerican humanistic tradition" results in critics' resistance to "the notion that the land has a life of its own and tends instead to proceed as though vitality were a quality imposed on the land by human imagination but not vice-versa" (*Place and Vision* 7). By contrast, the poets in this book, as well as many others of the West not mentioned here, illustrate the mature concern of the informed—informed by science, experience, and spirit—for the land around them, understanding that "around them" is a convenience of speech. They, the poets, and it, the land, are part and parcel of the same phenomenon, the universe. This is the voice we hear over and over in the poets, past and present, of the American West.

Another historical problem is that Americans have always been ambivalent about nature, wilderness, and the outdoors. The Puritans considered anything outside the town limits as Satan's lair, a "hidious & desolate wildernes," as William Bradford put it, "full of wild beasts & wild men" (*Of Plymouth Plantation* 60), both of whom needed some good Christianizing before one could safely consort with them. In the seventeenth and early eighteenth centuries, as Roderick Nash points out, the Puritans conceived of themselves as engaged in a cosmic "manichean battle" (*Wilderness and the American Mind* 36) between light (cultivation, city) and darkness (the wild), so the westward expansion was a great moral as well as practical endeavor. Later, the settling of the open lands validated democracy and independence and gave Americans an "achievement" to compare to Europe's culture and history (*Wilderness and the American Mind* 42). Independence brought with it the need to point to something distinctly American and valuable, something Europeans did not have, as we did not have the

Europeans' culture, a fact ably illustrated by Henry James when listing all the things Nathaniel Hawthorne did not have available to him—all "the items of high civilization" including everything from the aristocracy to castles and manors to the sporting class—that seemed to James to be required before any author could get started (*Hawthorne* 43).

What America did have, however, was nature. Even Washington Irving, in his account of the cultural glories of Europe (*The Sketch Book,* originally published in 1820), had to acknowledge America's superiority in matters of natural splendor:

> Her mighty lakes, like oceans of liquid silver; her mountains, with their bright aerial tints; her valleys, teeming with wild fertility; her boundless plains, waving with spontaneous verdure; her broad, deep rivers, rolling in solemn silence to the ocean; her trackless forests, where vegetation puts forth all its magnificence; her skies, kindling with the magic of summer clouds and glorious sunshine— no, never need an American look beyond his own country for the sublime and beautiful of natural scenery (14).

Irving was more impressed with Europe's "accumulated treasures of age" (14) than with America's lakes and mountains, and James saw no great value in America's natural glories ("In the United States . . . there were no great things to look at (save forests and rivers . . . [85]), but at least in some nineteenth-century quarters, America's wilderness became a source of national pride, a revaluation urged on not only by nationalistic forces but also by Romanticism's fascination with the primitive and Edmund Burke's recognition that beauty—the sublime—can reside in the awesome as well as the well-ordered landscape. As Nash says, "While other nations might have an occasional wild

peak or patch of heath, there was no equivalent of a wild conti-
nent" (*Wilderness and the American Mind* 69).

The gradual disappearance of the wilderness only made it
more valued, as often happens when scarce resources become
scarcer, and Frederick Jackson Turner's declaration in 1893 that
the frontier no longer existed guaranteed that, despite the fact
that most Americans are land developers at heart, the outdoors
will always be the magnet for Americans who want to escape
the ironic barbarism of the city and regenerate themselves spiritually. The ambivalence—development and conquest versus
preservation and reverence—remains strong and can be illustrated by a July visit to a Montana trout stream. The preservers
and reverencers battle for enough streamside space to make a
decent back-cast, while the developers and conquerors turn the
adjacent banks into small housing developments for the rich.
The depth of our ambivalence is highlighted by the fact that,
when the fishermen put away their rods, they often turn out to
be the developers. We revere wilderness while wondering just
which direction to orient our new house after we save enough
money to buy some river-view property.

To complicate matters, too often we Americans assume
that the only "real" way to respect nature is to escape into it, to
live permanently, or semi-permanently, as Thoreau lived for
two years at Walden Pond. We feel hypocritical claiming to
value place and nature while sitting in the office or on the
couch. We seem to think that if we are "truly" going to experience nature, even temporarily, we have to be on vacation in a
tent, suffering deprivation, dirt, and a little fear. Neither willing
nor able to change our lives to accommodate those possibilities,
we try to ignore nature and pretend we have nothing to do with
it. The value—one value—of the poets discussed here, and
their brother and sister poets of the West and elsewhere (one

thinks immediately of Mary Oliver, a New Englander with one of the finest natural sensibilities in verse today) is that they show us that we are in nature all the time, that we need not feel guilty about not being "out" in nature daily, and that as human beings we already enjoy a profound relationship with the natural world. The flip side of this new benefit is responsibility. We could modify Sartre and say that we are "doomed" to be natural creatures, whether we like that or not, and that status commits us to be aware that non-human nature's concerns are our concerns, and the non-human nature's future (or lack of it) is also ours. Hence, the poets of this study are more worthy of being read now than ever before, all the more shame that too many of them do not enjoy a wider audience.

One unexpected, and very non-western, source for this same awareness of the ongoing relationship between the human and the non-human is the German philosopher Georg Hegel, as explicated by philosopher Thomas Auxter in his article "Poetry and Self-Knowledge in Rural Life." In our culture, the self most commonly "establishes and recognizes its capacities and powers" ("Poetry and Self-Knowledge in Rural Life" 17), that is, acquires self-knowledge, by establishing control over what is outside itself, by "conquering a new world or surpassing a previous record" (17). Hegel, in *Enzyklopadie* (*Logik* 94), calls this the attitude of a "naïve consciousness" (17) destined to produce nothing more than what he calls a "wrong (or false) infinite" (17), a simple quantitative measure of itself, "a false god [that] like all false gods . . . lures us into vain and fruitless endeavors that undermine our ability to live well, squandering life energies on an unreachable goal" (17), that is, the goal of total mastery and security. As a result of such a naïve conscious-ness, we "limit . . . what we can know of [others'] lives and what we can know of ourselves because the investigation has been narrowed to the terms of knowledge of abilities exercised in competition" (18).

The normally prescribed alternative to this dead-end method of conquering the outside world is introspection, which, Hegel warns, simply shifts "the theater of human activ-ity . . . from exteriority to interiority" (19), substituting escaping the world for mastering the world. Based as it is in rejection of and alienation from the external, introspection as a path to self-knowledge and self-awareness is doomed to reflect "the impov-erished world it rejects," for "the terms and conditions of flight are dictated by that from which one is fleeing" (19).

Both methods suggest a hostile relationship to the other, resulting in a desire to conquer or escape the world, and nei-ther method will ever be able to produce a life or a self-knowl-edge that goes beyond frustration. Hegel suggests another method. He argues that the most beneficial relationship to the world outside requires giving up egoistic claims to victory over the other or self-definition in opposition to the other, affirming instead one's essential connection with the rest of life, and seek-ing integration into the networks of relationships with other liv-ing beings (19-20), which we are here taking to be all things human and non-human.

This affirmation of a "shared identity" with all around one, other people and the entire world, is the only true path to what Hegel calls the "genuine infinite" (20), a process that allows us "to be at home with ourselves in the other because it is no longer alien" (20). We and all others are cohabitants of one reality and identity. The prescription is not for a mystical one-ness that denies differences, but for an awareness of how "diverse beings fit into an organic unity" (20). Appreciating our likeness to others is therefore bound up in appreciating all beings' differences. Finding ourselves at home in the world and properly oriented to it, we have achieved the satisfaction of knowing ourselves, the goal of true and mature self-knowledge. The artists discussed here acknowledge the Other as not-Other, as one "no longer alien," in Hegel's words, and make that premise the basis of their self-knowledge, which becomes the basis of their art, which affirms the possibility of working within the "Euroamerican humanistic tradition" while continuing to respect and understand the profound value of place in their lives and work. Such a mature understanding should recommend poets of the American West to a much larger audience.

CHAPTER ONE

1. With her family, Church moved in her first year from New Mexico to Detroit and lived there until 1910. She attended boarding schools in Connecticut and California, enrolled for two years at Smith College, and lived a year in Berkeley with her husband. In a 1979 review of *New and Selected Poems*, Rodney Nelson asks a provocative question and makes a good point about Church's choice of residence and her relative obscurity:

   > Did she choose obscurity by remaining close to her New Mexico birthplace, living there, publishing there, joined to the soul of that landscape while other poets of her age were establishing Greenwich Village as a spiritual home detached from place? The curricula of modern American literature evolved in New York, reflecting the concerns of those who were published by the great houses; only in the last decade has an alternative denomination begun to appear in the regions, and Peggy Church just happened to do long ago what others are doing now (36).

2. The statement is written in the margin of a 1982 paper on the poem "Ultimatum for Man" by James Maguire in Box 3, Folder 24 of the Peggy Pond Church Papers, Center for Southwest Research, General Library, University of New Mexico (hereafter referred to as Papers).

3. For biographical information, I am indebted to Shelley Armitage's *Peggy Pond Church*, Boise: Boise State University, 1993; to Armitage's introduction to Church's collected poems, *This Dancing Ground of Sky;* and to the Papers.

4. From "Autobiographical Outline," a letter Church wrote in response to a request for biographical information, Box 3, Folder 34, Papers.

5. From "The Environment," a typed nine-page mediation written to Lawrence Clark Powell in response to Powell's letter of March 16, 1978, Box 4, Folder 59, Papers.

6. Journal entry for February 7, 1972, Box 4, Folder 13, Papers.

7. From "Meditation" of May 28, 1968, Box 4, Folder 40, Papers.

8. Ibid., July 23, 1969, Box 4, Folder 24, Papers.

9. Ibid., June 25, 1967, Box 4, Folder 96, Papers.

10. Ibid., May 28, 1968, Box 4, Folder 40, Papers.

11. Ibid., April 29, 1968, Box 4, Folder 24, Papers.

12. In the margin of the 1982 Maguire paper, Church hand-writes, "I loathe poetry that makes 'statements.' (I think.)" Box 3, Folder 24, Papers.

13. Rodney Nelson's remark should be noted here. Nelson says that "Church's vision of nature is one that is totally, if not painfully, fused with the existence of the visionary: there is no dualism of self and the world, of humans and earth, or of Mother Nature as against a pitiless, fanged devourer" ("The Necessity of Love" 36). Nelson uses the word "dualism" slightly differently, however.

14. Poli-kota is the Pueblo word for butterfly (Armitage, *Church* 28).

CHAPTER TWO

1. Even the connotations of the term "cowboy" have been transformed from derisive to laudatory to suit the culture's needs. As Don Russell notes,

    > . . . less than a century ago, the very word cowboy was derogatory, disreputable, opprobrious, even infamous. Early notable use of "Cowboys" in American annals was to denote bands of irregulars, banditti, or outlaws operating in the Neutral Ground between the British forces occupying New York City during the American Revolution and the American forces hovering about the upper Hudson in ineffective but persistent siege ("The Cowboy" 7).

    Russell goes on to note a report in a Las Vegas newspaper of 1881:

    > It is possible that there is not a wilder or more lawless set of men in any country that pretends to be civilized than the gangs of nomads that live in some of our frontier states and territories and are referred to in our dispatches as "the cow boys" (8).

The President, Chester A. Arthur, in the same year "denounced" a band of "armed desperadoes known as 'Cowboys'" ("The Cowboy" 8) for their role in disrupting the peace of Arizona Territory. Clearly, the cowboy has not always been our national hero. The poets, often eastern transplants, helped create the image of the noble individual, with the help of dime novels, B-Westerns, rodeos, and, above all, the American need for a hero.

Regardless of the connotations attached to the word "cowboy," it seems that the term was not even used widely as a purely descriptive term for an occupation until the 1880s. Earlier, the term "drover" was preferred for a herdsman (Jordan 62-63). The switch came about because editors of dime novels needed a romantic term to use in the increasingly popular Westerns (Jordan 63).

2. Exceptions to the rule exist, and the rule itself may be changing as miners and cowboys find themselves with more common ground, and less ground to call their own, as they lose more and more of it to real-estate developers, a group who remain anathema to both cowboy poets and miner poets. A recent book of mining poems, *Rhymes of the Mines: Life in the Underground,* is published by a Phoenix couple named Mason and Janice Coggin. They call their operation Cowboy Miner Productions. The first Gathering of Mining Poets was held in November, 1999, at the Western Folklife Center in Elko, Nevada, which is the home of the largest cowboy poetry gathering, and dates to 1985.

3. Ramsey's poem carries an interesting echo of an earlier ballad, "Song of the Bottle," by E. A. Brubacker:

>   They smile a little thinkin'
>   Of times that used to be,
>   When they were free and a-ridin',
>   A-ridin' the herd like me.

4. Another possible angle on the cowboy's relative indifference to female companionship is that the cowboy's knowledge, earned in labor on the land, is consolation for his enforced solitude, also a result of laboring on the land. The cowboy is forced to live alone, so he turns that deprivation into an honor and a virtue; he elevates a deprivation into a valued feature he acts as if he has chosen. The one who is set apart by economic necessity learns to value being set apart as a mark of virtue freely chosen.

5. An extreme example of cowboy poets' respect for Native Americans is Wesley Beggs' poem, "Twenty Years Ago," which lays all burdens at the white man's feet:

> The white man did it all, old Pard,
>   On him I lay the wrong
> In forcing the Red Man's heritage
>   To sing the white man's song.

6. The hostility toward "book larnin" is not unique to McRae. In "Cowboyology," Dan Bradshaw takes a swipe at Ph.D.s, but goes on to question the value of education in general:

> Most schools won't have a single class
> Much less a credit course
> Ta teach a guy what he can learn
> Watchin' cows from a horse.

Bad grammar becomes a sign of having passed the cowboy initiation ritual.

7. The word "nostalgia" comes up several times in this chapter, so perhaps a definition is in order. Steven Heller and Julie Lasky, in their book *Borrowed Design: Use and Abuse of Historical Form*, a history of modern design, offer this analysis and definition of the word:

> With each new century—and now, a new millennium—the past is neatly, if artificially, severed from the future. This phenomenon can produce apocalyptic fever; but more often it produces a case of nerves. . . .
>
> Making its first appearance in print in 1770, at the dawn of the Industrial Revolution, *nostalgia* describes an acute longing for a past one may never have experienced, or that in all probability never existed. The idea of a particular home from which one has departed has been transferred to the idea of a general (indeed, over-general) history that is unrecoverable. But the attributes of both realms are the same: comfort, security, beauty, and innocence (*Borrowed Design* 68).

CHAPTER THREE

1. Haines' academic training is in art at the National Art School (1946-47), American University (1948-49), and the School of

Fine Art in New York (1950-52), where he studied with Hans Hoffman. In 1948 he won a sculpture prize given by the Corcoran Gallery.

2. Haines describes his formative years as a poet, both in and out of Alaska, in more detail in "Within the Words: An Apprenticeship" (*Fables* 3-15).

3. James R. Wilson has done the work of counting images in *Winter News:* "I count twenty direct references to darkness and fifty-seven references to that which is cold, icy, snowy, or frozen" ("Relentless Self-Scrutiny: The Poetry of John Haines" 21).

4. Oddly enough, John R. Carpenter, in a review of *The Stone Harp,* declares that "John Haines's manner of looking at animals is diametrically opposed to that of Gary Snyder" ("Comment" 167).

5. Haines' "solid bottom" may be an allusion to Thoreau's famous description, in the "Where I Lived, and What I Lived For" section of *Walden,* of the Realometer, the "hard bottom" underneath "the mud and slush of opinion, and prejudice, and tradition, and delusion, and appearance," upon which one may build a life.

6. James Wilson also notes that in Haines' first book, red dominates the color image.

7. The elemental diction and spare sentence structure have been noted by several readers, including Hecht ("Poetry Chronicle" 333), C. Allen ("Death and Dreams" 35), and Wilson ("Relentless Self-Scrutiny: The Poetry of John Haines" 21, 23-24).

8. Haines' desire for wholeness perhaps partially explains his profound dislike for much postmodern poetry and art. For example, in criticizing the work of John Ashbery, Haines says, "Poetry like this arises from a fundamental immaturity in the culture. Games, wordplay, snickers, nose-thumbing—a tabloid equivalent of the art; the equal in verse of a Warhol in painting, closer to a media event than an artistic one" ("Turning Inward" 71). By "immaturity," it seems, he means something roughly the opposite of or at least opposed to wholeness.

9. It would be unfair to suggest that there was complete consensus in the critical response to Haines' poems of the seventies. For example, Lawrence Raab concludes that "particularly weak are

the political poems of 'America'" (*The American Scholar* 538) from the 1971 book, *The Stone Harp*, while James Healey calls those same poems "the most powerful in the volume because Haines has a clear notion of the beliefs which he is rejecting" ("Roots" 271). Peter Stitt calls the work of *Cicada* (1977), "a book of changes" (*The Georgia Review* 476), while Hayden Carruth calls the poems of the same book "the mature work of one of our best nature poets, or for that matter one of our best nature writers of any kind . . ." ("Passionate" 87). Peter Wild asserts that the poems of *Cicada* are somewhat different, incorporating "history, home life, politics, and geography" (*John Haines* 30) and hypothesizes that the poet's divorce and new marriage, his growing into middle age, his experiences teaching, the Vietnam War, his travel within the country, and perhaps other facts "may have served to shake him out of his insularity" (*John Haines* 30).

10. Haines says: "The motivation in art is always the same: to renew contact with the world, to maintain a creative flow between the inner and the outer worlds—to have them, in fact one" (*Fables* 81).

CHAPTER FOUR

1. Adrian C. Louis published a new book of poems while this manuscript was in press: *Ancient Acid Flashes Back* (Reno: University of Nevada Press, 2000).

   On another issue, some readers may still object to a non-Indian writing about an American Indian's poetry. For example, before calling Louis' language "flaccid" (an interesting choice of words, given the poet's sexual preoccupations) and accusing Louis of being irresponsible, Rhoda Carroll almost declares herself unfit to pass judgment: "What can a New England *wasicu* professor understand about a Paiute teaching composition at Oglala Lakota College on the Pine Ridge Reservation of South Dakota?" (Review of *Among the Dog-Eaters* 92) For a persuasive and informed discussion of the issue, see Arnold Krupat, "Criticism and Native American Literature" in his *The Turn to the Native*.

2. Woody Kipp, reviewing *Ceremonies of the Damned*, admits that reading too much Louis is a bit masochistic: "Given the choice

of more of Louis' poetry of this type or staring at the sun through a high-powered telescope, I might take the telescope" ("Review" 42).

3. Leslie Ullman comes close to the same point when she says, in a review of *Among the Dog-Eaters*, that "it is a kind of insanity that Louis embraces as necessary to a maintenance of vital boundaries within himself—thorny barbed-wire boundaries hold him intact even as they tear at his skin" ("Betrayals and Boundaries" 190).

4. Further examples: Roger Weaver, reviewing *Fire Water World*, mentions the "clarifying and purging quality" ("Review" 72) of the poetry, as well as the poet's "unflinching severity of vision, the merciless eye upon the dreadful toll that has been exacted" (73). Craig Womack, in *American Indian Quarterly*, also reviewing *Fire Water World*, calls the poems, "starkly realistic" as well as "bleak and honest and appropriate" ("Review" 106). Denise Low, in a review of *Among the Dog-Eaters*, describes the poems as "grisly tales of poverty, prejudice, violence . . ." ("Review" 189). An unsigned review of the same book in *The Beloit Poetry Journal* calls the poems a record of "what brutal conflicts ravage an American Indian in this society that co-opts and corrupts" (44). Reviewing *Ceremonies of the Damned* as one of the "Best Books of 1997," Matthew Rothschild warns the reader that "There is no sentimentalizing here" ("Review" 42). Louis' prose fiction is no easier. In a review of *Wild Indians and Other Creatures*, Howard Meredith says that the book of stories "depicts a world so cruel that even such a mythical figure as Coyote cannot add his own destructive force to the chilling aspect of people's lives" ("Review" 431).

5. Having mentioned the darkness of Louis' work, it is only fair to mention that he can also be quite humorous. Several reviewers have noted the poet's "ironic humor" and its role as a "survival strategy." See, for example, the unsigned *Beloit* review (44) and Low ("Review" 190, 191).

6. In his poetry Louis resembles the Trickster, whose traits are identified by Laura Makarius ("Ritual Clowns" 66): exhibits an independence from and an ignoring of temporal and spatial boundaries (i.e., the Trickster wanders aimlessly and lives

beyond communities); is usually situated between the social cosmos and the other world or chaos; frequently exhibits some mental and/or physical abnormality, especially exaggerated sexual characteristics; has an enormous libido; has an ability to disperse and to disguise himself and a tendency to be multiform and ambiguous; may appear as a human with animal characteristics or vice versa; is involved in episodes that are creative, destructive, or simply amusing (i.e., is both creative and destructive); in keeping with trait #7, the Trickster tends to be ambiguously situated between life and death as well as between good and evil; is often ascribed to a role in which an individual normally has privileged freedom from some of the demands of the social code. Victor Turner ("Myth and Symbol" 578) supplies a similar list of traits.

7. In contrast to Ullman, Carroll disparages what she calls Louis' "continuing habit of externalizing blame" ("Review" 93).

CHAPTER FIVE

1. Sanford Pinsker agrees: "And for Hugo, the Pacific Northwest was the generating landscape" (*Three Pacific Northwest Poets* 57).

2. This point concurs with Dave Smith's assertion that "what [Hugo] has constantly in mind is survival and getting home" (*Local Assays* 106).

3. Again, this idea runs parallel to Smith's assertion that Hugo's "great theme is to speak of dispossession" (*Local Assays* 109), and, by implication, his great goal is to seek stability.

4. Hugo has said of himself that he feels like "a wrong thing in a right world" (*Town* 70). His work consists of eight books published between 1961 and 1980.

5. Smith, too, notes Hugo's antagonism to civilization, but he focuses on a different aspect of the conflict: "Hugo knows . . . that [civilization] is the anonymity which buries the fierce individual, and knows that the poet does not speak to crowds but to the single beleaguered spirit" (*Local Assays* 117).

6. Hugo was "fascinated with maps," as Dave Smith notes (*Local Assays* 112). Although his attitude toward contemporary culture places Hugo into what could be considered a liberal or leftist

tradition of cultural criticism, M. Allen is correct to note that the poet's desire for stability is essentially a "conservative impulse" (*Human* 40).

7.   Hugo has experience with simple madness, and it is not to his liking. As he describes the ordeal in an interview with Joe David Bellamy:

> My drinking became so heavy in Iowa City, when I taught back there in 1970 and 1971, that I ultimately suffered a kind of minor-league breakdown. I couldn't go on with my work. I had to be relieved of my teaching two weeks early. I had never done anything like that before—I'm an ultra-responsible kind of person in certain ways—and I was ashamed (*American Poetry Observed* 102).

The experience is alluded to in his poem, "Letter to Bell from Missoula":

> Dear Marvin: Months since I left broke down
>   and sobbing
> in the parking lot, grateful for the depth
> of your understanding and since I've been treated
> in Seattle and I'm in control like Genghis Khan.
> That was a hairy one, the drive west, my nerves
>   so strung
> I couldn't sign a recognizable name on credit slips.

Hugo's analyst reportedly interpreted the breakdown as being "motivated by the desire to keep alive the self-hatred that had for so many years been the psychological source of his poems, a self-hatred that was threatened by the public approval which his poems now earned him" (Holden 113-14). Holden, for reasons he does not specify, calls this a "suspiciously simple explanation" (*Landscapes of the Self* 114). Hugo, however, says in an interview that "I suppose that's why poets do drink, to keep alive a self worthy of rejection, deserving of rejection" (Bellamy 103), which seems to corroborate his analyst's interpretation of the incident.

8.   Smith says that Hugo "writes in a private code of the single confrontation of a man with an inevitable fate" (*Local Assays* 107) and later refers to the poet's "coded vocabulary" (114).

9. Zdenek Stribrny claims that the word "Kapowsin" is "Indian for 'lake-of-stumps'" ("The Poetry of Richard Hugo" 63). What tribal language the word is he does not specify.

10. This idea echoes Allen's assertion that "Hugo's towns are dominated by vast, unseen, and highly changeable economic and geographical forces" (*Human* 20).

11. Sanford Pinsker, when discussing this poem, knows that something must be ironic but stops short of asserting which line is the ironic one: "On which photograph does the sly shadow of irony fall" (*Three Pacific Northwest Poets* 84).

12. Hugo discusses this incident and others from his WWII experience in "*Ci Vediamo*" (*Town* 75-98).

13. Allen refers to the experience as a moment of "self-regeneration, and renewal" (*Human* 77).

14. Whether or not the moment's return is necessarily beneficial is a point of debate. Hugo says the moment "haunted me" as a kind of reproach "to remind me how we learn little from our positive experiences, how we slip back too easily into this ungenerous world of denial and possession" (*Town* 85).

15. In this way, his poetry resembles that of his friend, James Wright, whose first book was described by W. H. Auden as a celebration of "social outsiders."

16. Another poem, "Antiques in Ellettsville," contains a similar sentiment: "Here, the antiques/warn us to be tolerant of dust."

17. Another example of Hugo's lamenting the loss of something old that is judged worthless in the name of progress is "The End of Krim's Pad," in which the house of Krim suddenly finds itself in the path of a new freeway:

> When they plan a freeway thru a city
> they plan it deliberately thru places
> you love most. They take out houses people
> lived in years and people die in face
> of the fear of loss. We call this progress.

As the poem illustrates, the anti-progress theme can border on the paranoid or conspiratorial.

18. Pinsker mentions this Hugo persona: "Hugo adopted a 'fat man' persona early, partly from the girth his legendary appetite created (he could polish off a half-gallon carton of ice cream in a single sitting), partly from a need to see the world as an oddity, a comic outsider" (*Three Pacific Northwest Poets* 79). The fat man has also been noted by Gertsenberger (*Richard Hugo* 20) and Garber (Fat *passim*).

19. Smith, for example, notes that Hugo "does not show the radical alternation of style or thought which mark his contemporaries such as, say, Adrienne Rich, Robert Bly, James Wright, or Donald Hall. Indeed the poems he includes here [*Selected Poems*] reinforce the sense that Hugo was born to say one kind of poem and knew what it was from the start" (*Local Assays* 106).

20. Hugo is aware of his occasional tough-guy pose: "You'll notice that the men I wanted to be are strong men, men in control. Humphrey Bogart. Herbert Marshall. Each in his own way tough. My urge to be someone adequate didn't change after the war. When I gave up fiction as a bad job and settled back into poems for good, I seemed to use the poems to create some adequate self. A sissy in life, I would be tough in the poem" (*Town* 79).

21. 15th S. W. is the address of Hugo's boyhood home, the residence of his grandparents (*Human* 36).

22. Smith says that in Hugo's work, nature "is alien to man" (*Local Assays* 114), which is true in the sense that Hugo has no romantic illusions about nature's concern for humanity's plight. But Hugo insists on his love of nature and the influence of place on his work: "[I]f I were religious, I'd be an earth worshiper" (Bellamy 105).

23. Smith notes Hugo's ongoing "search for permanent, healthy, and reliable values" (*Local Assays* 108).

24. Smith asserts that Hugo "is not unaware of the fisherman's traditional role as a quasi-religious art figure, a visionary" (*Local Assays* 114).

25. As Allen says of *White Center:* "It is as if [Hugo] were trying to put something right . . ." (*Human* 133).

26. Along this line, Hugo has said that, "I'm inclined more and more to believe that writing, like sex, is psychogenic," but then

he qualifies that quickly with, "though I could probably be argued out of it" (*Town* xi).

27.   Hugo repeats the idea in another poem in *White Center:*

> And I feel nothing now except the faint dream
> time to time that had I stayed there
> in my makeshift room my poems would still be
> personal as doom, ring wild with fear
> until some troubled reader pounded on the door.
>   "Beaverbank"

Perhaps one could conclude that the speaker is pleased that his poems no longer are "personal as doom" nor "ring wild with fear," but the tone suggests a lament that by leaving this "makeshift room" the poet has lost some of his poetic potency, a type of fear that reveals the relationship between Hugo's persistent sexism and his fear of losing his creative power.

28.   Hugo's marriage to his first wife, Barbara Williams, ended in 1955 after fourteen years together. He married for the second time to Ripley Schemm on July 12, 1974 (Holden 16, 20).

29.   Rivers wash clean, too: "The cruel things I did I took to the river./I begged the current: make me better" ("The Towns We Know and Leave Behind, the Rivers We Carry with Us"). Later in the poem, Hugo says, "The river is there to forgive what I did," implying that he has reason to believe the river will answer his earlier prayer.

30.   About the direction north, Hugo says, "As a child, I believed life was a northern journey and at some unknown point in the north, all things end" (*Real West* 116).

31.   In one instance of his reconciliatory mood in *White Center,* he apologizes to the women he has turned into enemies in his poetry: "We have misused you,/invested you with primal sin. You bleed/for our regret we are not more" ("To Women"). Some critics ignore or seem not to notice Hugo's sexism. Others, like Hayden Carruth, find it so obvious that he allots it only an undefended, parenthetical remark: ("Masochism and sexism are conspicuous threads through all his work.") ("Here Today" 285). Adrienne Rich reportedly found Hugo "more honest" about his sexist attitudes than most men (Allen, *Human* 89).

CHAPTER SIX

1. While this manuscript was in press, Jane Hirshfield published a new book of poems: *Given Sugar, Given Salt*, New York: HarperCollins, 2001.

2. In *Imagining the Earth*, John Elder notes that Gary Snyder "has asserted on several occasions that Zen arises from the same emptying of self as hunting does" (*Imagining the Earth* 45). In a rather circuitous way, then, Hirshfield and Haines find themselves on common ground.

3. Elder also quotes from a Wendell Berry poem, "The Current," and a Robert Pack poem, "Rondo of the Familiar," in which the relationship between human and earth is captured by the marriage metaphor (*Imagining the Earth* 61, 63-64).

4. I want to suggest that this caution to not praise too much is different from the suggestion in James Harris' 1995 review of *The October Palace*, which is published in *The Antioch Review*, and states that, "These poems know the ruins, and place them lovingly beside the pristine and restored, all to be praised" ("Review" 122). The point is that "all" is not praised, but all is acknowledged.

5. In this attitude, Hirshfield can be compared to Peggy Church, who writes, "I do not believe in trying to save the earth but to understand it and endure it" (Box 3, Folder 24, Papers).

6. Defined by Joseph Campbell as a doctrine that says, "Everything, all the time, is causing everything else. . . . [The Doctrine] implies that no one—nobody and no thing—is to blame for anything that ever occurs, because all is mutually arising" (144).

7. In a review of *The October Palace*, James Harris makes a similar point:

   > Although the prevailing consciousness is Buddhist, the presiding influence is Dickinson. Like Dickinson, Hirshfield often manages to yoke the inner and the outer worlds into close quarters through the use of metaphysical conceits and surprising metaphors ("Review" 122).

8. Hirshfield's use of "extravagant" seems reminiscent of Thoreau's remark that he never feared being extravagant but only worried about not being extravagant enough.

WORKS CITED AND CONSULTED

Many of the works of cowboy poetry below, especially those limited-edition books, were found in the Fife Folklore Archives in the library of Utah State University, Logan, Utah. Many of the collections of cowboy verse are self-published, and therefore data about city and date of publication and publisher (often a local printer) are frequently unavailable. Any data found in the volume cited have been included.

Abe, Masao. *Zen and Western Thought*. Ed. William R. La Fleur. Honolulu: University of Hawaii Press, 1985.

Allen, Carolyn J. "Death and Dreams in John Haines' *Winter News*." *Alaskan Review* (Fall-Winter, 1969): 28-36.

Allen, Michael S. "'Because Poems Are People': An Interview with Richard Hugo." *The Ohio Review* 19.1 (Winter 1978): 73-90.

_____. "'License for Defeat': Richard Hugo's Turning Point." *Contemporary Poetry* 3.4 (Winter 1978): 59-74.

_____. "'Only the Eternal Nothing of Space': Richard Hugo's West." *Western American Literature* 15 (1980): 25-35.

_____. *We Are Called Human: The Poetry of Richard Hugo*. Fayetteville: University of Arkansas Press, 1982.

Allen, Paula Gunn. "Iyani: It Goes This Way." *The Remembered Earth: An Anthology of Contemporary American Indian Literature*. Ed. Geary Hobson. Albuquerque: University of New Mexico Press, 1980.

_____. "The Sacred Hoop: A Contemporary Perspective." *Studies in Indian Literature: Critical Essays and Course Designs*. Ed. Paula Gunn Allen. New York: The Modern Language Association of America, 1983.

Allmendinger, Blake. *The Cowboy: Representations of Labor in an American Work Culture*. New York: Oxford University Press, 1992.

American Poetry Observed. Ed. Joe David Bellamy. Urbana: University of Illinois Press, 1988.

Armitage, Shelley. "New Mexico's Literary Heritage." *El Palacio* 90. 2 (1984): 21-29.

_____. *Peggy Pond Church*. Boise: Boise State University, 1993.

Auxter, Thomas. "Poetry and Self-Knowledge in Rural Life." *Agriculture and Human Values* (Spring 1985): 15-27.

Babcock, Barbara and Jay Cox. "The Native American Trickster." Ed. Andrew Wiget. *Dictionary of Native American Literature*. New York: Garland, 1994.

Barsness, John. "The Dying Cowboy Song." *Western American Literature* 2 (Spring 1967): 50-7.

Barton, Owen J. *Saddle Talk*. 1984.

Basho, Matsuo. *The Narrow Road to the Deep North, and Other Travel Sketches*. Trans. Nobuyuki Yuasa. New York: Penguin, 1966.

Beggs, Wesley. *Rhymes from the Rangeland*. Denver: The Eastwood-Kirchner Printing Company, 1912.

Berry, Wendell. "The State of Letters: Speech After Long Silence." *Sewanee Review* (Winter 1996): 108-10.

Black, Baxter. *A Rider, A Roper, and a Heck'uva Windmill Man*. Denver: Coyote Cowboy Company, 1982.

Blair, Rob. *Poems of a Desert Cowboy*. 1984.

Blodgett, E. D. "Richard F. Hugo: Poet of the Third Dimension." *Modern Poetry Studies* 1 (1970): 268-72.

Bolick, Katie. "Some Place Not Yet Known: An Interview with Jane Hirshfield." The Atlantic Online <http://www.theatlantic.com/unbound/bookauth/jhirsh.htm>, unpaginated. Copyright 1997, The Atlantic Monthly Company.

Boruch, Marianne. "Comment: Blessed Knock." *American Poetry Review* (July-August, 1988): 39.

Bradford, William *Of Plymouth Plantation*. Ed. Harvey Wish. New York: Capricorn Books, 1962.

Bradshaw, Dan, *The Science of Cowboyology*. 1993.

Brininstool, E. A. *Trail Dust of a Maverick*. Los Angeles, 1921.

Brisendine, Everett. *One Man of a Kind.* 1976.

Brubacher, E. A. *Songs of the Saddle and Trails into Lonesome Lands.* Idaho Verse Series, vol. IV. Bess Foster Smith, Publisher.

Bruchac, Joseph. Back cover of Adrian Louis' *Fire Water World.* Albuquerque: West End Press, 1989.

Campbell, Joseph. *Myths to Live By.* New York: Penguin, 1972.

Cannon, Hal, ed. *New Cowboy Poetry.* Layton, Utah: Peregrine Smith Books, 1990.

Carnes, Rebecca. "Cowboy Poetry: A Sentimental Journey." *The Catch-Pen: A Selection of Essays from the First Two Years of the National Cowboy Symposium and Celebration.* Ed. Lew Ainsworth and Kenneth W. Davis. Lubbock: Ranching Heritage Center, Texas Tech University, 1991: 45-51.

Carpenter, John R. "Comment: Revalues." *Poetry* 120.3 (June 1972): 164-69.

Carr, Robert V. *Cowboy Lyrics.* Chicago: W. B. Conkey Company, 1908.

Carroll, Rhoda. Review of Adrian Louis' *Among the Dog-Eaters.* *American Indian Quarterly* 18.1 (Winter 1994): 92-94.

Carruth, Hayden. "Here Today: A Poetry Chronicle." *The Hudson Review* 24.2 (Summer 1971): 320-36.

_____. "The Passionate Few," *Harper's* 256 (June 1978): 86-89.

_____. "Richard Hugo." *Selected Essays and Reviews.* Port Townsend, Washington: Copper Canyon Press, 1996.

The Catch-Pen: A Selection of Essays from the First Two Years of the National Cowboy Symposium and Celebration. Ed. Lew Ainsworth and Kenneth W. Davis. Lubbock: Ranching Heritage Center, Texas Tech University, 1991.

Cattle, Horses, Sky, and Grass: Cowboy Poetry of the Late Twentieth Century. Ed. Warren Miller. Illustrated by Joe Beeler. Flagstaff: Northland Publishing, 1994.

Chapman, Arthur. *Out Where the West Begins.* Boston: Houghton and Mifflin Company, 1917.

Chappell, Fred. "Wise Saws When Last Seen." *The Georgia Review* 48.4 (Winter 1994): 784-99.

Church, Peggy Pond. *Birds of Daybreak: Landscapes and Elegies.* Santa Fe: William Gannon, 1985.

_____. *The Burro of Angelitos.* Los Angeles: Suttonhouse, 1936.

_____. *This Dancing Ground of Sky: The Selected Poetry of Peggy Pond Church.* Santa Fe: Red Crane Books, 1993.

_____. *Familiar Journey.* Santa Fe: Writers' Editions, 1936.

_____. *Foretaste.* Santa Fe: Writers' Editions, 1933.

_____. *The House at Otowi Bridge: The Story of Edith Warner and Los Alamos.* Albuquerque: University of New Mexico Press, 1959.

_____. *A Lament on Tsankawi Mesa.* Santa Fe: The Thistle Press, 1980.

_____. *New and Selected Poems.* Boise: Ahsahta Press, 1976.

_____. Papers, Center for Southwest Research, General Library, University of New Mexico, Albuquerque.

_____. *The Ripened Fields: Fifteen Sonnets of a Marriage.* Santa Fe: The Lightning Tree, 1978.

_____. *A Rustle of Angels.* Denver: Peartree Press, 1981.

_____. *Ultimatum for Man.* Stanford: James Ladd Delkin, 1946.

_____. *Wind's Trail: The Early Life of Mary Austin.* Santa Fe: Museum of New Mexico Press, 1990.

Clayton, Lawrence. "Elements of Realism in the Songs of the Cowboy." *Proceedings of the Second University of Wyoming American Studies Conference.* Laramie: University of Wyoming, 1982.

Cotter, James Finn. "Poets, Poems, and University Presses." *America* 138.13 (8 April 1978): 282-84.

Cowboy Poetry: A Gathering. Ed. Hal Cannon. Salt Lake City: Peregrine Smith Books, 1985.

The Cowboy: Six-Shooters, Songs, and Sex. Ed. Charles W. Harris and Buck Rainey. Norman: University of Oklahoma Press, 1976.

Cowboy Songs and other Frontier Ballads, Revised and Enlarged edition. Ed. John A. Lomax and Alan Lomax. New York: The Macmillan Company, 1938.

Crowley, Marcus. *Bunkhouse Ballads.* North Bend, Oregon: Wegferd Publications, 1972.

Dickey, James. "Public and Private Poetry." *The Hudson Review* 25.2 (Summer 1972): 295-308.

Doerry, Karl. "The American West: Conventions and Inventions in Art and Literature." *Essays on the Changing Images of the Southwest.* Ed. Richard Francaviglia and David Narrett. College Station: Texas A&M University Press, 1994: 127-53.

Dunsmore, Roger. *Earth's Mind: Essays in Native Literature.* Albuquerque: University of New Mexico Press, 1997.

The Ecocriticism Reader. Ed. Cheryll Glotfelty and Harold Fromm. Athens: University of Georgia Press, 1996.

Ehrenzweig, Anton. *The Hidden Order of Art.* Berkeley: University of California Press, 1967.

Elder, John. *Imagining the Earth: Poetry and the Vision of Nature.* 2nd edition. Athens: University of Georgia Press, 1996.

Elkins, Andrew. "'So Strangely Married': Peggy Pond Church's *The Ripened Fields: Fifteen Sonnets of a Marriage.*" *Western American Literature* 30.4 (1996): 353-72.

Espada, Martin. Review of Adrian C. Louis' *Among the Dog-Eaters. MELUS.* 20.3 (Fall 1995):160-62.

Essays on the Changing Images of the Southwest. Ed. Richard Francaviglia and David Narrett. College Station: Texas A&M University Press, 1994.

Eye on the Future: *Popular Culture Scholarship into the Twenty-First Century,* Eds, Marilyn F. Motz, John G. Nachbar, Michael T. Marsden, Ronald J. Ambrosetti. Bowling Green State Univeristy Popular Press, OH 1994. "The Heart of the Wise Is in the House of Mourning." Stephen Tatum (62).

Fife, Austin and Alta Fife. "Spurs and Saddlebags: Ballads of the Cowboys." *The American West* 7 (September 1970): 44-45.

Five Poets of the Pacific Northwest: Kenneth O. Hanson, Richard Hugo, Carolyn Kizer, William Stafford, David Wagoner. Ed. Robin Skelton. Seattle: University of Washington Press, 1964.

Fletcher, Bob. *Corral Dust.* Helena: State Publishing Co.

Garber, Frederick. "Fat Man at the Margin: The Poetry of Richard Hugo." *Iowa Review* 3.4 (1972): 58-69.

_____. "Large Man in the Mountains: The Recent Work of Richard Hugo." *Western American Literature* 4 (1975): 205-18.

Gardner, Gail. *Orejana Bull for Cowboys Only.* 1935.

Gardner, Thomas. "An Interview with Richard Hugo." *Contemporary Literature* 22.2 (1981): 139-52.

Geographies of the Mind: Essays in Historical Geosophy in Honor of John Kirtland Wright. Ed. David Lowenthal and Martyn J. Bowden. New York: Oxford University Press, 1976.

Gertsenberger, Donna. *Richard Hugo.* Boise: Boise State University, 1983.

Gough, L. *Spur Jingles and Saddle Songs: Rhymes and Miscellany of Cow Camp and Cattle Trails in the Early Eighties.* Amarillo: Russel Stationery, 1935.

Graining the Mare: The Poetry of Ranch Women. Ed. Teresa Jordan. Layton, Utah: Peregrine Smith Books, 1994.

Hadella, Paul. Review of Adrian Louis' *Vortex of Indian Fevers. Western American Literature* 31.3 (Fall 1996): 285-56.

"Roderick Haig-Brown: Angling and the Craft of Nature Writing in North America." *ISLE: Interdisciplinary Studies in Literature and the Environment* 51 (Winter 1998). 1-11.

Haines, John. *At the End of This Summer: Poems, 1948-1954.* Port Townsend, Washington: Copper Canyon Press, 1997.

_____. *Cicada.* Middletown, Connecticut: Wesleyan University Press, 1977.

_____. *Fables and Distances: New and Selected Essays*. St. Paul: Graywolf Press, 1996.

_____. "Homage to the Chinese." *The Ark* (1980): 41-44.

_____. *In a Dusty Light*. St. Paul: Graywolf Press, 1977.

_____. "In and Out of the Loop." *The Hudson Review* 46.2 (Summer 1973): 425-31.

_____. *In Five Years Time*. Missoula: SmokeRoot Press, 1976.

_____. *Leaves and Ashes*. Santa Cruz: Kayak Books, 1974.

_____. *The Legend of Paper Plates*. Santa Barbara: Unicorn Press, 1970.

_____. *Living Off the Country: Essays on Poetry and Place*. Ann Arbor: University of Michigan Press, 1981.

_____. "The Lure of the Hunt." *New York Times Book Review*. 142 (15 August 1993): 16.

_____. *The Mirror*. Santa Barbara: Unicorn Press, 1971.

_____. "The Nature of Art." *NEA Explore: Writer's Corner*. <http://arts.endow.gov/explore/writers/Haines.html>, unpaginated.

_____. *New Poems: 1980-88*. Brownsville, Oregon: Story Line Press, 1990.

_____. *News From the Glacier: Selected Poems, 1960-1980*. Middletown, Connecticut: Wesleyan University Press, 1982.

_____. "On a Certain Attention to the World." *The Ohio Review* 49 (1993): 75-84.

_____. *The Owl in the Mask of the Dreamer: Collected Poems*. St. Paul: Graywolf Press, 1993.

_____. *The Stars, the Snow, the Fire: A Memoir*. St. Paul: Graywolf Press, 1989.

_____. *The Stone Harp*. Middletown, Connecticut: Wesleyan University Press. 1971.

_____. *Suite for the Pied Piper*. Menomonie, Wisconsin: Ox Head Press, 196

_____. *The Sun on Your Shoulder*. St. Paul: Graywolf Press, 1976.

_____. "Turning Inward into Poetry." *The New Criterion* (June 1995): 68-72.

_____. *Twenty Poems*. Santa Barbara: Unicorn Press, 1971.

_____. *Winter News*. Middletown, Connecticut: Wesleyan University Press, 1966.

Hall, Donald. "The Lenore Marshall/*Nation* Poetry Prize, 1991." *The Nation* 253.18 (25 November 1991): 677.

Harris, James. Review of Jane Hirshfield's *The October Palace*. Antioch Review 53 (Winter 1995): 121-22.

Hatcher, Ashley. "Interview with Jane Hirshfield." *The University of Arizona Poetry Center Newsletter* 20.1 (Fall 1995) <http://www.coh.modlang.arizona.edu/poetry/nwsfl95.html>, unpaginated.

Healey, James. "Roots," *The Prairie Schooner* 46 (Fall 1972): 270-71.

Heath, Anne. "Cowboy Poetry." *Parabola* 17.3 (August, 1992): 42-48.

Hecht, Anthony. "Poetry Chronicle." *The Hudson Review* 19.2 (Summer 1966): 330-38.

Hedin, Robert. Review of John Haines' *The Owl in the Mask of the Dreamer*. *North Dakota Quarterly* 61.2 (Spring 1993): 190-94.

Heller, Steven and Julie Lasky. *Borrowed Design: Use and Abuse of Historical Form*. New York: Van Nostrand Reinhold, 1993.

Helms, Alan. "Writing Hurt: The Poetry of Richard Hugo." *Modern Poetry Studies* 9 (1978): 106-18.

Hirshfield, Jane. *Alaya*. New Jersey: *The Quarterly Review of Literature*, 1982.

_____. *Given Sugar, Given Salt*. New York: HarperCollins, 2001.

_____. *The Lives of the Heart*. New York: HarperCollins, 1997.

_____. *Nine Gates: Entering the Mind of Poetry*. New York: HarperCollins, 1997.

_____. *The October Palace*. New York: HarperCollins, 1994.

_____. *Of Gravity & Angels*. Hanover, New Hampshire: Wesleyan University Press, 1988.

Holden, Jonathan. *Landscapes of the Self: The Development of Richard Hugo's Poetry.* New York: Associated Faculty Press, 1986.

Howard, Richard. "Richard Hugo: Why Track Down Unity When the Diffuse is So Exacting." *Alone with America: Essays on the Art of Poetry in the United States since 1950.* New York: Atheneum, 1969: 232-46.

Howarth, William. "Some Principles of Ecocriticism." *The Ecocriticism Reader.* Athens, Georgia: University of Georgia Press, 1996.

Hudson, Marc. Review of John Haines' *The Owl in the Mask of the Dreamer. North Dakota Quarterly* 62.3 (Summer 1994): 210-18.

Hugo, Richard. *Making Certain It Goes On: The Collected Poems of Richard Hugo.* New York: W. W. Norton, 1984.

_____. "The Real West Marginal Way." *American Poets in 1976.* Ed. William Heyen. Indianapolis: Bobbs-Merril, 1976: 106-27.

_____. *The Real West Marginal Way: A Poet's Autobiography.* Ed. Ripley S. Hugo, Lois Welch, and James Welch. New York: W. W. Norton, 1986.

_____. *The Triggering Town: Lectures and Essays on Poetry and Writing.* New York: W. W. Norton, 1979.

_____. "The Writer's Situation." *New American Review* 11 (1971): 221-24.

Hurst, Mary Jane. "Connections Between Cowboy Poetry and Other Developments in American Literature and in American Culture." *The Catch-Pen: A Selection of Essays from the First Two Years of the National Cowboy Symposium and Celebration.* Ed. Lew Ainsworth and Kenneth W. Davis. Lubbock: Ranching Heritage Center, Texas Tech University, 1991: 31-37.

_____. "Linguistic Innovation & Conservatism: Dialect in Cowboy Poetry." *New Mexico Humanities Review* 36 (1992): 103-12.

The Interpretation of Ordinary Landscapes: Geographical Essays. Ed. D. W. Meinig. New York: Oxford University Press, 1979.

Irving, Washington. *The Sketch Book of Geoffrey Crayon, Gent.* New York: New American Library, 1961.

James, Henry. *Hawthorne.* London: Macmillan and Company, 1879.

Jones, Bill and Rod McQueary. *Blood Trails.* Lemon Cove, California: Dry Crik Press, 1993.

Jordan, Philip D. "The Pistol Packin' Cowboy." *The Cowboy: Six-Shooters, Songs, and Sex.* Ed. Charles W. Harris and Buck Rainey. Norman: University of Oklahoma Press, 1976: 57-84.

Jung, Carl. *Analytical Psychology: Its Theory and Practice,* The Tavistock Lectures. New York: Random House, 1968.

_____. *The Essential Jung.* Ed. Anthony Storr. Princeton: Princeton University Press, 1983.

_____. *Psyche and Symbol: A Selection from the Writings of C. G. Jung.* Ed. Violet S. de Laszlo. New York: Bollingen Foundation, 1958.

_____. Commentary and Introduction to *The Secret of the Golden Flower: A Chinese Book of Life.* New York: Harcourt, Brace and World, 1931.

_____. *Two Essays on Analytical Psychology.* New York: Meridian Books, 1956.

Kipp, Woody. Review of Adrian Louis' *Ceremonies of the Damned. Tribal College* 10.1 (Fall 1998): 42.

Kiskaddon, Bruce. *Rhymes of the Ranges and Other Poems.* 1947.

_____. *Rhymes of the Ranges: A New Collection of the Poems of Bruce Kiskaddon.* Ed. Hal Cannon. Layton, Utah: Gibbs-Smith, 1987.

Kittredge, William. "Introduction." *Outside* 20.4 (April, 1995): 66-67.

Klapp, Orrin. "The Clever Hero." *Journal of American Folklore* 67 (1954): 21-34.

_____. *Heroes, Villains, and Fools.* Englewood Cliffs: Prentice-Hall, 1962.

Krupat, Arnold. *The Turn to the Native: Studies in Criticism and Culture*. Lincoln: University of Nebraska Press, 1996.

de Laszlo, ed. *Psyche and Symbol: A Selection from the Writings of C. G. Jung*. New York: Bollingen Foundation, 1958.

Levinger, Larry. "Poet Richard Hugo: The Open Field Beyond." *Ploughshares* 18.1 (Spring 1992): 44-59.

Lincoln, Kenneth. *Native American Renaissance*. Berkley, California: University of California Press, 1983.

Logsdon, Guy. "The Cowboy's Bawdy Music." *The Cowboy: Six-Shooters, Songs, and Sex*. Ed. Charles W. Harris and Buck Rainey. Norman: University of Oklahoma Press, 1976: 127-38.

Louis, Adrian C. *Among the Dog-Eaters*. Albuquerque: West End Press, 1992.

_____. *Ancient Acid Flashes Back*. Reno: University of Nevada Press, 2000.

_____. *Blood Thirsty Savages*. St Louis: Time Being Books, 1994.

_____. *Ceremonies of the Damned*. Reno: University of Nevada Press, 1997.

_____. *Fire Water World*. Albuquerque: West End Press, 1989.

_____. *Vortex of Indian Fevers*. Evanston: TriQuarterly Books, 1995.

Love, Glen A. "Revaluing Nature: Toward an Ecological Criticism." *Western American Literature* 25.3 (Fall 1990): 201-15.

_____. "Roderick Haig-Brown: Angling and the Craft of Nature Writing in North America." *ISLE: Interdisciplinary Studies in Literature and the Environment* 51 (Winter 1998): 1-11.

Low, Denise. Review of Adrian Louis' *Among the Dog-Eaters*. *American Indian Culture and Research Journal* 17.2 (1993): 189-92.

Lutwack, Leonard. *The Role of Place in Literature*. Syracuse: Syracuse University Press, 1984.

Makarius, Laura. "Ritual Clowns and Symbolic Behavior." *Diogenes* 69 (1970): 44-73.

Maverick Western Verse. Ed. John C. Dofflemeyer. Layton, Utah: Peregrine Smith Books, 1994.

McClure, Arthur F. and Ken D. Jones. *Heroes, Heavies, and Sagebrush.* New Jersey: A. S. Barnes, 1972.

McMurtry, Larry. "How the West Was Won or Lost." *The New Republic* (22 October 1990): 32-38.

_____. "Take My Saddle from the Wall." *Harper's* 237 (September 1968): 37-46.

McRae, Wallace. *It's Just Grass and Water.* Spokane: Shawn Higgins, Publisher, 1979.

Meier, C. A. *Soul and Body: Essays on the Theories of C. G. Jung.* San Francisco: The Lapis Press, 1986.

Meredith, Howard. Review of Adrian C. Louis' *Wild Indians & Other Creatures. World Literature Today* 71.2 (Spring 1997): 431.

Miller, Warren. Ed. *Cattle, Horses, Sky, and Grass: Cowboy Poetry of the Late Twentieth Century.* Illustrated by Joe Beeler. Northland Publishing Company, 1994.

Mills, Kathryn Mary. "Jane Hirshfield and the Mind of Poetry." *The Montserrat Review.* <http://www.themontserratreview.com/issue-02-98/interview-01.html>, unpaginated.

Mitchell, Waddie. *Waddie's Whole Load: The Cowboy Poetry of Waddie Mitchell.* Layton, Utah: Gibbs-Smith, Publisher, 1984.

Molesworth, Charles. "Some Locals." *Poetry* 120.2 (May 1972): 107-12.

Moore, Judith. "A Conversation with Jane Hirshfield." *Poetry Daily.* <http://www.poems.com/hirinter.htm>, unpaginated.

Nash, Roderick. *Wilderness and the American Mind.* New Haven: Yale University Press, 1973.

Nelson, Robert. *Place and Vision: The Function of Landscape in Native American Fiction.* New York: Peter Lang Publishing, 1993.

Nelson, Rodney. "The Necessity of Love." *Anvil* (Winter 1979): 36-37.

New Cowboy Poetry. Ed. Hal Cannon. Layton, Utah: Peregrine Smith Books, 1990.

Norskog, Howard. *Yesterday's Trails.* St. Anthony, Idaho: High Country Enterprises, 1989.

O'Brien, Chip. *Downwind O'Cows: A Collection of California Cowboy Poetry.* Arizona: Coyote Cowboy Company Record Stockman Press, 1990.

Olson, Ray. Review of Adrian Louis' *Blood Thirsty Savages. Booklist* 90.21 (July 1994): 1917.

_____. Review of Adrian C. Louis' "Vortex of Indian Fevers." *Booklist* 91.15 (1 April 1995): 1374.

Olson, Steven. *The Prairie in Nineteenth-Century American Poetry.* Norman: University of Oklahoma Press, 1994.

Paul, Sherman. *For Love of the World: Essays on Nature Writing.* Iowa City: University of Iowa Press, 1992.

Pinsker, Sanford. *Three Pacific Northwest Poets: Stafford, Hugo, and Wagoner.* Boston: Twayne, 1987.

Plato. *The Dialogues of Plato.* New York: Bantam Books, 1986.

Raab, Lawrence. *The American Scholar* 40 (Summer 1971): 538-42.

Radin, Paul. *The Trickster: A Study in American Indian Mythology.* New York: Bell Publishing Company, 1956.

Rainey, Buck. "The 'Reel' Cowboy." *The Cowboy: Six-Shooters, Songs, and Sex.* Ed. Charles W. Harris and Buck Rainey. Norman: University of Oklahoma Press, 1976: 17-56.

Rhymes of the Mines: Life in the Underground. Ed. Mason and Janice Coggin. Phoenix: Cowboy Miner Productions, 1999.

Rothschild, Matthew. Review of Adrian Louis' *Ceremonies of the Damned. Progressive* 62.1 (January 1998): 41-2.

Russell, Don. "The Cowboy: from Black Hat to White." *The Cowboy, Six-Shooters, Songs, and Sex.* Ed. Charles W. Harris and Buck Rainey. Norman: University of Oklahoma Press, 1976: 5-15.

Russell, Sharman Apt. *Kill the Cowboy: A Battle of Mythology in the New West.* New York: Addison-Wesley, 1993.

Savage, William W., Jr. "The Cowboy Myth." *The Cowboy: Six-Shooters, Songs, and Sex.* Ed. Charles W. Harris and Buck Rainey. Norman: University of Oklahoma Press, 1976: 154-63.

Schein, Harry. "The Olympian Cowboy." *American Scholar* 24 (Summer 1955): 309-20.

Schramm, Richard. "A Gathering of Poets." *Western Humanities Review* 26.4 (Fall 1972): 389-99.

Scott, Nathan A, Jr. *Visions of Presence in Modern American Poetry.* Baltimore: Johns Hopkins University Press, 1993.

Shearer, Mike. "Peggy Pond Church: An 'Octogeranium' Speaks." *New Mexico Magazine* (February 1985): 23, 58-59.

Shepperson, Wilbur S. and Judith K. Winzeler. "Cowboy Poetry: The New Folk Art." *Nevada Historical Society Quarterly* 29 (Winter 1986): 254-65.

Sherwin, Elizabeth. "Poet Hirshfield Produces Private Words for Public Feast." May 12, 1996. <http://www.dcn.davis.ca.us/go/gizmo/hirshfl.html>, unpaginated.

Shortridge, James R. "The Concept of the Place-Defining Novel in American Popular Culture." *Professional Geographer* 43 (August 1991): 280-91.

Silko, Leslie Marmon. *Ceremony.* New York: Penguin Books, 1977.

Sims, Grant. "Leaving Alaska," *Alaska* (December 1992): 32-35.

Singing Cowboy: A Book of Western Songs. 1931. Ed. Margaret Larkin. New York: Oak Publications, 1963.

Smith, Dave. *Local Assays: On Contemporary American Poetry.* Urbana: University of Illinois Press, 1985.

Smith, William Jay. "The New Books." *Harper's* 233 (August 1966): 89-92.

Songs of the Cattle Trail and Cow Camp. Ed. John A. Lomax. New York: Macmillan Company, 1931.

Songs of the Cowboys. Ed. N. Howard (Jack) Thorp. 1908. Lincoln: University of Nebraska Press, 1984.

Stitt, Peter. *The Georgia Review* 32 (Summer 1978): 474-80.

Stonequist, Everett. *The Marginal Man: A Study in Personality and Culture Conflict.* New York: Charles Scribner's Sons, 1937.

Storr, Anthony, ed. *The Essential Jung.* Princeton: Princeton University Press, 1983.

Stribrny, Zdenek. "The Poetry of Richard Hugo and Tony Harrison." *Challenge of the Century: Proceedings of the Third Symposium on Twentieth-Century English and American Poetry in its International Context.* Germany: Wilhelm-Pieck-Universiätt Rostock, 1985.

Summers, Al. *Where Cattle Roam: A Book of Cowboy and Western Rhymes and Lyrics.* Dallas: Mathis, Van Nort and Co., 1944.

Suzuki, D. T. *An Introduction to Zen Buddhism.* New York: Grove Press, 1964.

Tatum, Stephen. "The Heart of the Wise Is in the House of Mourning." (62). *Eye on the Future: Popular Culture Scholarship into the Twenty-First Century,* Eds, Marilyn F. Motz, John G. Nachbar, Michael T. Marsden, Ronald J. Ambrosetti, Ohio: Bowling Green State University Popular Press, 1994.

Tillinghast, Richard. "A Prizewinner, The Real Thing, and Two Others." *Poetry* 109.2 (November 1966): 118-22.

A Trout in the Milk: A Composite Picture of Richard Hugo. Ed. Jack Myers. Lewiston, Idaho: Confluence Press, 1982.

Tuan, Yi-Fu. "Language and the Making of Place: A Narrative-Descriptive Approach." *Annals of the Association of American Geographers* 81.4 (December 1991): 684-96.

Turner, Victor. "Myth and Symbol." *International Encyclopedia of the Social Sciences.* New York: Macmillan, 1968.

Ullman, Leslie. "Betrayals and Boundaries: A Question of Balance." *Kenyon Review* 15.3 (Summer 1993): 182-97.

Unsigned article. "Peggy Pond Church." *The New Mexico Pasatiempo* (9 December 1983): 4-5.

Unsigned article. "Poet Can't Eat Laurels." *Alaska Magazine* (April 1991): 12.

Unsigned article. Review of Adrian Louis' *Among the Dog-Eaters.* *The Beloit Poetry Journal* 43.3 (Spring 1993): 44-55.

Vizenor, Gerald. *The Trickster of Liberty: Tribal Heirs to a Wild Baronage.* Minneapolis: University of Minnesota Press, 1988.

Weaver, Roger. Review of Adrian Louis' *Fire Water World.* S.A.I.L. 3.4 (Winter 1991): 72-74.

The Well-Tended Tree: Essays into the Spirit of our Time. Ed. Hilde Kirsch. New York: G. P. Putnam's Sons, 1971.

White, Lynn, Jr., "The Historical Roots of Our Ecological Crisis," *The Ecocriticism Reader: Landmarks in Literary Ecology.* Ed. Cheryll Glotfelty and Harold Fromm, University of Georgia Press, Athens, Georgia, 1996.

"The Whorehouse Bells Were Ringing" and Other Songs Cowboys Sing. Ed. Guy Logsdon. Urbana: University of Illinois Press, 1989.

Wild, Peter. *John Haines.* Boise: Boise State University, 1985.

Wilhelm, Stephen R. *Cowboy Poet.* 1944.

Williams, Norm. "Richard Hugo and the Politics of Failure." *Yale Literary Magazine* 146: 4-5.

Wilson, James R. "Relentless Self-Scrutiny: The Poetry of John Haines." *Winter News* 16-27.

Womack, Craig. Review of Adrian Louis' *Fire Water World. American Indian Quarterly* 17.1 (Winter 1993): 102-09.

Worster, Donald. *Under Western Skies: Nature and History in the American West.* New York: Oxford University Press, 1992.

Wright, James. "Hugo: Secrets of the Inner Landscape." *American Poetry Review* 2.3 (1973): 13.

Young, William. "Traveling through the Dark: The Wilderness Surrealism of the Far West." Midwest Quarterly 39.2 (Winter 1998): 187-202.

Ziff, Larzer. *Puritanism in America: New Culture in a New World.* New York: The Viking Press, 1973.

Zweig, Paul. "Messages in a Bottle." *The Nation* 204 (27 February 1967): 281-83.

embodiment of spirit(s), xii; history of, 8; identification with, 6–7, 103; invalid claim to, 71; Native Americans, loss of, 151–153; psychic wholeness with, 118, 119, 157; respect for, xi; validation of Americans, 292, 293

"Land of Magic (The)" (Blair), 61

landscapes: California, 3; mysterious, 11; Pacific Northwest, 199; past incorporated in, 6; reflection of self, 8

"Land (The)" (McRae), 60

Language and the Making of Place (Tuan), xiii

Lasky, Julie, Borrowed Design: *Use and Abuse of Historical Form,* 302 n.7

"Last Buckaroo (The)" (Gibford), 92

life: battle of civilization vs. nature, 201; boundaries of, 247–249; circle of, 144; continuum of, 254, 258–260, 273; cowboy's way, 58; critique by poets, 125; emergence, 121; hidden by nature, 117, 118; inevitability of failures, 262; instability of, 200, 202, 203; interaction with imagination, 135–140; mysteries of, 109, 145, 179; reflection on, 264, 265;

responsibility for, 174, 188; return to origins, 200; self-destructive, 155; union of man and nature, 116; unpredictability of, 202. *See also* union of self and nature.

limitations, mental and spiritual, 15–16

"Loafer Mountain" (Bradshaw), 63, 64

"Lost on the Road" (Real Bird), 77, 78

Louis, Adrian C.: criticism of work, 305–306 ns.2–6; cultural debt, 180, 181; dependent on the land, 156; distrust of relationships, 172, 176, 178; lack of vision, 155; need of love, 197; personal style, 192; power of poetry, 178–180, 182, 183, 187; relationship to culture, 195; subjects of poetry, 155, 156, 161, 169, 171

Louis Adrian C., works by: "After Long Silence Marilyn Returns," 180; "Among the Dog-Eaters," 181; "Ancient Acid Flashes Back," 304n. 1; "Another Indian Murder," 161, 162; "A Post Card from Devils Tower," 153–155; "A Prayer for the Lost," 185; "Betrayals and Boundaries," 182; "Black Crow Dreams," 196, 197; "Blame It on the Dog, He's Dead," 165, 166;

Andrew Elkins

*A*ndrew Elkins, who holds the Ph.D. degree from North-western University, is former dean of the School of Arts and Sciences at Peru State University in Nebraska. Elkins is the author of numerous essays on western poets and two books, *The Poetry of James Wright* (1991) and *The Great Poem of the Earth: A Study of the Poetry of Thomas Hornsby Ferril* (1997). He and his wife, Mary Ellen, make their home in Peru, Nebraska.